MR. INSIDE

and

MR. OUTSIDE

*World War II, Army's Undefeated Teams, and
College Football's Greatest Backfield Duo*

JACK CAVANAUGH

TRIUMPH
BOOKS

Library of Congress Cataloging-in-Publication Data has been applied for.

This book is available in quantity at special discounts for your group or organization. For further information, contact:

Triumph Books
814 North Franklin Street
Chicago, Illinois 60610
(312) 337-0747
Fax (312) 280-5470
www.triumphbooks.com

Printed in U.S.A.
ISBN: 978-1-60078-929-8
Book design by Alex Lubertozzi

*To the members of the unbeaten 1944, 1945, and 1946
Army football teams, and to all the other cadets who have since
been part of Army's great football tradition*

"We have stopped the war to celebrate your magnificent success."

—General Douglas MacArthur

in a telegram to Army coach Red Blaik after
Army had beaten Navy in 1944 to win its first
of two consecutive national championships

CONTENTS

FOREWORD

M R. INSIDE" AND "MR. OUTSIDE"—THE FABLED "TOUCHDOWN Twins"—hold a very special place, both in the lexicon, and in the annals, of college football. For three tumultuous years, at the end of the Second World War, the Army team went undefeated. For football fans all across the country, these West Point teams represented a sterling standard of success. And the two icons of their fortune—Felix "Doc" Blanchard and Glenn Davis—seemed to embody General Douglas MacArthur's dictum that, "There is no substitute for victory!"

I can speak, personally, of the excitement and drama of those heralded Army teams and, more particularly, of Blanchard and Davis, as I was an impressionable 8-year-old at the time. I knew little of the sport of football more broadly, but my youthful wonder was piqued by these two truly larger-than-life gridiron heroes. Little did I know that, a decade and a half later, the seed they planted in my youthful imagination would lead me in a similar direction.

Anyone with a love of the game will find Jack Cavanaugh's story of those times, and those teams, to be intoxicating. He folds intriguing personal vignettes into detailed game descriptions, in a recipe that is, frankly, delicious. Chapters on "Two Good to be True," "The Racial Divide Even During Wartime," "Changing the Game," and "The Colonel as Coach" carry you across the rich terrain of a treasured period of college football in America.

A climactic high point of the saga occurred in the 1946 Army-Navy game—what Cavanaugh labels, the "Game of the Century." Army's three-year undefeated status was at stake, and an underdog Navy team rose to the occasion to play the game of its life. Late in the contest, with Army clinging to a narrow three-point lead, Navy gained the advantage and moved impressively down the field. With the final seconds ticking away and the ball on the Army 8-yard line, there was time for just one final play.

Navy handed the ball to their star half-back, Pete Williams, who rounded right end and darted toward the end zone. It was "now or never." As Williams reached the plain of the goal line he was met head-on by Army's Barney Poole. The sound of their thunderous clash reverberated throughout the stadium. At that moment, it wasn't clear whether Williams would fall forward into the end zone, or be pushed back. In the following two or three seconds—but in what seemed to be an extended period of suspended time and motion—Army players suddenly appeared from every direction. Hank Foldberg attacked from outside. Then, Goble Bryant muscled in to lift Williams off his feet. Next it was Jim Enos, followed by Joe Steffy and what seemed like the entire Army team. Williams was lifted upward, higher and higher, and ultimately thrown back, away from the goal line. He crashed to the turf, and it was over! The victory preserved the storybook tale of Blanchard and Davis, and Army's third undefeated season was entered into the record books for all time.

Jack Cavanaugh's fascinating book is the story of the remarkable exploits of, arguably, the two best college football players who ever played together on the same team. But that climactic ending of the 1946 Army-Navy game deserves being highlighted because it under-scores the book's important and enduring sub-plot. Blanchard and Davis excelled by their spectacular individual performances. Time and again, what they did produced the essential margin of victory. They were respected, indeed lionized, for their manifold on-field exploits.

That said, it's worth remembering that these Army teams were groups of young men who, as World War II came to a close, were brought together by circumstance and fate. The bonds that developed among them were strong and enduring. By every measure, they were a team. Not just any team, but the Army team. At its heart, Cavanaugh's book is, indeed, the story of the genius of two of their number. But its lasting legacy is what all of those players accomplished together.

Pete Dawkins
Brigadier General, U.S. Army (Ret'd)
Heisman Trophy 1958

INTRODUCTION

T HERE THEY WERE, THE FABLED "MR. INSIDE" AND THE equally storied "Mr. Outside," former teammates, Heisman Trophy winners, and three-time All-Americans, standing in front of the football-shaped headstone of their legendary coach, Earl "Red" Blaik, not far from Michie Stadium at the United States Military Academy in West Point, New York, where Felix "Doc" Blanchard and Glenn Davis became the most famous running back tandem in college football history. There, too, at the grave site at the Academy cemetery on Saturday, September 30, 1995, was Barney Poole, one of the few players to have been named an All-American at two different schools—the United States Military Academy and the University of Mississippi—before spending six years in the NFL. Close by were three other former All-Americans, quarterbacks Arnold Tucker and Doug Kenna and guard Joe Steffy, along with 41 other players who had played on at least one or all three undefeated Army teams in the mid-1940s, the Academy's most glorious football era when Army teams won outright national championships in 1944 and 1945 while the 1946 team was picked in some pools for a third national title. Indeed, it's safe to say that to millions of sports fans, Army was "America's team" during World War II, both because of the military connection and the Cadets' outstanding football teams.

Fifty years after winning the second championship in 1945 with what Blaik proclaimed as his best team, and, in his estimation, very likely the best college team of all time—a claim that could very well stand the test of time. Most of the former players gathered for what would be their final reunion were in their seventies, and at this writing in 2014 only Tucker, like Blanchard a retired Air Force colonel, of those mentioned above was still alive. After placing a wreath on Blaik's grave, the players later stood as guests of honor to a round of applause at the parade ground on campus at the traditional pregame march of the Corps of Cadets, and then were introduced, again to a huge collective cheer, at halftime of the Army-Rice game at Michie Stadium, which I was covering for the *New York Times.* The game, which ended in a 21–21 tie, was an afterthought to me and also in the story I filed late that afternoon that highlighted the homecoming of players from Army's best-ever team and its two greatest players during the military academy's most glorious football era.

For a sportswriter already somewhat inured to interviewing celebrity athletes, including such sporting legends as Muhammad Ali, Sugar Ray Robinson, Ted Williams, Joe DiMaggio, Gene Tunney, Arnold Palmer, Jack Nicklaus, Bjorn Borg, John McEnroe, the great Olympian Jesse Owens, and Roger Bannister, the first runner to cover a mile in less than four minutes, meeting and talking to those Army players of a half-century earlier was particularly special, perhaps because of the setting and my memories of hearing their exploits on radio broadcasts as a boy growing up in Connecticut—especially Davis, the 5'9" 170-lb. Golden Boy, unstoppable in the open field, and the husky hard-driving and equally unstoppable 6'1" 210-lb. Blanchard capable of running over or through would-be tacklers.

For three golden years from 1944 through 1946, Blanchard and Davis emerged as America's biggest sports stars, even overshadowing such superb athletes as Louis, Williams, DiMaggio, and Ben Hogan after they returned from military service at the war's end. How good were they? Well, though they rarely played more than half of a game because of Army's superiority over most of its opponents and usually only carried the ball about 15 times each, together they scored a total of 97 touchdowns, more than any other two backs in the same backfield in college football history, while also excelling on defense at a time when most players played both offense and defense.

"It was a wonderful period that I'll never forget," Davis, then a graying 70 but looking considerably younger while carrying about 15 lbs. more than during his playing days, told me on that golden autumnal day. "My days at West Point stay with me everywhere I go. And they mean more than anything to me." Others in the group expressed similar sentiments about their time at West Point when the Army team's success seemed to give a lift to many Americans, including GIs abroad, during some of the country's darkest days in large measure because of the spectacular accomplishments of Blanchard and Davis, who in 2014 still held National Collegiate Athletic Association (NCAA) records for rushing average at 8.3 yards per carry over a four-year period and an astounding 11.5 yards a carry rushing average in 1944 and 1945. Blanchard, who played one less season, averaged a remarkable 5.9 yards on running plays while, like Davis, excelling on defense as a two-way player. Because of his remarkable open-field running and long touchdown runs, a hallmark of his career at Army, Davis was the more spectacular of the Touchdown Twins, as they were also called, a dazzling lightning-fast runner, equally unstoppable whether he ran around end or bolted through the line, always with what appeared to be a minimalistic effort. Though Davis was a more multi-faceted athlete, who also excelled at West Point in baseball, track, and basketball, Blanchard was also an outstanding shot-put thrower and, despite his size, a sprinter on the indoor track team. "There are words to describe how good an athlete Doc Blanchard was, but there aren't words to describe how good Glenn Davis was," said Bill Yeoman, a center and linebacker and teammate of both players in 1946 and later the head coach at the University of Houston. "He's the most phenomenal athlete I ever saw."

The Blanchard-Davis heroics at West Point occurred during a tumultuous period in American history because 1944, their first season as teammates, was the last full year of U.S. involvement in World War II. The war ended in August 1945, four months after the death of President Franklin Delano Roosevelt and two weeks after American bombers dropped atomic bombs on the Japanese port cities of Hiroshima and Nagasaki. President Harry Truman, who had succeeded Roosevelt in April, and Congress struggled to find adequate housing and jobs for hundreds of thousands of American GIs and deal with crippling strikes by steelworkers, coal miners, and railroad workers in 1945 and 1946. With the National Football League still struggling for acceptance and larger attendance and a major professional basketball league (the Basketball Association of America, the forerunner of the National Basketball Association) still a year away, college football and Major League Baseball were arguably the two most popular forms of recreation and entertainment for people in need of a break from the travails of the real world, and Davis, Blanchard, and their teammates certainly did their part to thrill millions of Americans on fall Saturday afternoons from 1944 through 1946.

More than six decades later, it's still practically impossible to mention Blanchard without mentioning Davis or vice versa. It would be like mentioning Gilbert but not Sullivan, or Abbott and not Costello, or Rogers without adding Hammerstein or Hart. Apart, perhaps, from Babe Ruth and Lou Gehrig, never have two athletes on the same team been more inextricably linked and yet so different in personality. Indeed, the Blanchard-Davis twosome more than holds its own in the company of any famed duo in sports or entertainment because of a three-year team relationship that established them as the best running tandem in football history and the biggest names on the American sports scene in the mid-1940s.

Starting in 1944, renowned sportswriters including Damon Runyon and Grantland Rice glamorized the spectacular exploits of Blanchard and Davis, who piled up huge amounts of yardage as Army's victory streak grew and their fame resonated throughout the country. Indeed, even casual sports fans knew the identities of "Mr. Inside" and "Mr. Outside," nicknames that were bestowed on them by well-known New York sportswriter George Trevor. Other appellations applied to Blanchard and Davis were "the Touchdown Twins" and, simply, "B and D," as sports columnist Joe Williams of the *New York World-Telegram* called them. Both because it was for the national championship and also the final Notre Dame game for Blanchard and Davis, the meeting between Army and the Fighting Irish at Yankee Stadium in New York on November 9, 1946, outdrew in both attendance and attention the NFL Championship Game at the Polo Grounds in New York a month later between the New York Giants and the Chicago Bears, and it overshadowed Joe Louis' return to the ring after serving in the army and a stirring seven-game World Series between the Boston Red Sox and the St. Louis Cardinals, which included two of baseball's best players, Ted Williams and Stan Musial, both just back from World War II.

Capitalizing on their immense fame and popularity, Hollywood, in an extraordinarily rare production, had the handsome Davis and ruggedly good-looking Blanchard play themselves as stars of a movie entitled *The Spirit of West Point*, which was made and released in 1947, the year they graduated from West Point as second lieutenants in the U.S. Army and before they went on active duty. Davis' celebrity status continued when he began to date actress Elizabeth Taylor in 1948 when he was 23 and still in the army and Taylor was 16 and already a star after her performances in *National Velvet* and *Courage of Lassie*, going so far as to give her a gold football pin emblematic of his All-American status. Gossip columnists and photographers seized on the brief romance between the teenage starlet who was fast becoming much of America's sweetheart and the All-American football star and army lieutenant, whose humility, good looks, and athleticism had seemed to have made him the quintessential All-American boy. A *Life* magazine photo of Taylor brushing her lipstick off Davis after kissing him on his arrival back from Korea made front pages in many papers across the country, sparking rumors that the relationship had become serious. For those Americans who feasted on celebrity romance stories in the late forties, this one was as good as it got.

What made Davis and Blanchard's football achievements all the more remarkable was that, although nationally known athletes, they were not exempt from the rigorous academic grind and traditional and time-consuming routines at West Point, including the notorious "Beast Barracks" that prompted many cadets to drop out after the first or second year at West Point and has led to at least one suicide. Once cadets reach the third year at the military academy, they are committed to complete the exacting four-year curriculum and then spend five years on active duty in the army, two years more than cadets who graduated in the mid-1940s. That commitment in the twenty-first century is responsible for deterring many outstanding high school and prep school football players bent on playing in the National Football League from accepting appointments to West Point, but was not the case during World War II when the academic term was reduced from four to three years, making the studying grind all the more arduous. Davis is among the few former West Point players who have played in the NFL, having spent the 1950 and 1951 seasons with the Los Angeles Rams following his discharge in 1949 and, despite a bad knee, still managing to lead one of the best NFL teams of all time in rushing in 1950 before retiring because of the knee injury sustained while making *The Spirit of West Point*.

Though college teams like Notre Dame had huge followings in the forties, both graduates and so-called "Subway Alumni," the name bestowed on ardent fans, many of them Irish, who had not attended the South Bend school, the Army team enjoyed tremendous support during the war years because its football players, like other cadets, were being trained to become officers in the army, which almost all of them did. That was also true at the U.S. Naval Academy, Army's main football rival, where most players eventually became naval officers during or after World War II. At the same time, both football teams, and West Point in particular, benefitted by recruiting highly skilled players from other schools, including Blanchard, mainly because of the charm and persuasive powers of one of Blaik's assistant coaches, the colorful, highly literate, and ample-sized Herman Hickman, a former All-American lineman at Tennessee, an All-Pro tackle with the old Brooklyn Dodgers of the NFL, and a professional wrestler who later became the head football coach at Yale. By transferring to the U.S. Military Academy, those players became exempt from the military draft as long as they stayed at West Point, as did younger players like Davis, who entered West Point at the age of 18 although they were still committed to multi-year tours of army duty after graduating from the Academy.

But if Army benefitted from those transfers and draft exemptions, so did a number of well-known college football powers under navy programs that enabled enlisted service personnel, many of whom had starred at other colleges, to play football while training at their own schools. However, none of the players in those V-5 and V-12 programs had to endure the severe regimen that members of the Army football team did during the war years and still do today. "Practice was always the easiest part of the day," said former Army guard Al Joy. However, by 1943 many of the navy personnel and Marines in the V-5 and V-12 programs who were playing college football were called to active duty, including such All-American stars as Notre Dame quarterback Angelo Bertelli. By contrast, so long as football players kept up to speed on their studies, players at West Point were exempt from active duty.

How good were the Army football teams of 1944, 1945, and 1946? Tackle Tex Coulter, who went on to play six seasons with the New York Giants, said he thought the Army teams he had played on in 1944 and

1945 had more depth than the Giants' team that had won the Eastern Division NFL championship in 1946, the year he joined the team. "I think our Army teams of those years could have beaten the Giants," Coulter said. Famed sportswriter Grantland Rice went even farther, saying that he thought the 1944 Army team was the best one in the country, college or professional. Indeed, the 1944 team had so many first-rate players that Blaik alternated two separate units throughout the season that each played two alternating quarters of a game. Although he rarely played more than half of a game, Davis scored 20 touchdowns that season while averaging a remarkable 11.5 yards rushing, a feat that he duplicated in 1945 when it became an NCAA record that still stands (it hadn't been accepted as a record the previous year because Davis had not carried the ball at least 75 times, which was an NCAA requirement). Despite that, Davis finished second to Les Horvath of Ohio State in the voting for the Heisman Trophy in 1944, as he would again, behind Blanchard, in 1945. Blanchard, who finished third in the voting for the Heisman in 1944, scored nine touchdowns that season while averaging 7.1 yards a carry and, like Davis, rarely played more than half of a game.

★   ★   ★

As to how those Army teams of the mid-1940s would have fared against outstanding college teams in later years, Red Blaik felt that they would have more than held their own, and many of those former Army players tended to agree. "I think we could have beaten most of them," said Roland Catarinella, a lineman and briefly a running back from 1943 through 1945 who seemed to sum up the feelings of most of the Army players from the unbeaten teams of the 1940s. "Our talent was that good. We were loaded with Hall of Famers and All-Americans, and had great coaching." Another former player, Robert Woods, thought, however, that the size, speed, and strength of current-day players might give collegiate teams a significant if not insuperable edge over the Army teams of the 1940s. Like many of his former teammates, though, Woods felt that, assuming those Army teams were as big, fast, and strong, Army could more than hold its own.

Not surprisingly, there were skeptics who felt that Army, with a team loaded with star players from other schools who had been recruited to play at West Point during the war years, had a huge advantage against most of its opponents who had been weakened by the military draft. While valid, that argument did not seem to stand up entirely since the Cadets remained unbeaten during the first post–World War II peacetime year of 1946, and after losing two games in 1947 went unbeaten again in 1948 and 1949 and lost only one game in 1950. However, many of the players on the 1946 and 1947 teams had been recruited during the war and thus were exempt from the draft.

So how did Army become so good so fast during World War II while most other college teams were in decline? The main explanation seems to be that the army hierarchy beyond West Point was behind the team's ascendance and dominance during the war years and even beyond. Two of the country's best-known generals, Dwight Eisenhower, the head of Allied forces in Europe during the war and himself a former Army halfback, and Douglas MacArthur, a onetime baseball player and later an innovative, albeit controversial, superintendant at the Academy, were huge fans of the Cadet football team, and MacArthur often exchanged letters with Blaik about the team's progress. Whether Eisenhower or MacArthur or any other high-ranking military officials had anything to do with the recruitment of proven players from other schools to enhance Cadet teams is conjecture and was never proven, although Herman Hickman, an assistant coach under Blaik, was known to have told prospective recruits that prominent alums like Eisenhower and MacArthur felt that a powerful Army football team would boost the morale of West Point alumni and other soldiers along with many sports fans in general.

At any rate, it seems entirely possible, and even understandable, that top army officials perhaps extending all the way to Secretary of War Henry Stimson could have felt that powerful West Point football teams during the war would be a metaphor for a powerful U.S. military. If so, they may have succeeded, since Army's long string of victories during most of the war seemed to have created more fans than ever for West Point football teams and perhaps made those fans feel that those successes on the football field would be a harbinger of victories by U.S. troops abroad. Yet, as the austere and autocratic Blaik was to say years later, some of those wartime Army teams had to endure taunts of "slackers"— most notably, Blaik claimed, from Notre Dame's so-called Subway Alumni—during games against the Irish at Yankee Stadium, which were at least partially responsible for temporarily ending the traditional series following the 1947 game, the first one ever played in South Bend. That, of course, would have been ironic, since Notre Dame players in the Knute Rockne era before and after World War I were often subjected to taunts of "harps," "micks," and "papists," among other derogatory terms, even though most of the Notre Dame players at the time were not Irish.

★   ★   ★

Not surprisingly, many people felt that Blanchard, Davis, and a number of other Army players had no intention of becoming career officers, let alone future Eisenhowers, MacArthurs, or Pattons. That suspicion was somewhat manifested when Blanchard and Davis tried to delay going on active duty after they graduated in 1947 when they asked for five four-month furloughs every year in order to spend five seasons in the National Football League, after which they would each spend 20 years in the army or Air Force. When that effort became public, Blanchard and Davis in particular came under fire in the media on the grounds that they were using their reputations to seek favoritism and exceptions that would enable them to avoid military service and make far more money playing football then serving in the army like the other graduates in the West Point Class of 1947.

With their proposal denied and their reputations somewhat sullied, Davis became an officer in the infantry while Blanchard earned his wings as a pilot in the Air Force, as did Arnold Tucker. Most of their teammates also served for at least a few years in the army or Air Force, while a number of others who, like Blanchard, Davis, and Tucker, had gone to West Point expressly to play football, decided to make the army a career.

Army's football teams of the mid-forties indisputably benefitted from the transfers of highly talented players from other schools. But that seemed to matter not at all to a legion of American sports fans, along with untold thousands of GIs, especially those in the U.S. Army, who felt that those wondrous Army football teams took their minds off far more serious matters as they cheered for what had become truly America's team and indeed one of the best college football teams of all time, if not *the* best.

1

★ ★ ★

The Professor's Recruit

IKE MANY COLLEGE FOOTBALL COACHES, EARL "RED" BLAIK received plenty of tips on potentially good college football players—even from a few generals—but never before had he gotten one from a college dramatics professor, as he did in early 1943, his third year as the head coach at the United States Military Academy in West Point, New York. The tip came from a friend, Warren Bentley, a drama professor at Dartmouth, where Blaik had coached for seven years before returning to West Point, his alma mater, as head coach in 1941. Bentley had attended college in Pomona in Southern California and along with occasionally vacationing in the area, had relatives there, one of whom, a grocer, told him about a football player in Los Angeles County whose mother had told him her son was interested in going to West Point.

"Everybody in California talks about a football player at Bonita High School in La Verne, which is not far from Pomona," Professor Bentley wrote to Blaik. "They say that this kid is the fastest halfback ever seen out there. He's an all-round athlete: baseball, basketball, and track, as well as football. Since I'm told he is interested in going to West Point, I thought you would want to know about him. His name is Glenn Davis."

Not only had Blaik never heard of Davis, he had never even tried to recruit a player from the West Coast, either while he was at Dartmouth or since his arrival at West Point. "I didn't know anything about West Coast football," Blaik said years later. Even if he had, Blaik knew recruiting would be difficult. For one thing, most people still traveled by train in the 1940s, and the transcontinental trip from the West Coast to New York took at least four days. For another, it was hard enough recruiting players from the Northeast, the South, and the Midwest because of the rigorous academic schedule at West Point and the commitment after graduation to serve three years on active duty.

However, in 1943 it was considerably easier to recruit players since they knew that by enrolling at the military academy they would be exempt from the draft, which the previous year had been lowered from 21 years old to 18, the age many high school students usually graduate. So long as a high school or prep school student could get a Congressional appointment, usually from a congressman or congresswoman in his congressional district, and pass the somewhat exacting entrance examination, he would in effect be getting a four-year all-expenses-paid scholarship at an outstanding, albeit very demanding, educational institution where athletes were shown no favors.

The young Davis, who had broken every offensive football record at Bonita Union High School, had been considering accepting an offer from the University of Southern California, as had his twin brother and football and track teammate, Ralph, both of whom had thought of applying for the navy's V-12 program at USC, which would have provided free tuition and eventually commissions in the navy. After receiving Professor Bentley's letter, Blaik checked with some friends and West Point alums in the Los Angeles area and was assured by those who had seen or heard about Davis that he not only had been an outstanding high school running back at Bonita High but probably could already start in the backfield at both USC and UCLA.

Indeed, a West Coast scout had told Davis' coach, John Price, "I have seen every one of the Coast Conference college teams play, and not one of them has a back as good as Davis." Not only was Davis an outstanding all-round athlete, he also seemed to have been a real-life All-American boy in the mold of Jack Armstrong, the fictitious and heroic star of the popular 1930s and 1940s radio program *Jack Armstrong, The All-American Boy*. Handsome, unpretentious, soft-spoken, totally without ego, and well-liked by his classmates, Davis, as he was to say some years later, "I was the kind of guy who dated one girl all the way through high school and West Point," which he did.

In an era when high school football games were rarely filmed, as was the case at Bonita High, college coaches usually had to rely on unpaid scouts or assistant coaches to check on potential recruits. But by early 1943 it was too late to do that with Davis, since he had already played his last high school football game. Thus, apart from the glowing verbal and written reports he had received on the 5'9" 160-lb. Davis, Blaik had little else to go on, and thereupon wrote to Davis' parents in the spring of 1943, and after talking to them by phone later, succeeded in convincing the 18-year-old Davis to come east to take the entrance examination at the military academy—but only after Blaik agreed that Davis' twin brother also could take the same exam.

What Blaik heard about Davis during his research was almost too good to be true, though he was somewhat concerned about Davis' relatively small size. During his senior year, Davis had accounted for a California state record of 236 points, an average of 26 points per game over nine games, the equivalent of almost 40 touchdowns. In one game, Davis, playing left halfback out of the single-wing formation, scored three touchdowns on runs of more than 50 yards. Then in the California Interscholastic Federation Southern Division championship game against Newport Harbor High School, Davis, playing quarterback in the T formation, which Price also occasionally used, threw three touchdown passes, one to his brother, on three consecutive plays, but all three were nullified by offensive penalties. On the next play, which was sent in by Price, Davis faked another pass and then sprinted almost 50 yards for one of his three touchdowns—he threw for two others—en route to a 39–6 Bonita victory. Not surprisingly, Davis was unanimously voted conference Player of the Year.

Once past the line of scrimmage, Davis was virtually unstoppable because of his speed and his body control. Though he usually was at his best on an end sweep, Davis, though never heavier than 160 lbs. in high school, also bolted through holes in the line and avoided linebackers by swerving left or right without losing any speed. When frustrated opponents were able to tackle Davis, Price said, some of them often tried to keep him down with their knees in his back. "But he never gave them a second look," Price said. "He'd just get up and grin, and never complained about anyone playing dirty against him."

Donald St. Claire, a former teammate who played in the backfield with Davis, recalled blocking for Davis—or at least trying to block for the speedy Bonita High star. "Quite often, I'd just start to block a lineman for him, and he was already past me and in the clear," said St. Claire, a medical doctor in La Verne, in 2013. "Glenn was just unbelievably fast." Another former football teammate, Charles Creighton, said the same year that Davis was also an outstanding baseball player. "He was a very good hitter, very good in the outfield, and a terrific base-stealer," said Creighton, who played right field alongside Davis in center field. "If anything was hit to right-center, or even in my territory, Glenn could almost always get to it." So much so that in a much later Army game against the Montreal Royals, the Brooklyn Dodgers' Triple A farm team, at West Point in April 1945, Davis stole second, third, and home to the astonishment of the Royals and to the delight of Army fans long accustomed to Davis' speed and heroics on the base paths, the football field, the basketball court, and as a sprinter and broad jumper on the track team.

Years later, Davis said he became aware of his ability as a football player and his speed while attending junior high school in Claremont, California, where he was born the day after Christmas in 1924, just minutes after his twin, but not identical, brother had preceded him. "We had a team that played other junior highs in a league, and I'd say that was when I felt I could compete pretty well," Davis recalled. "I was blessed with speed, and I was just faster than everyone else."

In the early 1930s the Davis family moved to nearby La Verne, a citrus-growing town of 3,000 residents about 35 miles east of Los Angeles. They lived on a 14-acre spread that included scores of orange and citrus trees and afforded Glenn and Ralph plenty of room to play and throw footballs and baseballs. "Glenn's father was a banker and a very pleasant man," Charles Creighton said. "Like Glenn, while he was nice, he wasn't particularly outgoing. As kids, we always wanted Glenn on our football and baseball teams because he was so good. Ralph, who was always bigger than Glenn, was also a good athlete and more outgoing than Glenn, but nowhere near as good as his brother."

At Bonita High coaches of the football, basketball, baseball, and track teams also wanted Glenn Davis on their teams in a big way. What struck all of them at first glance was Davis' blazing speed, which, coupled with his all-around athleticism, intelligence, and determination made him a pleasure to coach. By Davis' junior year at Bonita Union High, even some major California newspapers like the *Los Angeles Times* began to pay considerable attention to the sensational Bonita High halfback and quarterback who could also run the 100-yard dash in less than 10 seconds and rarely ever lost a race at that distance or in the 220-yard dash while also starring in the broad jump and pole vault. He consistently hit well over .300 as a speedy outfielder in baseball, and he excelled as a guard on the school's basketball team.

Always gracious and self-effacing, Davis once said, "In high school I only weighed about 160 lbs. So it wasn't my size, it was my speed. And God gave me that. I didn't have to work for it."

When Davis was in high school, then, as now, would-be cadets were required to get congressional appointments, usually from congressmen in their congressional districts. A well-known Democratic congressman named Jerry Voorhis, perhaps best known for having lost his seat to Richard Nixon in 1946 after serving five terms, nominated Davis, while his brother received his nomination from another Southern California member of Congress. That seemed more kosher than the 1945 West Point appointment of tackle Goble Bryant, an all-conference lineman at Texas A&M that came from congressman Emanuel Cellar in whose Brooklyn district Bryant, a Texan, most definitely did not live. As Bryant was to say some years later, "There was no subterfuge in how the Army coaches got their appointments. They went to Washington, knocked on the doors, and said, 'If you don't have anybody for an appointment to West Point, we've got one whose got the mental and physical capability not only to fill the appointment but to play football, too.'"

With their appointments assured, Glenn and Ralph Davis, loaded down with sandwiches and reference books, were seen off by their parents at the train station in San Bernardino for a four-day train trip to West Point in early May, more than a month before their scheduled graduations from Bonita Union High. Aware of the strict entrance examination, Ralph and Ima Davis had made it clear to their twin sons that it was extremely important that they study the books on the long trip East and continue to do so from the time they settled in at West Point and took the validating examination, as it's called. For two 18-year-olds who had never been out of California, it was the trip of a lifetime and a golden opportunity to see much of the country, and to study, as their train wound through the Rockies, the wheat fields of Kansas, on to Chicago, and finally to West Point. They would be met at the train station by Coach Red Blaik and driven to the Blaik's home near the famous West Point Plain, where they would stay until July 1 when they moved into rooms on the Academy grounds. While staying with Blaik, his wife, Merle, and their two teenage sons, Bob and Bill, the Davis brothers would meet with tutors, study at night and on weekends, and eventually take the entrance examination, which they passed and, perforce, became cadets. (Bob, who became a starting quarterback for Army in 1949 and 1950, came to idolize Glenn Davis while he was playing football at Highland Falls High School near West Point.)

While staying with the Blaik family, Glenn and Ralph had ample time to roam around the Academy grounds, to view its stately gray Gothic buildings, and to savor the spectacular view from a bluff on the edge of the famous Plain where the Hudson River bends. There, facing the river, they could see a statue of the Polish General Thaddeus Kosciuszko who was commissioned by President George Washington in 1778 to build a garrison at West Point from where American colonial forces could repulse any passing British ships. (The garrison was not converted into a military academy until 1802 when Thomas Jefferson was president.) Nearby at Trophy Point, they could see a collection of assorted captured weaponry, including artillery cannons, dating from the Revolutionary War, along with a section of the great massive chain that Kosciuszko had stretched across the Hudson, making it impossible for British ships to pass through. Nearby, too, was the 45'-high Battle Monument where several cannons carry the names of the more than 2,000 officers and soldiers who died during the Civil War, and not far away was a statue of George Washington on horseback. For teenagers from the West Coast it was heady stuff that Glenn Davis said years later had moved him and his brother and that they had never forgotten.

Far less memorable for the Davis brothers were the so-called "Beast Barracks," a form of basic training and hazing for incoming cadets that starts on July 1, the day cadets are scheduled to report to the Academy.

For six weeks, the plebes—the term for first-year cadets—were subjected to a variety of hardships and indignities that include harsh
questioning about West Point traditions and sights, an assortment of
excessive physical challenges, extensive marching while loaded down
with gear, and even being awakened at all hours of the night. It may not
have been the main factor, which very likely was the academic grind and
rigidly structured daily routine, but until the 1920s, about 40 percent of
the plebes left West Point after the first year, a percentage that dropped
to around the current figure of around 20 percent after MacArthur, who
was the Academy's youngest ever superintendent from 1919 until 1922,
decreed that Beast Barracks be toned down and the curriculum liber-
alized to include psychology and other social studies courses. Though
both of the Davis brothers endured Beast Barracks without complaint
unlike some of the older players who had been recruited from other
schools, Glenn privately derided some of the West Point customs, and
in light of his eventual stature at the Academy along with his likeability
he avoided even further harassment directed at other plebes. In fact,
most of the football players were accorded "recognition," a West Point
term that in effect meant special treatment, at least from upperclassmen
if not from their instructors, as is often the case at many big-time football universities. Nevertheless, even in the 1940s it was not uncommon
for an upperclassman to peremptorily order a plebe to do 100 or more
sit-ups or push-ups on the spot.

Davis may have won over some of the "yearlings" (second-year
cadets), "cows" (the equivalent of a college junior), and "firsties" (cadets
in their fourth and final year) by his performance in the rigorous physical
test required of all plebes that included a 300-yard run, standing broad
and vertical jumps, a rope climb, chin-ups, sit-ups, parallel bar dips,
and a softball throw. In 1942, Dale Hall, an outstanding running back at
West Point and an All-American basketball player, had broken the record
when he scored 865 out of a possible 1,000 points. A year later, Davis

demonstrated his remarkable athletic versatility when he smashed Hall's mark by scoring 962½ points. None of his football teammates during that first year, or thereafter, ever came close to topping Davis' record mark.

After Army had won only 1-of-9 football games in 1940, Blaik turned the team's fortunes around, as he had at Dartmouth, when his first Cadets team went 5–3–1 in 1941. In 1942, the Cadets went 6–3, though they were again shut out by Notre Dame and losing to Navy for the fourth time in a row. By then, the freshman rule that restricted first-year college players, including those at West Point and at Annapolis, to playing on freshman teams, had been suspended, and at Army plebes such as quarterbacks Doug Kenna, who had played one season at Mississippi, and Tom Lombardo, halfback Dale Hall, and linemen Ed "Rafe" Rafalko, Joe Stanowicz, and Bob St. Onge found their way into the starting lineup.

Because of the war, cadets enrolled in the fall of 1942 would graduate in 1945 rather than 1946. Before the 1942 season began, Blaik was promoted to colonel, a quantum leap from his rank as a second lieutenant when he resigned from the army in 1922. After receiving his promotion in February, Blaik requested active duty in the Pacific, preferably under General MacArthur with whom he had remained close since his graduation from West Point. However, both the new superintendent, Major General Francis Wilby, and Wilby's predecessor, General Robert Eichelberger, who had been instrumental in luring Blaik to West Point as Army's head coach, convinced Blaik that he was needed at the military academy. "Keep driving ahead on your job for it's a top-flight project in our war effort," Eichelberger wrote to Blaik, "and don't let anyone tell you anything else." At that point, Blaik realized he had to resign himself to remaining at West Point as the head football coach and that the chances of him being placed on active duty in a war zone were out of the question. Even ardent Army football fan Douglas MacArthur, no doubt would have agreed.

★ ★ ★

Apart from Davis and a dozen newcomers, most of whom had been recruited from other schools, the most significant addition in 1943 was Herman Hickman, who was hired away from North Carolina State, where he had been an assistant coach, as much for recruiting purposes as to be the head line coach. Blaik knew that Hickman, a Tennessean who had previously coached at West Forest, was aware of college football talent in the South as well as anyone, and it was hoped that he could induce some top-tier players to attend West Point. The former All-American guard did not disappoint. A self-deprecating raconteur whose ample build bespoke of his prodigious appetite, Hickman was a polished and popular after-dinner speaker who delighted in quoting Rudyard Kipling, William Shakespeare, Edgar Lee Masters, and other legendary writers and poets.

During their first meeting at the Vanderbilt Hotel in Manhattan during the summer of 1943, Hickman delighted Blaik with his seriousness about coaching, his love of literature and poetry, and his homespun humor. "Colonel, I have three loves: my wife, football, and my belly," he said to Blaik, "and I don't rightfully know which I love the most." Even the disciplined Blaik, whose life revolved around his wife and two sons and football, had to smile on hearing that. From the time Hickman was hired in the spring of 1943 until the beginning of the football season that year, the Poet Laureate of the Smokies, as Hickman was sometimes called, had recruited a half dozen outstanding players from Southern schools. "I love to hear those Southern voices," he often said after luring players from Southern schools.

But for a while it looked as if Davis and Hickman's recruits, unless they changed their minds, would not be playing football at West Point in 1943. In November, General George C. Marshall, the army chief of staff and later the architect of the Marshall Plan, wrote a letter to West Point superintendent Wilby, saying that while college football had a morale value, it was not essential during the war and directed that Army cancel its 1943 football schedule. For whatever reason, Marshall never mailed the letter, but both he and secretary of war Henry Stimson favored canceling football at West Point in 1943. Also, by the end of the 1942 season, the minimum draft age was lowered in November from 21 to 18, meaning that most college football players would now be eligible for conscription into the armed forces.

Making matters more difficult for college football programs, in February 1943 the War Department announced that college students in its Specialized Training Program for prospective army officers would not be eligible to play varsity football. That ruling, coupled with the drafting of thousands of college-age students, prompted more than 100 football-playing schools, including Stanford, Auburn, Baylor, and Michigan State, to suspend varsity football in 1943. That, no doubt, was good news to former heavyweight champion Gene Tunney, who had been named head of the navy's physical fitness program during the war. "Football has no place in war or training for war," said Tunney who had served with the Marines in World War I before upsetting Jack Dempsey in 1926 to win the heavyweight title. "It has to be done the hard way with special calisthenics and road work to build stamina, and bayonet drill and handling of weapons to develop a warrior psychology."

In spite of Tunney's comments, the navy cruised to the rescue of about 100 varsity sports programs by starting V-12 and V-5 programs for prospective officers, many of them varsity football players who were sent to campuses where the program was offered and where, unlike students in the army's Specialized Training Program, they were eligible to take part in varsity sports, which gave many of those schools a huge competitive edge during the first two years of the war. A classic example was at Northwestern whose V-12 program in 1943 included eight starting players from Minnesota's 1942 team. By chance, the two schools met that year in a Big Ten game in which the loaded Wildcats crushed the Golden Gophers 42–6.

By the time Davis began preseason practice in early September 1943, another dozen or so transfers from other colleges had been lured to West Point, and in almost every instance not because they were bent on becoming career army officers, but because they realized that it would be a haven from the military draft or, if they eventually graduated and had to serve in the army, it would be as officers and not enlisted men. For one thing, Red Blaik had amassed a staff of assistants, most of whom, including Herman Hickman, eventually would become head coaches at top-tier football schools. Secondly, on the basis of Army's strong 1942 season, Army was definitely on the rise as a football power. Third, and perhaps most important, West Point was a haven where student-athletes, like those in the army and navy college-based programs for eventual officers, were exempt from the draft so long as they remained in good academic standing.

By early 1943, the tide in the war had shifted to where the Allies, in such dire straits a year earlier, had gained the upper hand both in Europe and in the Pacific. After more than two years of fighting that had taken several million lives, Russia finally repulsed German forces in the battle for Stalingrad while American and British forces invaded Sicily, forcing Italy to surrender during the summer. In the Pacific, following six months of fierce ground fighting that had claimed more than 10,000 American lives, the United States could finally claim victory in the battle for the Solomon Islands in the southwestern Pacific, while U.S. forces continued to make successful landings on Japanese-held islands despite heavy death tolls. By April, the Selective Service System was calling up around 400,000 men a month, and food rationing had been extended to cover meats, coffee, sugar, shoes, and some other apparel, including nylon stockings.

Army started the 1943 season with a strong nucleus that included Lombardo, Kenna, and Hall, along with most members of the previous year's line, led by eventual All-American center Casimir Myslinski, who had started out as a quarterback at West Point. Supplementing those letter-winners was an influx that included backs Max Minor, who had already played at Texas and Tulsa; Dick Walterhouse, also an outstanding placekicker, who had spent one year at Michigan; Bob Chabot and Johnny Sauer; and linemen and future All-Americans Jack Green, who had played at Tulane, Frank Merritt, and Al Nemetz, who had played one season at Wake Forest; tackle Bob Wayne, also from Wake Forest; and guard and occasional running back Roland Catarinella, who had played one season at Pittsburgh; and Bill Webb. Among the returning backs was Robert Woods from America's glass capital of Corning in upstate New York, who had scored three touchdowns against Princeton at Yankee Stadium in 1942 after having played the year before for Navy but not lasting at Annapolis because of academic issues. That did not deter Red Blaik from recruiting the 22-year-old Woods on the pre-condition that the former Midshipman pass the entrance examination, which he did, making him the rarest of recruits, who played on a different side in two Army-Navy games, and consecutive ones at that, and who, while at West Point, also served during the 1944–45 academic year as the First Captain of the United States Corps of Cadets, the highest leadership post for a cadet at West Point.

In such an experienced and older group, Davis was a novelty, a player right out of high school. Even members of the squad who had not first played elsewhere had spent at least a year at West Point Prep or at another preparatory school. (The current one on the Academy grounds did not exist at the time.) Thus it was not surprising that Kenna pinned the nickname of Junior on the 18-year-old Davis, whom neither Kenna nor the rest of the players, who were mostly from the

South, knew anything about. But they would find out a lot about him soon, very soon.

Though the 1943 team was loaded with veterans, it was relatively light, with only four of the 40 members of the squad weighing at least 200 lbs., two of them starting tackles, Frank Merritt and eventual All-American Joe Stanowicz, who both weighed 215 lbs., which made them the heaviest players on the team. That was hardly a problem, Blaik felt, knowing that the T formation favored quick and relatively light linemen rather than behemoths not inclined to move as well. Even by 1943 standards, the backfield was also light, averaging about 175 lbs. None of the dozen backs weighed more than 185 lbs., and that was Lombardo, the senior quarterback. Still, with a plethora of veteran— and good—running backs, Blaik felt that it was extremely unlikely that even a wunderkind halfback from a California high school with 350 students was going to play much in 1943 even though during scrimmages he consistently bolted through the line or raced around end for long gains, displayed a very good passing touch, and showed excellent moves and hands as a pass receiver. Moreover, Blaik saw that Davis was equally effective on defense, lining up at left halfback, and blanketing would-be receivers repeatedly, and constantly intercepting passes. Still, with so many veteran backs on the squad, Blaik did not expect to use Davis that often during his plebe year. However, his plans changed after Kenna tore ligaments in his right knee during a preseason scrimmage. With Lombardo taking over at quarterback, Blaik then inserted Davis into the starting lineup at fullback, a position he had never played in high school, which, given his obvious skills as a runner, did not phase Blaik at all.

In its opening game, Army faced a Villanova team that was strengthened by more than a dozen navy V-12 players who had already played at other colleges, but they never had a chance against the Cadets. In addition to breaking loose for several long gains, Davis scored Army's, and his, first touchdown on a five-yard sweep around end after taking a pitch-out from Lombardo en route to a 27–0 Army victory at Michie Stadium before a small crowd of about 10,000—about a quarter of the spectators were cadets—in the picturesque stadium that at the time had a capacity of around 16,000 seats. Apparently the word hadn't got around that the 1943 Army team included a legend in the making. (The stadium was named for Dennis Michie, who organized and coached the first-ever football team at West Point while a cadet in 1890, and it was expanded in 1969 so that it could hold slightly more than 40,000 spectators.)

If Davis was nervous before or during his first college game, neither his teammates nor his coaches could discern it, but then his calm demeanor would become a hallmark of Davis' persona throughout his football career at West Point. In his account of the game for *The New York Times*, sportswriter Lou Effrat wrote, "In filling in for the ailing Edgar Kenna [Doug Kenna's actual first name], Davis, a product of Hollywood, California, ran wild and proved himself quite a shifty young man." Effrat may have been wrong about Davis' hometown, but he was right about his inaugural performance for Army. However, Army's impressive victory and Davis' scintillating debut were overshadowed in the New York Sunday papers by a New York Yankees 2–1 win over the Detroit Tigers that gave the Yankees their third straight American League pennant and seventh pennant in the last eight years even though they had lost regulars Joe DiMaggio, Tommy Henrich, Phil Rizzuto, Red Rolfe, and Buddy Hassett, along with pitcher Red Ruffing, to the military since the 1942 season.

Overshadowed by the Yankees' pennant-clinching win were front-page stories about Russian forces continuing to push back German troops from the Russian front in suburbs of Kiev, the country's third largest city after the Germans had previously been driven out of Stalingrad, and American and British forces on the verge of a breaking through German defenses near Salerno three weeks after Italy had surrendered to the Allies. To get their minds off the war, New Yorkers could see long-standing shows like *Tobacco Road*, in its eighth year on Broadway in 1943; *Arsenic and Old Lace*, *Oklahoma*, Helen Hayes in *Harriet*, and Ethel Merman in *Something for the Boys*. If you chose to go to a movie, you could catch Jimmy Cagney, fresh off making *Yankee Doodle Dandy*, or in *Johnny Come Lately* at the Capitol Theater on Broadway along with Morton Gould and his Orchestra, teenage actress Virginia O'Brien, and Henny Youngman on stage, all for less than a dollar. Other movies included *So Proudly We Hail* at Radio City Music Hall with Claudette Colbert, Paulette Goddard, and Virginia Lake, plus a stage show featuring the famed Rockettes, and the quintessential World War II musical, *This Is the Army*, with George Murphy, Ronald Reagan, Joan Leslie, and Irving Berlin, who wrote the classic score that included "Oh How I Hate to Get Up in the Morning" and the show's signature song, "This Is the Army."

By 1943, rationing had increased to the point where Americans had to apply to local rationing boards to buy a kitchen stove. Under the nationwide rationing program, most drivers could only buy three gallons of gasoline a week, just enough for a short Sunday drive, although you weren't supposed to drive for pleasure. Among the other items rationed were fuel oil, meats, sugar, butter, cheese, coffee, most canned vegetables and all canned fish, soups, fruit juices, prunes, raisins, peas, dried beans, shoes, and tires, which were almost impossible to get, along with some types of clothing apparel. Few people complained, though, since the U.S. mainland, unlike England and France, had not come under attack or been invaded, apart from the abortive landing of German saboteurs off Long Island and the east coast of Florida in June 1942. If you couldn't get coffee, the government advised Americans to drink Ovaltine Postum, or a beverage made of okra, a somewhat esoteric green vegetable that contained dietary fiber and was good for the skin but, without caffeine, was hardly a good substitute for coffee. Cadets at West Point need not have worried, though, since the military academy was exempt from food rationing and so the cadets were guaranteed to have coffee in the morning if they so desired along with some food items that were hard to come by in civilian life.

* * *

Army's triumph over Villanova marked the first time that the Cadets had used the T formation, wherein the quarterback lines up behind the center with one hand on his posterior, while the fullback is about five yards directly behind the quarterback, and the halfbacks are around four and a half yards back of the tackles. In the formation, which approximates a T, the quarterback either hands off to or pitches out to a halfback or the fullback, or he runs or passes. By contrast, in the long conventional single-wing formation, the halfbacks and fullback line up about five yards behind the center, with the quarterback a few yards back on either side of the center. In the single-wing, the left halfback, who is called the tailback, is generally the best runner and passer, and he is quite often the most efficient punter, who at times surprises the defense with a so-called "quick kick" on third down. Famed tailbacks of the past had included such great runners as Red Grange, George Gipp, and Tom Harmon, while other backs who had thrived on the single-wing included the great passer Sammy Baugh, Bronko Nagurski, and Nile Kinnick, a Phi Beta Kappa student at Iowa, who, while a navy pilot, was killed while making an emergency landing in 1943 during World War II.

Where the quarterback is the central figure in the T formation, he is usually used primarily as a blocker in the single-wing, although he is sometimes used as a passer. Essentially a conservative coach—apart from using Bill Carpenter as a "lonely end" who never went into a huddle during Blaik's last year at West Point in 1958—Blaik had no intention of adopting the T after the innovative Clark Shaughnessy had introduced it during his first year at Stanford after having used it with an inept team at the University of Chicago until the school dropped football following the 1939 season. With most of the same personnel, Stanford, which had won only 1-of-8 games in 1939, proceeded to go unbeaten with its new formation in 1940, under the deft guidance of left-handed quarterback Frankie Albert, and then beat Nebraska in the Rose Bowl.

Further bolstering the appeal of the T formation, only three weeks before the Rose Bowl game on New Year's Day, the Chicago Bears, with Hall of Famer Sid Luckman at quarterback, crushed the Washington Redskins 73-0 in the National Football League championship game in Washington, D.C. No less than Clark Shaughnessy had been brought in by the Bears' coach and owner George Halas to teach the T formation to Luckman and the rest of the Monsters of the Midway, as the Bears were known. Soon, a number of college and other NFL teams switched to the more complex but more wide-open T, including Notre Dame, which used it to beat Army in 1942. By the mid-1950s most college and high school teams had adopted the T. As for the peripatetic, and much in demand, Shaughnessy, in 1943 he had moved on to Pittsburgh to introduce the T, which did not help the Panthers in their opening game when they were routed by Notre Dame 41-0.

In preparing for the 1943 Notre Dame game, Blaik had his "scout" team emulate the Irish by using the T formation against Army's starters and was startled by how well the formation worked against the confused Cadets starting team. Indeed, those scrimmages, followed by a 13-0 Notre Dame victory, convinced Blaik to switch to the T formation in 1943. Actually, the formation had been around for years but was never used to any great effect by a well-known college or NFL team until Shaughnessy, one of football's most innovative coaches, refined it while at the University of Chicago, where it made no difference, and then at Stanford and with the Chicago Bears where it made all the difference in the world. A prerequisite to its success, however, is a good passing quarterback, and in 1943 Red Blaik had three of them—veterans Tom Lombardo and Doug Kenna, both bright and quick learners, and Glenn Davis who had run and passed out of the T formation at Bonita Union High School.

Actually, the T formation had been used on and off for many years but was usually abandoned because of its complexity. Like so much in football, Walter Camp, the coach at Yale from 1882 to 1892, and the so-called "Father of American Football," had invented the "line of scrimmage," devised a specific number of downs, and a seven-man line and four-man backfield, is said by some football historians to have employed the T formation for a while at Yale while football was still in its infancy. Once, asked where or how he had come up with the famous box formation he used, Notre Dame's iconic coach Knute Rockne said, "I got it from where everything else in football came from—Yale and Walter Camp." Rockne, though, never employed the T, probably feeling that he didn't need it with backs like George Gipp, Elmer Layden, Jim Crowley, Don Miller, and Marchy Schwartz.

In Army's next two games, both at Michie Stadium, the Cadets routed Colgate 42–0, despite nine fumbles, and Temple 51–0, with Davis scoring touchdowns on runs of 47 and 38 yards against Colgate, and from 11 yards out in the victory over Temple, while also throwing a touchdown pass in the Colgate game. In that game, Davis completed all four passes he threw for 69 total yards, caught two passes for 22 yards, and gained 147 yards on 11 carries, an average of a staggering 13 yards per carry, which was inflated by Davis' long runs. "No Army team in years, if ever, has struck with such lightning fury as did Lieutenant Colonel Earl Blaik's Cadets in one of the worst defeats suffered by an Andy Kerr [the Colgate coach] 11," Allison Danzig wrote in *The New York Times*.

After Army had run up an insurmountable lead against Temple at Michie Stadium, Blaik instructed his team not to score again, not to pass, and to punt on third, instead of fourth, down. That created a ticklish, and even laughable, situation in the third quarter when Army substitute guard Charles Sampson intercepted a pass and raced toward the Temple goal line with no one in front of him. Suddenly aware of Blaik's dictum that Army was not to score, Sampson stopped and put down the ball at the 1-yard line. "The concession to my order was an unintentional insult to Temple," Blaik said, "far worse than if he had actually scored, yet Sampson looked over toward me with a self-satisfied smile, as if to say, 'Mission accomplished, sir.'" On the ensuing play Blaik decided to go for a field goal rather than a touchdown and picked Sampson, who Blaik said that to his knowledge had never kicked a three-pointer. "Much to the surprise of the team, myself, and himself, Charlie kicked the field goal," Blaik said. "After the game, I hastened to assure Temple's coach, my old friend Ray Morrison, that Sampson's performance was no preconceived coaching gem but an abortive attempt to exemplify West Point discipline."

Davis' performances in Army's first three games turned out to be mere appetizers to his accomplishments in Army's first road game of the season against Columbia at Baker Field in New York, when he scored three touchdowns on dazzling runs of 82, 46, and 12 yards as the Cadets crushed the Lions 52–0 before a press corps that included the country's best-known sportswriter, Grantland Rice. By now, sportswriters, coaches, and fans throughout the United States had become aware of the teenage halfback from Southern California, who because of his speed and uncanny body control, was virtually impossible to tackle once he got past the line of scrimmage.

In writing about Davis' performance against Columbia in *The New York Times*, columnist Arthur Daley said, "Davis is so terrific that the opinion in this corner is that he could move into the Chicago Bear backfield and immediately operate with the explosive efficiency of a George McAfee," a star halfback for the Bears. By now, too, Red Blaik knew that Davis was already Army's best runner and that there was no way he could keep the talented plebe out of the starting lineup. As for Davis, despite his instant success on the football field, he knew his future as a player was not assured given his struggles with geometry and algebra. Cadets were tested on their five courses every week, and a failing grade could make a student ineligible for varsity sports. Davis knew that he had no aptitude for mathematics and that a course in trigonometry was scheduled during the fall semester.

As intense and serious as Davis was about football, he was doubly so about his class work, which, for him, was far more of a challenge and far more worrisome than an upcoming football game. Although it was only October, Davis already had serious concerns as to whether he would survive the fall semester that ended in December. Flunking a course, Davis knew, would make him "founded deficient," a West Point term that meant expulsion from the military academy for failing a course. Unlike the policies at many big-time football schools, athletes received no preferential treatment at West Point and were hardly held in awe by their fellow cadets. At many of those other schools, Glenn Davis, in light of his emerging stardom, would be a very big man on campus, but at West Point he was just a struggling cadet, trying to pass several very hard math courses with next to no aptitude for such subjects.

Though Army was unbeaten, it had committed a dozen fumbles in the first four games, stemming from the team's unfamiliarity with the T formation, which requires so many more quick exchanges of the football. In addition to changing the way the backfield operated and far quicker ball handling, the formation required linemen to revise their blocking patterns. With the new, wide-open offensive system, offensive linemen had to shift from the double blocking system primarily used under the single-wing to brush and trap blocking, which often required a tackle or guard to brush-block both a defensive end and a linebacker on the same play.

Through four games, Army had scored 172 points, an average of 43 points a game, was un-scored on, and was ranked second in the country behind Notre Dame, the eventual national champion. Next up was Yale, which had taken in several thousand army, navy, and Marine personnel, all studying to become officers and, except for the soldiers, eligible to play varsity sports. Indeed, the military dominated on the Yale campus, occupying two of the six dormitories and most of the classrooms. "There were only a handful of regular students since most of them had been drafted," Judith Schiff, a Yale spokeswoman, said in 2013. "By the end of the war, around 20,000 military personnel, including a number of WACS [Women's Army Corps], had studied at Yale." It was almost as if Yale had been leased to the government.

As a result of the military influx, the 1943 Eli football team was stronger than it had been in years, with a 40-man squad dominated by servicemen, almost all of whom had already played at other colleges, and with only six lettermen back from 1942. Indeed, the military presence was so strong at Yale that, for a while, the campus even included the 50-piece 418th Army Forces Band formed by Glenn Miller, who had joined the army at the age of 38, three years beyond the maximum draft age. All of the musicians in the band, which was based at Yale from May 1943 to June 1944, were recruited by Miller, including a few who had played in his orchestra and many who had played for other well-known big-band orchestras. Not surprisingly, the orchestra had the famed Glenn Miller sound, even when it played marches, and in addition to playing at enlisted men's dances at Yale, also performed throughout Connecticut and on a nationwide radio broadcast every Saturday. At Miller's request, the band was sent to Europe to play for American troops in the summer of 1944. A year later, Miller died at the age of 40 when a single-engine Air Corps plane he was aboard disappeared in bad weather and crashed on a flight from London to Paris.

The 1943 game marked the 19th time in a row that Army had played the Elis at the Yale Bowl, which was highly unusual since the Cadets had always played most of their games at home. The setting was somewhat special since, apart from the annual Navy game, Army had played its first "away" game at the Bowl in 1921. Before that, since its first football game in 1891, Army had played every one of its games at West Point except for the Navy games, most of which had been played on a neutral site, Franklin Field on the University of Pennsylvania campus, along with five games at the Polo Grounds in New York. Prior to the 1921 contest, Yale had played all 12 of its previous games against the Cadets at West Point. But that changed when General Douglas MacArthur, a onetime Army outfielder on the baseball team, became the superintendent and realized that such a one-sided scheduling system dissuaded other schools from playing Army. Following the resumption of the series in the 1921 game after an eight-year break in the rivalry, Army, apparently trying to re-pay Yale for all of those trips to West Point, visited the Yale Bowl 15 years in a row.

Opened in 1914, the Yale Bowl was the first stadium in the country shaped like a bowl with most of the structure below ground. Built about two miles from the Yale campus in downtown New Haven, it was also a precursor and model for similar bowl-shaped stadiums such as Los Angeles Memorial Stadium, the Rose Bowl, and the University of Michigan stadium. With a capacity of almost 71,000, it was also the largest college-owned football stadium in the country. Although he had not played there while he was a Cadet, Red Blaik certainly had some vivid memories of the Bowl. The worst one was from October 1931 while Blaik was an assistant coach at Army. With the score tied at 6–6 in the last quarter, Yale's Bob Lassiter took the kick off and was tackled head-on by 150-lb. Army end Dick Sheridan, who had scored the Cadets' touchdown on a fumble recovery in the Yale end zone. During the tackle, Lassiter's knee hit Sheridan in the back of the head, resulting in two skull fractures. The game continued after Sheridan was taken to a New Haven hospital, where he died two days later. Sheridan was one of seven college football players who died of game-related injuries in 1931. Coupled with 15 other football deaths, Sheridan's brought the total to 22, making 1931 the deadliest year yet in football. Those deaths and a number of serious injuries that season led to many rules changes, including the outlawing of the flying block and tackle and the flying wedge on kickoffs.

★ ★ ★

When the Army team arrived in New Haven in 1929, it was unbeaten through four games, the fourth of which was a 20–20 tie with Harvard. With All-American halfback Chris "Red" Cagle and fullback Johnny Murrell scoring touchdowns on long runs, Army took a 13–0 halftime lead. But in the second half, a relatively unknown sophomore named Albie Booth was sent into the game by Coach Mal Stevens, prompting a roar from the crowd since Booth had been born and grew up in New Haven. Only 5'6" and weighing about 145 lbs., Booth was small, even by the standards of the 1920s. The hometown boy proceeded to electrify the crowd, scoring three touchdowns, one on a 75-yard punt return, as he ran 33 times for 223 yards, and drop-kicked all three extra points to lead underdog Yale to a stunning 21–13 victory. "If ever one man beat a team all by himself, Albie Booth did it that day," Blaik said.

Booth easily outplayed Cagle, one of Army's greatest running backs, so good by 1929 that a month before the Yale game, he had been on the cover of *Time* magazine. But then at the age of 24 Cagle had a plenitude of experience, including four years as an All-American halfback at Southwestern Louisiana where Cagle had captained the team as a senior and graduated with a degree in arts and sciences, and in 1929, in his fourth season with Army where he was also captain of the team.

Using a star player who had already graduated from another school and played four seasons of a sport did not dissuade Army from recruiting the player, especially when he was already an All-American. When Red Blaik enrolled at West Point in 1918, he had already graduated from Miami of Ohio, where he had played four years of football and baseball. Before Blaik and Cagle, Army had also recruited a number of other outstanding running backs while they were seniors in college. Among them was Elmer Oliphant, who had been an All-American in football and basketball at Purdue before arriving at West Point in 1915, where he again was an All-American halfback while earning varsity letters in basketball and baseball and also competing on Army's hockey, boxing, and swim teams.

Other players who continued to earn All-American honors at West Point after graduating from another school included Harry "Light Horse" Wilson, who led Penn State in scoring in 1922 and 1923 and then did the same at Army in 1925 and 1926 while being named an All-American again and winning 12 letters at West Point in football, basketball, and lacrosse, and Harvey Jablonsky, who had been an All-American lineman at Washington University in Saint Louis from which he graduated in 1929 then played three more years at West Point, where he was also an All-American, and, as at St. Louis, captain of the Cadets' team in 1933 before graduating in 1933 and eventually rising to major general during World War II. Much earlier, quarterback Charles Daly starred at Harvard before becoming an All-American at West Point in 1901 and 1902 and later coached the Cadets for eight years over two spans interrupted by World War I. All of those players wound up in the College Football Hall of Fame, although Blaik went in as a coach, not as a player.

Remarkably, there were no rules against someone playing as many as eight varsity seasons in a sport, and Army more than anyone else, took advantage of that loophole. Because it did, a number of schools refused to play the Cadets, including Navy, which declined to play Army in 1928 and 1929. Following the end of the 1927 season, which ended when Army beat Navy 14–9, Navy announced it would no longer use players who had played three football seasons elsewhere and that, henceforth, it would only play teams that adhered to that position. At the time, Navy had not beaten Army since 1922, with the Cadets winning four of the next six games and the other two games finishing in ties. In almost all of those games, Army had used players like Cagle and Wilson who had played at least three years of college football elsewhere before coming to West Point. The Army superintendent at the time, Major General Edwin Winans, rejected the Navy request, ending, albeit briefly, one of the biggest rivalries in sports.

Army finally adopted the three-year rule in 1938, on orders from President Franklin D. Roosevelt, a former assistant navy secretary with an affinity for Navy teams. Years later, Red Blaik said Army's tendency to accept players who had already played as many as four years of college football elsewhere was necessary in order to compete with major football schools like Notre Dame, Yale, and Harvard because, as a military institution, West Point had more difficultly recruiting football players. Navy, by contrast, Blaik said, usually had between 200 and 700 more students. Of course, the necessary military commitment following graduation also made recruiting more difficult, although Navy faced the same problem.

★   ★   ★

After savoring the sight of the huge stadium during pregame practice before a crowd of 33,000, the largest of the season at the Bowl, the 1943 Army team wasted no time in demonstrating its dominance over the Eli, strengthened as Yale was by the aspiring navy and Marine officers on its squad. After Army had taken a 26–0 halftime lead, Yale managed to score a touchdown in the third quarter, the first one against the Cadets during the 1943 season, but Army tacked on another 13 points to win 39–7. On the three-hour bus ride home, while most of his teammates exulted over their fifth straight victory, Glenn Davis sat in the back of the team bus, studying for his next math exam. By then Davis knew that, try as he might to fathom the material, he was failing both his solid analytical geometry and spherical trigonometry courses, and that he might not last out the season. Cadets received grades every week for the previous week's work, and every week it was the same for Davis: he was flunking math. "It wasn't easy for me academically," Davis said years later. "I had one hell of a time. I was competing with guys who had already graduated from college. Others had two or three years of college. Going in there from a little old school of 350 kids and 18 years old, and I had never studied hard in my life because it wasn't that difficult, so I wasn't really prepared for that type of shock. I had to work my tail off."

Joe Steffy, an All-American guard and teammate of Davis in 1945 and 1946, understood Davis' academic plight. "Practically everybody at the time went to prep school or college before they went to West Point," said Steffy, who had gone to a prep school and then spent a year at Tennessee before being recruited by Herman Hickman. "They did not go from high school to West Point. The academic preparation was just too great."

Losing Davis, Red Blaik knew, would be a serious blow to the Cadets, but there was nothing he could do to keep the California teenager eligible. And he was well aware that while Davis could not be expelled until the end of the fall semester, he could be suspended from the football team if his grades continued to remain poor. Though Army had gone through the first half of its season unbeaten, Blaik felt that, with or without Davis, an unbeaten season was extremely unlikely given that games with three nationally ranked teams—Pennsylvania, Notre Dame, and Navy—lie ahead. But with Doug Kenna, Blaik's best runner coming into the season sidelined with an injury, Davis was now the best and chances of winning any of those games without Davis would be slim and probably even none.

Next to his brother, Ralph, probably no one knew Davis better during the fall semester than his roommate, Dick Walterhouse, who had the advantage of a year at Michigan in his hometown of Ann Arbor before coming to West Point. While most transfers said the academic rigors at West Point were much harder than at their previous schools, Walterhouse said that with him, the opposite was true. "I found it harder academically at Michigan," said Walterhouse, who had played halfback on the freshman team at Michigan in 1942. "Glenn was always worrying about his math, and he studied very hard," Walterhouse said. "And as a roommate, he was a great guy. Everybody liked Glenn."

Like all cadets at the time, Davis and Walterhouse roomed together because of their similar height; Davis was 5'9" and Walterhouse was an inch taller. At West Point, where there were around 2,500 cadets in the early 1940s, cadets were matched according to height. "The tallest cadets, over 6', would be in A company. Then those from about 5'10" to 6' would be in B company, and those at 5'10" and under would be in C company and were called runts," Robert Woods, the 6-footer who had first played for Navy, recalled in 2013. As to why the cadets were matched by height, Woods said, "I think it was because of the matching formations, where you'd want men the same height together." That system changed in 1957 after which cadets were no longer assigned to barracks based on their height.

Davis' relatively short stature certainly wasn't a factor during Army's first five games, not when he could run 100 yards in as fast as 9.7 seconds, as he was to do on the Army track team, establishing himself as one of the fastest athletes ever to attend West Point. But in Army's sixth game—against sixth-ranked Pennsylvania before a crowd of about 70,000 at Franklin Field on the Penn campus—Davis was slowed by a muddy field and never gained any substantial yardage. Further, a fumble by Davis, still playing fullback, deep in Army territory set up Penn's first touchdown, but the Cadets still led 7-6 at halftime and 13-6 at the end of the third quarter. Late in the fourth period, Penn back Bob Odell, the brother of Yale coach Howard Odell, out-jumped two defenders to make a dazzling catch at the Army 45-yard line and then sprinted into the end zone for the second Quaker touchdown. Penn converted the extra point, and the game ended in a 13–13 tie. It was far and away the least impressive game yet for Glenn Davis.

An even bigger task lay ahead on November 6 when top-ranked and unbeaten Notre Dame was to meet second-ranked and also undefeated Army. Frank Leahy, the Notre Dame coach, had replaced the traditional Notre Dame box formation in 1943 with the T formation, prompting Red Blaik to prepare for the Irish by having his reserve players employ the T in a scrimmage against the starting team during the week leading up to the game. The result turned out to be a revelation to Blaik since the reserves, despite their unfamiliarity with the T, consistently made significant gains against the varsity starters. "After practice, I remarked to my assistants, 'If our plebes, with that little experience, can make the T go that way, what would an experienced varsity do with it?'" Blaik knew it was too late in the season to switch to the T, but in view of what he saw during the scrimmage, pretty much decided that week to adopt the T formation the following season.

★ ★ ★

The Army–Notre Dame game would seem to have paled in significance that year to the war and the thousands of Americans fighting in Europe and the Pacific. If anything, though, the U.S. military progress abroad had lifted the spirits of millions of Americans, including, no doubt, most of those in a huge capacity crowd of almost 80,000 that turned out at Yankee Stadium for the annual game between the Fighting Irish and the Cadets. Though it was considered a home game for Army, thousands of New Yorkers, many of them Irish immigrants or at least of Irish descent, had adopted Notre Dame as their team, prompting sportswriters to refer to Notre Dame fans in the New York metropolitan area as Notre Dame "Subway Alumni," an appropriate term since most fans at the time traveled to the stadium by subway and usually both out-numbered and cheered louder for the Irish than Army supporters who usually included about 2,000 cadets.

If many of Army's opponents in 1943 were weakened by the draft-ing and enlistment of players, that was not the case with Notre Dame, which had most of its starters back from the previous season along with a strong contingent of Marines from other colleges who were among the almost 2,000 navy V-12 personnel that had been sent to Notre Dame for training. Missing, though, was the team's best offensive player, All-American quarterback Angelo Bertelli, who along with about 100 other Marine trainees had been called to active duty because of the des-perate need for more Marines in the Pacific, where the United States was making significant progress but losing considerable lives during invasions in heretofore unknown islands such as Saipan and Okinawa. Runner-up to Heisman Trophy–winner Bruce Smith of Minnesota in 1941—and the eventual winner in 1943 even though he missed Notre Dame's last four games—Bertelli had completed 25-of-36 passes for 512 yards and 12 touchdowns in the six games he played in his war-in-terrupted year.

In Bertelli's place was 18-year-old Johnny Lujack, the youngest player on the team, who also would be called into service by the follow-ing season. Though Lujack had showed extraordinary promise in high school as a single-wing halfback in Connellsville, Pennsylvania, near Pittsburgh, he was not heavily recruited but did get an appointment to West Point by his congressman, J. Buell Snyder. "When I went to visit West Point when I was 17 and still in high school, Red Blaik, who had recruited me, never even met with me," Lujack recalled in August 2013. "Instead I met with the backfield coach, Gustafson [Andy Gustafson]. I checked out the campus but wasn't impressed, and when I heard of the four-year commitment after graduation, I definitely didn't want to go there."

In his autobiography, *You Have to Pay the Price*, Blaik wrote that Lujack planned to go to West Point but had been swayed from coming "by some persuasive emissaries from South Bend." To that, Lujack said in 2014, "That's a lot of crap. What happened was that a businessman in Connellsville who my father knew got in touch with Fritz Wilson, a recruiter for Notre Dame, who he knew, and Wilson arranged a try-out for me at Notre Dame in the spring of 1942. I guess I did all right because Frank Leahy, who watched me, offered me a scholarship."

Lujack, the first of a half-dozen Hall of Fame quarterbacks from western Pennsylvania, also played one season of basketball, baseball, and track at Notre Dame, winning letters in all four sports. "On one day in 1943, I got two singles and a triple in a baseball game and, in between innings, ran over to the nearby track field and won both the high jump and the javelin," Lujack said. Glenn Davis later was to compete successfully in the same two sports on the same day at West Point, albeit not in between innings.

"John was a great athlete in just about every sport, and in football he could have played almost anywhere—as a running back and as an end besides quarterback," said Terry Brennan, a halfback and teammate of Lujack's for three years who later coached the Irish for five seasons. "But Frank Leahy wouldn't let him play baseball and basketball or compete in track in his last two years. Once he became head coach, he wouldn't let any football player play any other sport. He was a selfish man, concerned only about his own team."

* * *

With three consensus All-Americans in the lineup—Bertelli, the fourth, was in training at Paris Island in South Carolina—Notre Dame was a slight favorite to beat an Army team that, like the Irish, had won all six of its games.

In the midst of U.S. involvement in World War II, New York in 1943, like many American cities, was a vastly different city than it had been in 1941 before Pearl Harbor on December 7. In Times Square, as in many parts of the city, one would see thousands of soldiers, sailors, Marines, Coast Guardsmen, and members of the Army Air Corps on leave or liberty, reveling in the still-prevalent pleasures on and around Broadway in particular. From time to time, the famed Great White Way would go dark during "dim-outs," tests that simulated conditions that were to prevail in the event of an enemy air attack, something that never happened in the United States during the war apart from a small unmolested Japanese plane that dropped propaganda leaflets on a remote section of Oregon in February 1942. During dim-out drills, Broadway theaters and most other businesses in the Times Square area, along with high-rise apartments and hotels, had to turn off, or in some cases, dim lights for approximately a half hour. During that time, air-raid wardens and police officers would scour Manhattan and New York's four other boroughs in search of violators who risked arrests and fines if they failed to turn off lights. Scores of factories in the city that had been converted to "defense plants," turning out everything from weaponry to shoes for GIs, operated around the clock, seven days a week, employing thousands of additional workers, many of whom had never worked on assembly lines or any type of manual labor in the past. Many were women who had been secretaries and housewives, as were the approximately 500 "Rosie the Riveters," wielding lathes, drills, and other heavy equipment at the Brooklyn Navy Yard, which in its 137-year existence had never before employed women for heavy-duty work on naval warships such as the battleships *Missouri* and *Iowa*, and the aircraft carrier

Franklin Delano Roosevelt. Elsewhere in the city, women could be seen where they had never been seen before, driving taxi cabs and trucks, working as ticket agents at airports and railroad stations, and even mixing drinks as bartenders.

★ ★ ★

Like the movies, Broadway shows, and other major sports events, big time college football games helped take the minds of defense plant workers and others engaged in the war effort on the home front off the war itself. And no sports event was bigger in 1943 than the Army-Notre Dame football game at the home of the New York Yankees, who in October had won another World Series even though they had lost Joe DiMaggio, Phil Rizzuto, and Tommy Henrich to the army, navy, and Coast Guard, respectively. At least half of the spectators, if not more, made their way to the 20-year-old stadium in the Bronx by subway, bus, and train at a time when few New Yorkers had cars and a subway ride cost a nickel (in early 2014 it cost $2.50).

The game was considered by most football experts to be a toss-up, although Notre Dame was a slight favorite in the betting. With three consensus All-Americans in the lineup—Bertelli, the fourth, was in training at Paris Island, South Carolina—the Irish came into the contest averaging 43.5 points per game, while having yielded only 31 points per game on defense. Army, which had given up only 20 points in six games, was averaging 37 points per game on offense and had two 1943 All-Americans in center and captain Casimir Myslinski and tackle Frank Merritt. However, most of the focus was on each team's 18-year-old star—Lujack and Glenn Davis. A remarkably poised Lujack won that showdown, running for one touchdown and passing for two others, while Davis fumbled away the football twice and threw an interception as Notre Dame crushed the Cadets 26–0. Army got inside the Irish 30-yard line three times but lost the ball on all three occasions on two fumbles and an interception while gaining only 150 yards on offense compared with 413 for Notre Dame. In a rivalry that had become totally one-sided, the outcome marked the fifth time in a row that Army had failed to score against Notre Dame and the 10th loss in the last 12 meetings for the Cadets who had not scored against the Irish since 1938 when Army lost 19–7.

Army would rebound to beat the Sampson Naval Station team 16–7 and routed Brown 59–0 on November 20, the same day that American Marines landed on Tarawa in the Marshall Islands in the Pacific, a stepping stone to the invasion of the Mariana Islands that the U.S. needed to establish air bases close enough to launch bombers for raids on Japan. During three days of fighting in one of the bloodiest battles of the war, more than 1,000 Marines were killed and almost 2,000 others were wounded before the Marines could secure the island. Fighting to the death, as they almost always did, more than 4,000 Japanese troops were killed during the fighting with only about 25 surrendering. The death toll during the three-day period came close to equaling the number of Americans killed during the wars in Iraq and Afghanistan, which together lasted almost 20 years.

★ ★ ★

Next up was Navy, to whom the Cadets had lost their last four games while scoring only six points. After having been played primarily in Philadelphia or New York (and once in Chicago, once at Princeton, and once in Baltimore) since 1899, the 1942 game was played at Annapolis because of war restrictions imposed by President Roosevelt with Navy prevailing 14–0 before a small crowd of about 15,000, including all 3,200 midshipmen—but no Army cadets—with about 300 of the midshipmen designated by Annapolis officials to cheer for Army, which not surprisingly, they frequently forgot to do. It also prompted Willard Mullin, the talented sports cartoonist for the *New York World-Telegram and Sun,* to do a drawing of a group of midshipmen singing "On, Brave Old Army Team," but with their fingers crossed.

In 1943, it was Army's turn to play host and to assign several hundred cadets to root for Navy while wearing non-regulation midshipmen-like white caps before a similar gathering of just less than 13,000 at Michie Stadium. In addition to cheering at least moderately for Navy, the cadets were also instructed to sing "Anchors Aweigh." Those turned out to be difficult orders to obey, since, for the second game in a row, Army failed to score as Navy, a decided underdog, beat the Cadets for the fifth time in a row 13–0. Glenn Davis again was held in check, with his mind more concerned about his difficulties with his mathematics courses than football. Indeed, before the Notre Dame game, Doug Kenna, who had returned for the last few games though he was still well below par, tried to boost Davis' spirits. Feeling that the teenage fullback was jittery about facing the Irish before the huge crowd, Kenna said to him, "Don't worry, Glenn. You're going to do fine." Whereupon, Davis replied, "It's not the game, Doug; it's the math test I took this week. I'm pretty sure I flunked it." Kenna found Davis' response ironic. "Here he was going to play the biggest game of his life up to then, and he was worrying about his math course. But that was Glenn, always worrying about how he was doing in his classes, especially in math."

Davis never blamed his below-par performances in Army's losses to Notre Dame and Navy on his academic problems, but it appeared to Kenna and some of his other teammates, along with Red Blaik, that those concerns may well have been a factor. However, years later Davis conceded that his lack of academic preparation in contrast to most of his older teammates probably affected his performance. "I was competing with some guys who had already graduated from college, while some others had already had two years of college elsewhere," he said. "Going in there from a little old school with 350 in La Verne at 18 years old. I'd never studied hard because it wasn't that difficult, so I wasn't prepared for that kind of shock. And the 1943 season wasn't a particularly fond memory for me because I was having trouble with my academics. So I never thought I played like I was capable of playing."

As it developed, Davis had good cause to be worried at the end of a season most college halfbacks would have been delighted to have had. By the end of the spring semester, Army's best running back had been "found deficient," West Point's term for flunking a course, and in effect expelled, at least temporarily. If Academy officials determined that a "deficient" cadet still had good potential and obvious leadership qualities, the cadet was given a second chance if he managed to improve his proficiency in a subject and then passed an examination relating to the course he had flunked. Davis, of course, had very good potential as a football player, if not as a mathematician, and that did not hurt his chances of being re-admitted to the Academy in the following fall after he had boned up elsewhere on geometry, algebra, and trigonometry, which Davis was determined to do near his Southern California home. Still, when Glenn and his twin brother, Ralph, returned home in June, only Ralph was assured of returning to West Point as a cadet in the late summer of 1944 while Glenn would not be eligible to return unless he passed another "validating" examination. If Davis couldn't make it back to West Point, given his very impressive start as a football player for Army, there would be a host of schools eager to lure him to their campuses to play, his mathematics deficiency notwithstanding. Davis knew that, of course, but he was determined to make it back to West Point.

2

★ ★ ★

"I Love Hearin' Those Southern Voices"

FTER BIDDING SOME OF HIS TEAMMATES AND OTHER FRIENDS at the Academy good-bye, Glenn Davis left West Point in March for the long train ride back to California not knowing whether he would ever return. His brother, Ralph, a junior varsity end and a shot-putter on the Army track team, fared well in all of his courses and was certain of returning. While staying at home with his parents in Claremont, Davis enrolled at the Webb School for Boys, a private prep school in Claremont, to bone up on geometry and trigonometry, subjects he would have to improve on if he were to be accepted back at the Academy for the fall semester in 1944.

On returning home, Glenn found himself a celebrity since the *Los Angeles Times* and other newspapers in Southern California had carried stories about his spectacular first season on the Army football team. Indeed, no high school football player from California had received so much publicity during a first season on the college level in memory. While glad to be back in La Verne with his family and high school friends, Davis, still shy despite all of the accolades heaped on him by sportswriters, disliked much of the adulation he received during his months at home and declined repeated invitations to appear at various sports banquets and other functions. Determined to keep in shape, Glenn played basketball with former teammates and other friends several times a week at Bonita Union High, and he threw passes to brother Ralph and a few former high school teammates on the field where he first attracted attention only a few years earlier.

Meanwhile, Red Blaik phoned Glenn several times during the late spring and early summer to see how he was doing, especially in his math classes. Blaik, of course, had a lot to lose if Davis did not make it back to West Point in the late summer of 1944. Davis, by then 19, had even more to lose because if he was not accepted as a "turnback," the term for a cadet re-entering West Point, he would be eligible for the military draft. Though the tide had turned and the U.S. was doing far better in both the Pacific and in Europe than it was in 1942 and 1943, the military still needed men, and as the war went on, more and more 18- and 19-year-olds were being drafted into the army and the navy, some right out of high school. Failure to make it back to West Point almost assuredly would result in Davis being conscripted and sent off to war, while another three years at West Point very likely would exempt him from the draft, assuming the war would end before he graduated in 1947. While Davis was waiting to see whether he would be accepted back, which was highly likely, more than 2,000 Americans had been killed and about 5,000 wounded during the D-Day invasion of France in early June 1944.

During the four-day train trip back to West Point, Glenn, in a constant state of anxiety about his pending re-entrance examination, spent much of the time poring over several math books he had brought along. En route to New York, the Davis twins had a chance encounter with legendary football coach Clark Shaughnessy, the architect of the modern-day version of the T formation and a longtime college coach who also helped inaugurate the T for the Chicago Bears team in 1940. Sitting across from Glenn and Ralph Davis on the train, Shaughnessy overheard the brothers talking about Army's football prospects during the coming fall and recalled having read and heard about Glenn Davis' exploits for Army in 1943. After introducing himself, Shaughnessy, then the head coach at Pittsburgh, the third team on the Army schedule in 1944, told the twins that Army was fortunate in gaining a new fullback in Felix "Doc" Blanchard. Having seen Blanchard play in prep school, Shaughnessy raved about every aspect of his game, and predicted that he would attain All-American status, possibly during his first year at West Point. "You'll be seeing him this fall," Shaughnessy said. "Remember the name, Felix Blanchard." Glenn, who had never heard of Blanchard, said they would. Shaughnessy also told the Davis twins that he had coached Blanchard's father, Felix Blanchard Sr., when he was a star fullback at Tulane in New Orleans shortly before World War I. "When he got mad," Shaughnessy once said, "old Doc Blanchard was one of the best players I ever saw."

Determined to have his son follow in his footsteps, the elder Blanchard had young Doc sleeping with a football in his crib when he was an infant and tossing a football back and forth with him when he was a toddler. Forsaking a professional football career for medical school, Blanchard's father became a medical doctor in South Carolina, where he and his wife raised "Little Doc," as Blanchard was called by his boyhood friends. Blanchard Sr. eventually enrolled Little Doc at his prep school alma mater, Saint Stanislaus in Bay St. Louis, Mississippi, where by his junior year young Blanchard, a solid 180 lbs., was attracting attention from a score of major football-playing schools, including Notre Dame and Army. Red Blaik said that he'd had his main assistant, Harry Ellinger, meet with Blanchard Sr. in 1941 when Little Doc was a senior but that the elder Blanchard was not interested in having his son attend West Point, something that eventually would change. Young

Doc chose North Carolina, both because it was relatively close to the family's South Carolina home and because Tar Heels coach Jim Tatum was a close cousin of the young Blanchard's mother.

At the time, first-year athletes usually had to play on freshman or junior varsity teams, while varsity players were only eligible to play for three years when Army adopted a three-year eligibility rule by order of President Franklin Roosevelt. Some skeptics felt that Roosevelt, a onetime undersecretary for the navy with an affinity for that branch of the U.S. military service, had issued that order to West Point because of Army's penchant for using star players, including a number of All-Americans, after they had already played three or four years of football elsewhere.

As a freshman at North Carolina, Blanchard was so good that he was able to run through the varsity's line during scrimmages and also fast enough to run around end. "Once he knocked out two varsity tacklers on the same play," R.A. White, the trainer for the freshmen team, recalled. "It got so bad that some of the boys wouldn't even try to tackle him." Another one who watched Blanchard in freshmen games and during scrimmages, Glenn Thistlethwaite, a former coach at Northwestern, Wisconsin, and Richmond, also raved about young Blanchard. "I've seen all the great fullbacks, including Nagurski, but this boy will be the greatest," Thistlethwaite said.

At the end of his freshman year, little Doc tried to enter the navy's V-12 program but was inexplicably rejected because of deficient eyesight, which neither Blanchard nor his parents could understand since he never had experienced any difficulty with his eyesight. A secondary reason for his rejection was that at around a muscular 210 lbs., Blanchard was deemed too heavy for V-12. Convinced he was going to be drafted, Blanchard, then 18, joined the army, underwent basic training in Miami Beach, and was assigned to the chemical warfare division at an Army Air Corps base in Clovis, New Mexico. By then,

Blanchard's father, apparently unhappy seeing his star football player attached to a chemical warfare unit, was doing his utmost to get Little Doc into West Point to the point of calling Red Blaik. To his delight, Blanchard Sr. found Blaik still interested in Little Doc and suggested that Blanchard try to get a congressional appointment for his highly regarded son. Blanchard Sr. wasted no time and contacted "Cotton Ed" Smith, a legendary conservative Democratic senator from South Carolina, who provided the necessary appointment. By then, Little Doc Blanchard had reconsidered his position about West Point and accepted the appointment to the military academy. That was great news to Red Blaik, who was well aware of Blanchard's achievements in prep schools and as a freshman at North Carolina. What made it even better news was when Blaik learned that Blanchard had been turned down for the V-12 program, meaning that Army would not have to face a Navy team with Blanchard at fullback.

As it would develop, Navy's loss most certainly would become a huge gain for Army, where both Blanchard's eyesight and weight were found acceptable. His weight would not have been acceptable at West Point up until 1938, however, when Army football players could not weigh more than 208 lbs.—and only if they were at least 6′4″—under a directive that had been issued by the U.S. Surgeon General in 1931. Players 6′ and shorter could weigh no more than 176 lbs. The surgeon general explained his rationale by saying that slender men tended to live longer. In 1941, Red Blaik's first year as head coach at Army, a new surgeon general in effect overruled the 1931 directive, permitting players to weigh as much as 228 lbs. so long as the higher weight was the result of a robust athletic build and not obesity. "This meant we could get in some candidates who looked like football players as well as officers," Blaik said. Had the earlier directive still have been in force, in addition to Blanchard, Barney Poole, Tex Coulter, and most of the other Army linemen on the 1944 team would not have been eligible to play for Army.

As was common at the time, Blanchard, along with some of Army's other football recruits in the fall of 1943, were sent to Lafayette College in Pennsylvania—some others, including Barney Poole, were sent to Cornell in upstate New York—to study for the "validating" examination at West Point in late summer of that year, schools that Blanchard and Poole may have found it difficult to get into without the help of Blaik and the military academy. However, while at Lafayette during the 1943–44 academic year, Blanchard did not play football, meaning that when he got to West Point he had not played the game in two years.

Blanchard was hardly the only player to have attended another school or to have already been in the military to enroll at West Point in 1944, although he was one of only a few who hadn't already played varsity football, and at 19 one of the youngest. Gregarious talkative, and mature beyond his years, Blanchard, like many of the other new players, did not take kindly to West Point's infamous "Beast Barracks," which he and most of the other newcomers found degrading, demeaning, and sophomoric, but he still managed to abide by the hazing rituals during their first six weeks at the Academy in the summer of 1944. Sadly, a few weeks before his arrival at West Point, Blanchard's father, with whom he was very close and whom he idolized, passed away at the family's home in South Carolina.

As for his initial resistance to West Point, Blanchard was to say some years later, "Some people contacted me when I was in high school, but I'd already been down in Mississippi [in prep school], which is a long way from South Carolina, for four years. So when they started talking to me about going to West Point and told me a little bit about the place, I wasn't very interested because I wanted to be closer to home."

As it would develop, Blanchard was the prize recruit, followed by two other unlikely West Pointers from the South, end Barney Poole and tackle Dewitt "Tex" Coulter, along with quarterback Young (his actual first name) Arnold Tucker. "I love hearin' those Southern voices,"

Herman Hickman, who persuaded Poole and a number of other players from Southern schools to pursue at least brief military careers, was wont to say during the next two seasons. While still attending Lafayette, Blanchard visited West Point for the first time in the spring of 1944 to meet with Red Blaik and to tour the campus. While they were watching a spring practice session, Blaik asked Blanchard what he thought of the team. Not one to mince words, Blanchard both startled and amused the coach. "They don't look so hot to me, Colonel," Blanchard replied while referring to the coach's rank which he had been given during his second year as head coach. Blanchard's frankness also would be manifested another time when, during a team meeting, Blaik asked his players if any of them drank. The only hand that went up belonged to Blanchard. "I do, Coach," Blanchard said with a smile as the rest of his teammates let out a collective laugh. Even the normally stoic Blaik had to smile on both of those occasions.

Blaik and Blanchard's teammates soon became aware of the remarkable athleticism he displayed for a 210-lb. running back, which was relatively big for the time. During that visit, Johnny Sauer, an Army halfback, recalled seeing Blanchard at a pond that served as the Academy beach. "I was watching him from the sand beach, and he got up on a 30′ steel tower and did the most beautiful two-and-a-half pike I ever saw in my life," said Sauer, who at 5′7″ and 170 lbs. was the smallest man on the 1944 and 1945 teams. "And when they told me that big horse played football, I said, 'Hey, we got something here.'"

From the outset, Blanchard's teammates were amazed at how a player who was built like many linemen at the time could be so fast. "This is hard to believe, but Blanchard ran the first 60 yards [of the 100-yard dash] ahead of Glenn [Davis] or myself," said Thomas "Shorty" McWilliams, a starting Army halfback in 1945 who like Davis was also a sprinter on the Cadets track team. "For the first 60 yards he was a step or two faster than we were, but then we would pass him and beat him.

But for the first 60 yards he exploded out of the block like Buddy Young [a 5′4″ All-American halfback in the mid-1940s who later played with the New York Yankees of the All-America Football Conference, and the New York Yanks, Baltimore Colts, and Dallas Texans of the NFL]." As a sprinter on the indoor and outdoor track teams, Blanchard finished first in both the 60-yard and 100-yard dashes in a number of meets, along with starring in the shot put with the outdoor team in the spring.

Marveling at how fast Blanchard could run despite his size, McWilliams said, "You can't believe the size of his legs. I know his thighs were better than 28″, and he'd have to split his uniform pants to get them over his legs because they were so big." To Red Blaik, "Blanchard was the best-built athlete I ever saw, 6′ and 208 lbs. at his peak, not a suspicion of fat on him with a slim waist, Atlas shoulders, colossal legs. For a big man, Doc was the quickest starter I ever saw, and in the open he ran with the niftiness as well as the speed of a great halfback."

Blaik also soon noted that his new fullback was an outstanding tackler and blocker, a very good receiver, and a superb punter and kickoff man. During preseason practice sessions, Blanchard repeatedly boomed kickoffs into and even beyond the end zone, and a few times through the uprights from 70 yards away, as he would do during the 1944 season. On top of all that, Blaik said, Blanchard also had "great instinctive football sense, supreme confidence, and deep pride." Aware of his eventual prowess on the Army track team, Blaik said Blanchard could have become an Olympic decathlon star. In addition to his sprinter's speed—Blanchard was clocked in 10 seconds for the 100-yard dash, a staple of track meets at the time—he could put the 15-lb. shot more than 50′. That ability enabled him to win both of those events, along with the 60-yard dash, at a number of track meets during his three years at West Point.

Perhaps because he was already in the army when he enrolled at West Point, and due to his powerful build, along with a somewhat defiant presence, Blanchard did not confront the normal indignities that most cadets face during Beast Barracks. If anything, the new fullback ignored questions thrown at him by upperclassmen bent on reminding him of the Academy's caste system wherein plebes were held in extremely low esteem and were expected to show respect to first- and second-year men, who corresponded to seniors and juniors at a university. Not surprisingly, when some upperclassmen reported Blanchard's obvious lack of respect and refusal to abide by what had long become tradition, they were told by West Point officials that not only was he already an enlisted man in the army but an extremely promising fullback on the varsity football team.

Poole, by contrast, won over upperclassmen with his roguish charm and Southern drawl. The rangy end was the youngest of nine children in an illustrious Mississippi sports family, and by the time he reached West Point he already had played one season at Mississippi and one season at North Carolina, where he earned honorable All-America mention in 1943 but did not have to sit out a year before playing football with Army as NCAA rules require in the case of top-tier football schools today. One of his brothers, Jim "Buster" Poole, also an end, had already spent five seasons with the New York Giants of the National Football League, where he earned All-Pro honors three times and would play two more years in the league after service during World War II. Another brother, Ray, also an end, would play for the Giants for six seasons after serving as a lieutenant with the Marines. Barney Poole eventually became the third Poole brother to play for the Giants while also playing for three other teams during a six-year NFL career.

Poole spent one season on an Ole Miss freshman team that included Doug Kenna and Charlie Conerly, a long-time quarterback for the New York Giants, and one as a starting end on the varsity as a sophomore before signing up for the navy's V-12 program and spending a year at North Carolina, where he was an end in 1943 while playing with brother Ray, also a V-12 student. Ray, two years older than Barney, was named a third-team All-American, while Barney earned honorable mention while playing for a team loaded with V-12 talent. While at North Carolina in the spring of 1944, Barney received a visit from Herman Hickman, Red Blaik's new line coach and Tennessee native who was scouring the South for talented college players he thought could strengthen an already strong Army team.

"Herman had stopped by to see Peahead Walker at Wake Forest and asked him, 'Who are some good football players down in this area we could get on a real good football team at the military academy?'" Poole recalled in referring to the well-known Wake Forest coach. "He said, 'I'm not interested in ordinary athletes. I want some good athletes to play on a national championship–type team.' Herman also tells us that the impetus to put that team together didn't just come from Red Blaik but General Eisenhower and General MacArthur. He said that they had decided they had shifted too much to the brain [at West Point] and too much away from the physical on the officers to be. Herman Hickman also told us, 'This is not coming from us as football coaches and the colonel as head coach, or even the superintendent or commandant at the Academy,' but that it was coming from higher up. Of course, that caught my ear because I had spent a lifetime in athletics and was a fair to middling student because I didn't work at it like I could have. And I could have been an excellent student if I'd worked at it. Except for foreign languages. That damn Spanish still would give me trouble if I tried to master it now."

Poole conceded he was impressed by Hickman's pitch, both for its appeal to Poole's patriotic instincts and for hearing that no less than Eisenhower and MacArthur wanted players like him at West Point. "I think that what was being said wasn't made up by Herman Hickman, even though he was very capable of making up a good story. It seems that it was a tone that had gotten something from up top, and Eisenhower and MacArthur were the top cheeses right at the moment."

So far as is known, Barney Poole was the only player who had been told that West Point alums Eisenhower and MacArthur may have played a big part in ensuring that Army would have a standout football team during World War II. And whether or not they actually had done so was never really established. When he told his brother about Hickman's pitch, Ray Poole, by then a Marine officer about to go to war in the Pacific, urged Barney to accept the appointment because in addition to being able to play football for what apparently was going to be a dominant team during the next few seasons, he would get high-quality training to become an officer. "Ray told me, 'They say we're ready to go to war, and I guess we are, but we moved mighty fast, and if you've got a chance to go to the Academy, they say that's the best training in the world.' He thought he'd been pushed mighty fast to lead men into battle, and that weighed very heavy on my decision to take the appointment." Barney Poole, who had been on the verge of becoming a navy officer like his brother, would now begin training to become a lieutenant in the U.S. Army. Herman Hickman may have been very persuasive in extolling the benefits that he would enjoy at the U.S. Military Academy, but Ray Poole had convinced Barney Poole that he should go.

Following a month of preparation at West Point for the validating (entrance) examination that spring, Poole returned to start his plebe year in July 1944. On the way to the Point from Grand Central Terminal, offensive coach Andy Gustafson picked up Poole and issued a belated warning of sorts to the new Army end, who at 21 was at the age that most cadets graduate and are commissioned as second lieutenants. Few if any incoming cadets were or are ever picked up at railroad stations or airports by someone on the Academy staff, but a football player who had already earned honorable All-American honors was not a typical plebe. During their 50-mile hour-and-a-half drive, Gustafson, in Poole's words, "challenged" him. "He says that I was a pretty mature individual and might not like to put up with that childish type of hazing," Poole said. "But even after I started, you couldn't have pulled me out with a bulldozer."

Hazing turned out to be the least of Poole's concerns, mainly because, like Blanchard, he refused to be a target of upperclassmen, repeatedly ignoring their commands and getting away with it. When Poole was reported for his defiance and ridicule of a century-old tradition, Academy officials were inclined to tell the complaining upperclassmen that Poole would be urged to abide by the hazing and then let the matter drop. Whether or not they did is not known, but the upperclassmen soon gave up on hazing Poole. What particularly concerned and even startled Poole was when, after being sworn in, he became aware for the first time that following his three years at the Academy he would have to put in four years on active duty as an army officer. "I wasn't aware that that was mandatory until that time," Poole, inexplicably, said. Apparently in trying to recruit the former Mississippi and North Carolina football star, Herman Hickman had forgotten to mention the service commitment that all West Point graduates must serve as officers in the U.S. Army.

As it turned out, Poole needn't have worried about the required extended army service beyond his days at West Point. From the outset as a cadet, Barney Poole was one of a kind and seemingly unchallenged, perhaps because his defiance of Beast Barracks was usually comical, if not to First Class cadets. As a plebe during Poole's final year at West Point, Morris Herbert recalled how the entire Corps of Cadets dined together at Washington Hall during the Beast Barracks period during July and August. As part of the Beast Barracks ritual, upperclassmen fired questions at plebes about West Point trivia and history, but never at Poole, apparently because of his by then well known, and successful, defiance of the tradition.

As a further act of defiance, Poole would get up from his table and furtively leave the dining hall with First Classmen while the rest of the plebe class remained seated, including his plebe football teammates. "As he left, he walked out through the poop deck, an area where the officer in charge of the mess hall sits," said Herbert, a former consultant in the West Point Association of Graduates office at West Point. "Once he was out of sight of the officer in charge, Barney would toss his hat into the air so that it would do a complete somersault and then land, right side up, on his head while he was still walking in the mess hall, where you were not supposed to wear your hat. It was quite a trick, and all of the plebes loved seeing Barney do it, as he did often without ever being reprimanded, perhaps because of the way he did it."

Poole was also occasionally inclined to impersonate a "Firstie," as First Classmen are called at the Academy, Herbert said, and to call out instructions to companies of plebes massed outside their barracks waiting for official instructions from company commanders. "He'd call out, 'In battery!' which commands cadets to stand at attention and thrust out their chins, and then he would walk away," Herbert recalled. "The plebes then would hold that position until an actual company commander came along to give the next command of 'Rack that neck in!' which orders cadets to push their chins as low as possible into their necks."

After watching Poole, who was 6′2″ and weighed about 225 lbs., snare passes during preseason practice sessions in late August and early September, Red Blaik was not about to crack down on the Mississippian's antics, which would have gotten the average cadet in serious trouble. Poole's roommate as a plebe, Dewitt "Tex" Coulter, was also spared the hazing of Beast Barracks, if for no other reason than his physically impressive demeanor. At 6′4″ and a sinewy 230 lbs., Coulter was 2″ taller and a bit heavier than Poole. Like Poole, from the moment he first saw Coulter at practice, Blaik knew he had a potential All-American tackle who knew of no other way to play football but to go all-out, even at practice, to the point where Blaik, half in jest, told players to watch out for Coulter during scrimmage breaks lest he knock them off their feet.

Shorty McWilliams, one of Herman Hickman's Southern recruits, recalled Blaik telling him, "'If I blow the whistle and Tex Coulter is anywhere in your vicinity, lay down, because if you stand up, he's going to hit you.'" As a 170-lb. halfback, McWilliams found out how tough Coulter could be during Army scrimmages. "When Tex played football, he played to win," McWilliams said. "I mean, against his fellow cadets, against his rivals, it didn't matter who he played against; he played to win. It didn't take but one or two times to be standing up and get knocked 15 yards down the field by that big guy, till you learned to lay down."

In what may have been the most unusual pairing of cadets in the Academy's history, Poole and Coulter were roommates during their first year at West Point. Neither had the slightest bit of interest in an army career, and like most of Blaik's recruits from 1943 through 1945, the last three years of World War II, they were solely at West Point to play football and then hopefully continue to play in the NFL, which they both did. Although they were both bright, neither was a particularly good student and both needed counseling on class work while at the Academy. That neither of them made it to graduation and a commission in the army was hardly a surprise.

Like Poole, Coulter was a recalcitrant cadet, who had to work hard to control his temper during Beast Barracks and even beyond, unable as he was to conform to West Point traditions and rules, many of which he found incomprehensible. "I always felt like I had been able to keep Tex Coulter at the military academy," Poole said years later. "When we were plebes, Tex would always forget to shine his shoes. Then he'd be standing out there [in formation] and then some little guy way down the ranks would come along and chew old Tex out something unmercifully. They'd walk on down the line and old Tex, out of the corner of his mouth, would say, 'I wonder how far I could throw that little son of a bitch if I decided to hit him.' And I'd say, 'Cool it, Tex. We've got Notre Dame this week and can't do without you.'" Fortunately for Coulter, Poole's soothing and calm advice seemed to work every time Coulter was on the edge of losing his temper, or worse, at an arrogant upperclassman.

Given his background, Coulter's wellspring of anger against authority figures, and even teammates in scrimmages, was understandable. Along with his three older siblings, Coulter, then four, was placed in a Masonic home in Fort Worth, Texas, by their mother after their father died of tuberculosis. Army teammate and fellow Texan Goble Bryant, who had played against Coulter in high school, indicated that an episode involving one of Coulter's uncles may have been at least partially responsible for his inner anger. "The day their daddy was buried, the daddy's brother came over and took their only possession, which was a cow," Bryant said. "DeWitt told me about that, and I wish you could have seen his fingers on his desk. They were just white. And he said, 'Boy, if I could ever get ahold of him, I'd…' without finishing the sentence. And he could have pulled him apart because he was such a strong, well-coordinated man." Shortly after that, Bryant said, Coulter's mother put the children in what amounted to an orphanage because she was unable to care for them.

A grim, foreboding place, the Masonic Home also at times inflicted emotional scars on its young inmates, as they were called. "That was my home from first grade through 11th grade," Coulter said. "In effect we were orphans. That first night at the orphanage, well, I don't have a word that fits it," he said. "They put me in dorm one and my sisters, L.E. and Ima, God knows where. I thought I would never see them again." Not surprisingly, four-year-old Dewitt Coulter wound up crying himself to sleep, as he would often do. As time went on, the Coulter children adjusted to the harsh discipline at the Masonic Home where corporal punishment was often inflicted on children who failed to do assigned chores.

The saving grace for Dewitt Coulter turned out to be football. "Football gave us self-worth," Coulter said. "You started at the Masonic

Home on the 65-lb. team when you were about 10, and then you worked your way up to the 90-lb. and 110-lb. team, and then onto the high school team," Coulter said, referring to the high school, which like the other schools, was on the Masonic Home grounds. By the time Coulter reached the high school level, the team, which usually had less than 25 players and sometimes as few as a dozen, had achieved a measure of fame throughout the state not only for its talent but for its hard hitting and fierce blocking, both of which helped compensate for the relatively small quantity of players.

"We played a certain kind of football," Coulter said with a smile that indicated the team's style was more smash-mouth than finesse. "Our coach was 'Rusty' Russell, who was sort of a legend around Fort Worth and a very good coach. We didn't have many kids and were playing against schools that were tremendously populated in comparison with the Masonic Home. We couldn't make what we called the city guys admire us for our situation, but we could make them fear us. You know, a good healthy fear. And the city boys at the Fort Worth high schools were frightened as hell of us. The goddamn guys would be bleeding all over the place. We played a very tough brand of football. The ball was snapped, and you continued to hit people until the referee blew the whistle."

The Masonic Home school usually had only about 150 boys and girls ranging in age from four to 19, and the football team, usually vastly undersized compared to its opponents, played schools in Texas' top-tier A division, some of which had several thousand students. And the Mighty Mites, as they came to be known, rarely lost, with Russell achieving a winning percentage of 81 percent from 1926 until 1942 and reaching the Texas state championship game in 1932. Remarkably, despite the small number of football players that came out of the Masonic Home, three, including Coulter, made it to the NFL. The others were Hardy Brown, who spent 10 years in the league, and Allie White, a two-way lineman for the Philadelphia Eagles in 1939.

If Coulter was one of the toughest and hardest-hitting players ever, at Army and in the NFL, he was tame compared with Brown, who some football historians regard as the fiercest player ever to play in the league. Brown had left the Masonic Home in 1941, shortly before Pearl Harbor, to join the Marines and go on to fight the Japanese in the Pacific. After World War II, Brown attended Southern Methodist University and then the University of Tulsa, where he was a star blocking back and linebacker. Jim Finks, a quarterback and defensive back for the Pittsburgh Steelers from 1949 through 1955 and later president of the New Orleans Saints, roomed with Brown at Tulsa and remembered him well a half-century later. "I think it was in a game against Baylor that Hardy knocked out the two ends on consecutive plays," Fink said. "That's how hard he hit. But off the field he was generally intelligent, warm, and shy."

On the field, though, Brown was a hell-bent linebacker who leveled quarterbacks, running backs, receivers, and even opposing linebackers with his patented shoulder tackle, which started with a low crouch from which Brown sprang up and drove his right shoulder into an opponent's head. Hall of Fame quarterback Y.A. Tittle, who played with Brown on the Baltimore Colts and the San Francisco 49ers, called Brown the toughest football player he had ever met. "Hardy wasn't a great linebacker and missed a lot with his shoulder tackle, but when he hit you, you usually didn't get up," Tittle said. "He was a regular knockout artist and inspired us. I remember how in his first game with the Colts in 1951, he knocked out all three running backs. Altogether, he knocked out 21 players that season alone. And when I say knocked out, I mean knocked out cold with his shoulder tackle to the point that they had to be carried off on stretchers. All of his opponents hated him, and sometimes to get back at him, the quarterback would call a play that would let Hardy break through, and all 10 of the players would let him have it. But amazingly, I don't ever remember Hardy being hurt, although he sent a lot of players to the hospital."

Like Coulter, Brown's rage could have been attributable to traumatic boyhood experiences. When he was four years old in 1928, he looked on as his father was shot to death. Then a few months later, young Hardy witnessed a family friend shoot and kill one of Hardy's father's killers. Less than a year later, Brown's mother sent him and his three siblings to the Masonic Home, where he met Coulter, who was the same age. Off the field, Tittle said, "Hardy was quiet, soft-spoken, and very reserved. I used to look at him reading a book and wonder how he could be so tough out on the football field. But if you were in a bar with him, inevitably Hardy would wind up in a fight. He could be a good companion, but he could also be mean."

Coulter recalled lining up against his old Masonic Home teammate in an NFL game years later, in the early 1950s. "I came out of the huddle and thought I'd say hello to Hardy," Coulter said. "But when I came to the line of scrimmage and looked across at him at his linebacker spot, his eyes looked like they belonged to some caged animal. They were fiery and focused, so I kept my mouth shut."

So much for old childhood friendships at the Masonic Home in Fort Worth, Texas.

Considering that Brown had not heard from his mother for the 12 years he was at the Masonic Home orphanage—and then only when he had to get her permission to join the Marines—perhaps that deep-seated rage was understandable. Coulter, by contrast, though a fierce competitor even during practice sessions, managed to keep his temper in check and never exhibited a mean streak or sought to deliberately hurt or render opponents unconscious. Still, as teammate Joe Steffy, an eventual All-American guard at Army, said, "Compared to Dewitt, everybody on the team was a Sunday-school boy."

Sadly, Brown, one of only two players (placekicker Ben Agajanian was the other) to have played in the NFL, the All-America Football Conference, and the American Football League (AFL), spiraled out of control after his football career ended at the age of 36. He drank heavily and eventually was institutionalized by his wife in Stockton, California, where he was diagnosed with dementia and later died in a mental institution at the age of 67. Doctors said his condition probably was caused by excessive drinking, severe blows to the head while playing football, and traumatic experiences during childhood.

Coulter's lifetime path was much smoother and certainly much happier. From the time he first watched his new tackle in practice, Red Blaik knew Coulter was something special and no doubt a prospective All-American. But then Blaik had a special affinity for good tackles. "No football team can get anywhere without good tackles," he said. "Tackle is the position where most football games are lost." Along with Coulter, Blaik knew he had another outstanding one in Al Nemetz, a returning letterman and also a potential All-American.

Like Blanchard, Coulter was already in the army when he was lured to West Point in the summer of 1944. After earning All-State honors in Texas for three straight years along with winning the national high school championship in the shot put, Coulter was given a scholarship to Texas A&M. However, the draft intruded and the Masonic School graduate never did make it to the Texas A&M campus. Following basic training, Coulter was stationed at an air corps base in Texas when opportunity knocked. "The company commander came into the barracks and said, 'Where is Tex Coulter?' Or probably 'Where is Private Coulter?'" Coulter recollected. "I said to myself, *Oh my goodness. What have I done now? Or more important, what is it that I didn't do that I was supposed to have done?* The company commander then said, 'How would you like to go to West Point?' And I said, 'Me, sir?' And he said, 'Yes, you.' I said, 'Boy, I'd like that.'" Coulter said he thought the company commander had heard about his exploits as a high school player from an army captain stationed at Sheppard Air Base who had played under Red Blaik and did some scouting for Blaik.

Thus, after a year in the army, and never having given any thought to attending West Point, Coulter received an appointment from a prominent senator, Tom Connally of Texas, and was on his way to the U.S. Military Academy—another outstanding recruit who went from being an army private to a West Point cadet. First, though, Coulter had to spend a semester at Cornell preparing for the West Point validating examination. Still, like Glenn Davis, Coulter would find himself unprepared for the academic rigors of geometry and trigonometry that he would struggle with at the Academy while doing well in his other courses. "At the Masonic Home they didn't have good math courses, and we did not have trigonometry," Coulter was to recall. "And at West Point we were studying spherical trigonometry." That subject, Coulter no doubt was sure, wasn't being studied by freshmen football players at Texas A&M where he would have enrolled had he not been drafted.

As it was, Coulter was to find himself among the most outstanding group of plebe football players ever assembled at West Point. In addition to Blanchard and Poole, the newcomers included experienced players who were already in either the army or the navy or in V-5 and V-12 navy and Marine programs at colleges and universities. Of the 35 players recruited and who had received congressional appointments, 13 entered the Academy in July 1944 and became members of the varsity that year. Among those who would see considerable action during the next few years, on the football field if not the battlefield, were Young Arnold Tucker (University of Miami), Dean Sensanbaugher (Ohio State), Shelton Biles (Vanderbilt), Tom Hayes (Nebraska), Bill West (Dartmouth), Art Gerometta (Illinois), Harold Tavzel (Miami of Ohio), and from the army, Herschel "Ug" Fuson, who had attended Tennessee before going into the navy, Hank Foldberg, and Joe Starnes, who, like Coulter, had gone directly into the army from high school. They would join returning lettermen quarterbacks Doug Kenna and Tom Lombardo, running backs Davis, Dale Hall, Bob Chabot, Max Minor,

Bobby Dobbs, Dick Walterhouse, and Johnny Sauer, and linemen Dick Pitzer, Roland Catarinella, Bob Wayne, Bill LaMar, Jack Green, Bob St. Onge, Joe Stanowicz, Bill Webb, and Ed Rafalko.

Fuson was particularly special and not one of the many new players Blaik had to worry more about in the classroom than on the football field. Well-rounded and valedictorian of his high school class, Fuson was an excellent student also recruited by the ubiquitous Herman Hickman, who was as impressed by Fuson's breadth of interests and intelligence as he was with Fuson's football diversity in that he could play center, guard, and running back and do well in all three positions— although Blaik would primarily use him on the line. Listed at 6'2" and around 220 lbs., he looked taller and heavier, but then Blaik was always inclined to shave an inch or two off a player's height and as many as 20 lbs. in weight on the official roster and game programs.

"When Barney Poole and Ug Fuson came over to visit me when I was a plebe in 1945, I took a look at them and said to myself, *What on earth am I doing here?*" said Joe Steffy, a 5'11" 190-lb. guard. "They were big, huge men, you know, and here I am much smaller. Gee, I made a big mistake. I'll never be able to play with these people. Ug was also special as a student. In a group of very fine people, he was a little above, first in his class in French, and a very fine cadet who became a fine officer."

By then, Poole and Fuson had proven themselves as plebe players on the 1944 squad, which Red Blaik was to call the first of his "story book" teams at West Point, and a team so full of talented players that he planned to alternate two full teams throughout every game except perhaps the Navy game.

3

★ ★ ★

"Two Good to Be True"

I T HAD BEEN A WEST POINT TRADITION SINCE THE CIVIL WAR ERA, but Beast Barracks never before had included the likes of Barney Poole, Tex Coulter, Doc Blanchard, and some of the other already-grown men who encountered it when they reported for basic training as plebes in July 1944. Only a month after the D-Day invasion of France during which approximately 2,000 Americans were killed and about 5,000 wounded or missing, those three, along with a half dozen or so teammates, already had military ties before arriving at West Point and found it hard to reconcile some of the juvenile-like—and degrading—hazing tactics involved in the ritualistic Beast Barracks, which incoming plebes faced at the hands of upperclassmen during the six weeks of basic training that preceded the start of the fall semester and included interminable marching, sleep deprivation, and the uncompromising obedience to what at times were outrageous commands.

All the more outrageous was that the "tradition," despised by Douglas MacArthur both when he was a cadet and then superintendent at West Point, continued into World War II, although somewhat toned down at the order of West Point's top brass. The reaction of some of the older players who enrolled at the Point in 1944, not surprisingly, was to disdain "orders" from first and second classmen and refuse to answer questions from them on trivia pertaining to academy landmarks, statuary, and other West Point esoterica such as the amount of gallons of water in Lusk Lake or the number of pipes in the church organ in the cadet chapel.

"I think the word got around to take it easier on the football players," Dick Walterhouse, a teammate of Davis, Blanchard, Poole, and Coulter, said in September 2013. "As I remember it, it wasn't really too rough." That may have been easy to say for a football player at West Point, even one like Walterhouse who was much smaller and lighter at 5'10" and 175 lbs., although some of his teammates disagreed with his opinion on the hazing ritual. But in general, football players at West Point, in addition to getting no special favors from professors, were not looked upon by other cadets as being special but just as fellow cadets.

As for hazing, no less a West Point legend than Douglas MacArthur was called to testify during a congressional investigation into Beast Barracks in 1901 while he was a cadet, conceded that some tactics employed during the hazing were cruel. Years later, in his memoirs, MacArthur wrote that, "Hazing was practiced with a worthy goal, but with methods that were violent and uncontrolled." Apparently because his father was a general in the army, MacArthur had endured excessive hazing and on one occasion eventually collapsed to the floor exhausted after being forced to remain spread-eagled for more than an hour. That experience may have figured in to MacArthur's abortive effort to eliminate hazing when he became superintendent in 1919, a position he held until 1922, but he finally compromised so long as the hazing was less severe.

Defying hazing orders by upperclassmen did not work in the classroom at West Point where Blanchard and Coulter in particular struggled from the start of their plebe year, mainly in trying to understand the rudiments of advanced algebra and trigonometry. "When we got to West

Point, we had an academician trying to get us smart enough to pass the entrance examinations, which we both did," Blanchard recalled. "The academic side of it was very different for a lot of us. So I was not very interested academically, other than to do what you had to do."

Glenn Davis, a far more studious student than Blanchard, albeit with far more trouble with math courses, pointed out that cadets had to study for and attend five classes Monday through Friday. "We were graded every day in every subject," Davis said. "Every third day you have an exam over the past three days. And you have to be proficient to be eligible to play. And if you flunk one course, and it can be in physical efficiency, you flunk, you're out. And so everybody else was getting out of class at 3:30 every afternoon and they'd study from 3:30 to call for dinner. Well, I'm out there practicing football or practicing basketball or baseball or track. Then I come in dead tired, and I've got five classes to study for that night for the next day." That explained why Davis often dozed off when the Army team went to a movie in White Plains in Westchester County the night before a game in New York while staying at a country club in Westchester County about 15 miles from Yankee Stadium or the Polo Grounds.

Because of Army's remarkable depth in 1944, Blaik came up with a novel solution. Although coaches were able to use unlimited substitutions since 1941, none, so far as is known, were utilizing two separate platoons—one on offense and one on defense—until Fritz Crisler did so at Michigan starting in 1945. Blaik's plan was to use two separate teams that would play alternate quarters, meaning the players would play both offense and defense. One team would be made up of returning lettermen, while the other would include plebes—almost all of whom had already played at least a year of college football—with the exception of "firstie" (senior) quarterback and captain Tom Lombardo. Since the "veteran" team would play the first and third quarters, that meant that such promising new players as Blanchard, Poole, and Coulter, along with Davis, who was repeating his plebe year, would in effect be the second team and play the second and fourth periods. The only exception was Blanchard who always would be in to kick off. However, Blaik decided early on that in a close game he might change that pattern and have some players on the two teams playing together, at least for a while. Signifying the team's overall depth, Arnold Tucker, the heralded quarterback who had played one season at Miami after spending a few weeks as a student at Notre Dame and who would be the regular quarterback the next three seasons, was a backup on the plebe-oriented team. Indeed, the two teams also included six future All-Americans. No wonder that in later years, Blaik would refer to the 1944 Army squad as his first "story book" team and called the impressive group of plebes "probably the strongest in academy history." Normally reserved in assessing his teams in advance of a season, Blaik was downright effusive about the 1944 team. At the team's first practice in August, Blaik told the squad, "I expect you to be the greatest team in the history of West Point." Now all the Cadets had to do was live up to their potential and their coach's prediction.

If Army had the look of a potential national champion, so did Navy and Notre Dame, Army's traditionally big rivals. Like Army, Navy benefitted from the war by acquiring several outstanding players from other schools, particularly tackle Don Whitmire, who had been an All-American during his second season at Alabama and then in 1943 when he enrolled at Annapolis. Another transfer, back Dave Barksdale, had also played two years elsewhere, at North Carolina, where he had been the captain-elect when he decided to become a Midshipman. They were two of the reasons Navy was ranked first in most preseason polls. Notre Dame, on the other hand, was a beneficiary of football players from other schools now studying to become Marine officers under the navy's V-12 program, although most of those candidates had already been called to active duty by the fall of 1944, including All-American quarterback Angelo Bertelli. Also gone was Bertelli's replacement during the second half of the 1943 season, sophomore Johnny Lujack, who had joined the navy but would return in 1946. Still, Notre Dame, Army, and Navy were regarded as the top three college teams in the country at the beginning of the season. Chagrined at the fact that Army had not beaten Navy since 1938 and had scored only one touchdown in the last five Army-Navy games, Blaik contended that the Midshipmen had an edge because of less stringent academic standards and in view of what he maintained was a larger student body, when in fact the enrollments at both academies were about the same in the 1940s. Whether West Point's academic standards were more demanding is difficult to ascertain, although Robert Woods, who attended and played at both academies, said he thought the requirements were comparable but that the discipline was far more stringent at the U.S. Military Academy. Army's losing streak against Notre Dame was even longer. The Cadets hadn't defeated the Irish since 1931, and during the ensuing 12 years Army had lost 10 games and played two ties.

Blanchard, Poole, Coulter, and the other plebes soon found out that Blaik was both a perfectionist and a hard taskmaster during practice sessions. "Run that play again" was Blaik's mantra, heard again and again in practice until the play was run to perfection. Light moments were few and far between on the practice field, and when they occurred they were usually provided by Herman Hickman, the jovial and highly literate line coach. From time to time, though he was in his fifties and weighed in excess of 300 lbs., Hickman was inclined to line up against an Army player to demonstrate how he wanted a block or tackle to be executed. "Herman was still very quick and would fire off of his three-point stance right into a lineman in practice," Robert Woods recalled. "And as he did, his pet chihuahua, who he kept in one of his jacket pockets, would pop out of the pocket and onto the field with a stunned look on his face. You couldn't help but laugh at the scene."

* * *

Army's first four games were played at Michie Stadium, with the opener on September 30 (the college football season began much later at the time) against North Carolina, which by then had lost most of its V-12 players from the previous season, but included most of the players with whom Blanchard and Poole had played so it was also a chance to renew some acquaintances since Poole had played on the Tar Heels varsity in 1943 while Blanchard was a star fullback with the 1942 freshman team. Totally outplayed, North Carolina was able to gain only 14 yards rushing and 21 yards on three pass completions out of 16 thrown and was crushed 46–0.

The game marked the first time that Blanchard and Davis had played together, and their pairing was a bad omen for the Cadets' future opponents. Though Blaik employed his two-team pattern, Blanchard and Davis were limited to only 17:00 each, slightly more than a quarter, while playing on the second unit. Army, normally conservative in its approach under Blaik, surprisingly unveiled some razzle-dazzle including laterals on three touchdown plays.

Davis was spectacular, running for 125 yards and scoring three touchdowns on runs of 73 and 37 yards, two after grabbing laterals and one on a 38-yard pass from quarterback Tom Lombardo. Blanchard only carried the ball four times but averaged 4½ yards per carry while averaging almost 60 yards on five kickoffs. His one touchdown came on the game's most dazzling play, which included a lateral, and demonstrated the brilliance of Blanchard, Davis, and Barney Poole, like Blanchard playing in his first game for Army. With the ball on Army's 35-yard line early in the second quarter, Davis took a handoff from Lombardo and flipped an eight-yard pass to Poole who then ran for 10 yards to the North Carolina 47-yard line, where, about to be tackled, he lateraled to Blanchard who sprinted down the sideline for a touchdown. In his Michie Stadium debut, Blanchard also demonstrated his defensive prowess, making a half-dozen tackles from his left linebacker position and batting down several passes.

Sportswriters and fans who had been awed by Davis' brilliance in 1943 realized that, when paired with Blanchard's power and speed at fullback, Davis would be even more effective at left halfback on what Red Blaik had predicted would be his best team yet. Veteran football observers also realized that Army's remarkable depth would no doubt be able to wear down many, if indeed not most, of its opponents during the course of a game with Blaik's revolutionary two-team concept. Some writers assumed that the second unit, which played at least part of the second and fourth quarters and included Blanchard and Davis, was Blaik's "second team" and described it as such in their stories, as some of them also would do in subsequent games until Blaik made it clear that in his opinion, the two teams were equal in stature and talent. One of those he had to enlighten was Jesse Abramson of the *New York Herald Tribune* who was to write in the next day' paper, "Blanchard didn't play much, but while he was there with the so-called second team, he was more than slightly terrific."

Despite Army's impressive start, in New York newspapers the game was relegated well behind stories about the St. Louis Browns beating the defending World Series champion New York Yankees for the third time in a row in St. Louis on Saturday, which left the Browns in a first-place tie with the Detroit Tigers with only one game left to play. As it developed, the Browns beat the Yankees again on Sunday 5–2, while the Tigers were losing to knuckleball artist Dutch Leonard and the Washington Senators in Detroit to give the Browns their first—and last—American League pennant. That set up a "streetcar series" with the St. Louis Cardinals, who shared Sportsman's Park with the Browns and who had won the National League pennant for the third year in a row, this time by a whopping 14 ½ games. Far more significantly, Sunday newspapers played up an assault on the German Siegfried Line on

Saturday by infantrymen of America's First Army who had advanced across the Wurm River and two miles into Germany.

*   *   *

Army's second game was even more lopsided. On a scorching-hot Saturday before a crowd of about 6,000 spectators that only filled half of Michie Stadium, the Cadets demolished Brown 59–7. Blanchard and Davis again played less than half the game, but Davis still had enough time to score three touchdowns while Blanchard averaged eight yards on his eight carries. Demonstrating his versatility, Davis, by now obviously Army's fastest back—and indeed by now one of the fastest in the country—scored on a 16-yard run, a 60-yard punt return, and a 22-yard pass play. Like Blanchard, Davis was also an excellent receiver. The difference was that once Davis caught a pass on the run, it was almost impossible to keep up with him, while Blanchard, fast as he was for a big man, often fought off defenders to catch a pass or bowled over would-be tacklers in the open field.

Could Army score even more points against future opponents? The Cadets most assuredly could, trouncing Pittsburgh 69–7 the week after the Brown game and then the Coast Guard Academy 76–0 a week later in games also played at Michie Stadium. The Panthers' coach, Clark Shaughnessy, the master of the T formation who had predicted great things for Blanchard to Glenn and Ralph Davis in their chance meeting on a New York–bound train three months earlier, saw his predictions borne out as Blanchard scored twice on an 18-yard pass and on a 20-yard run after intercepting a pass. In addition, though he had played only 22 minutes, Army's new fullback had run four times for 44 yards, caught three passes for 108 yards, kicked off four times into the end zone, and punted once for 44 yards. All of that while playing left linebacker on defense.

Davis, who was also limited to 22 minutes and played right halfback on defense bolted through the line and around end while gaining

161 yards on nine carries, completed both passes he threw for 118 yards, and scored one touchdown on a dazzling 63-yard run during which he dodged past four defenders in the Pitt secondary. In all, the Cadets gained 606 yards on offense despite five fumbles. Pittsburgh's only touchdown came with shortly more than a minute left in the game, by which time Blaik had cleared his bench. After the game, Blanchard, remembering that his father had played under Shaughnessy at Tulane, crossed the field and told Shaughnessy, "Coach, I don't feel happy about this." Touched by Blanchard's comment, the veteran coach responded by telling Blanchard he was extremely impressed by his play. Later, Shaughnessy told writers that Blanchard had the potential to become the best college running back in the country, a remarkable tribute given that Blanchard had only played 22 minutes.

Army continued a pattern of scoring more points each week when the Cadets destroyed the Coast Guard Academy 76–0 in a game in which Blanchard played only 12 minutes and Davis 30, and in which reserve half-back and quarterback Dick Walterhouse kicked a record 11 extra points. Despite their limited time on the field, Davis and Blanchard each scored twice. Blanchard, who sportswriters were still calling Felix and not yet "Doc," crossed the goal line from one and 15 yards out, while Davis scored on runs of 58 and 44 yards. The statistics bore out the one-sided game as Army gained 443 yards rushing against 36 by Coast Guard, and 157 yards passing compared with 66 yards in the air by Coast Guard. Why the Cadets passed at all, as they did 13 times, was both a mystery and unnecessary, if not unsportsmanlike, as some observers thought. The question in the aftermath of those four one-sided games was whether Army could continue its better than a point-a-minute onslaught a week later at the Polo Grounds in Manhattan against a good Duke team, which Navy had barely beaten 7–0 and would go to the Sugar Bowl at the end of the season.

By then, though, Blaik had to worry as much about Blanchard, Poole, and Coulter's academics as he did about Duke and probably Army's three toughest, and last, opponents, Notre Dame, Pennsylvania, and Navy. In an academic milieu where a failing weekly grade could keep a player out of the following Saturday's game, all three players were barely keeping their heads above water in the classroom. Academic counselors were assigned to all three, but their tasks were virtually insuperable. In truth, it had become evident that Poole and Coulter, in particular, were not cut out to be West Point cadets, either in the classroom, the barracks, or almost anywhere else on the Academy grounds except for the football field. Much had also been expected from another newcomer, halfback Dean Sensanbaugher, a transfer from Ohio State, but he wound up playing very little mainly because of his struggles in the classroom, and he was gone by the end of the year. Meanwhile, Glenn Davis, studying as hard as ever, had become a good if not exemplary student—a far cry from his disastrous first academic year.

★   ★   ★

With Army now ranked second behind Notre Dame, the Cadets' first appearance of the season away from Michie Stadium drew a crowd of around 45,000 to the Polo Grounds, home of both the New York Giants baseball and football teams and the site of some of boxing's biggest fights, featuring such great heavyweights as Jack Dempsey, Gene Tunney, and Joe Louis. Living up to its reputation as one of the country's best defensive teams, Duke held Army scoreless in the first quarter before yielding the Cadets' only score of the half in the second period. On Army's third play of the second quarter, with Army's so-called B unit—still referred to by most sportswriters as Army's "second team"—now on the field, quarterback Tom Lombardo faked a handoff to Blanchard going left and then handed off to Davis headed to the right side. As Davis skirted Duke's left end, two Blue Devils had relatively clear shots at him but missed as he flew 53 yards down the right sideline for the game's first score. But then Dick Walterhouse, Army's normally accurate placekicker, missed the extra point attempt. That miss enabled Duke to take a 7–6 lead shortly before halftime when the Blue Devils blocked a punt and tackle John Kerns fell on the ball at the Army 13-yard line. Four plays later, following an interference call against Army on a pass by fullback Tom Davis that put the ball on the 2-yard line, Davis cracked through left tackle for a touchdown. Right end Harold Raether then kicked the extra point to give Duke a surprising 7–6 lead at the half.

Though Army had completed three of its eight passes for 30 yards in the first half, Blaik was convinced that the Cadets had to rely exclusively on their ground attack in the second half if they were to remain unbeaten. They did, totally eschewing the pass, and scored three touchdowns within a span of 15 minutes late in the third quarter and early in the fourth on drives of 50 and 74 yards and following a blocked punt by Barney Poole at the Duke 24-yard line. Halfbacks Dale Hall, Max Minor, and Blanchard eventually scored on runs of 28, 15, and one yards, with Walterhouse converting after all three touchdowns to put the game out of Duke's reach at 27–7. Blanchard's touchdown came on a one-yard plunge following a 23-yard run around right end. That run demonstrated both Blanchard's versatility and his speed. Mr. Inside, it had soon become apparent, could also go around end like a halfback. Conversely, Glenn Davis had clearly showed that, though labeled Mr. Outside, he could bolt through the slimmest of spaces in a defensive line and then out-run linebackers and defensive halfbacks, as they were called before the term "cornerback" entered the football lexicon.

Once again, Blaik's two-team concept proved highly effective. With both defenses well rested as the two units continued to play alternate quarters, Army held Duke scoreless in the second half in a game in which the Cadets gained 314 yards rushing against only 57 by the Blue Devils, who, by comparison, appeared to tire in the second half after holding their own against Army during the first two quarters.

Had Blaik fired up the Cadets at halftime? Apparently not. "That was not his way," said Ed "Rafe" Rafalko, an end from Stoughton, Massachusetts, a Boston suburb, who was prepared to accept a scholarship at Columbia (at least some, if not all, of the Ivy League schools offered scholarships to football players at the time) until he was recruited by Army during the spring of his senior year in high school in 1942. "He would just go over some of the things we did and then tell us that we knew what we had to do. That was about it."

Back at Michie Stadium the following Saturday, Army inflicted an 83–0 beating on a Villanova team that by then had lost most of its V-12 navy and Marine players who had been called to active duty. Convinced that he would not be missed on the sideline during the Villanova game, Blaik, accompanied by Herman Hickman and a few other assistant coaches, went to Baltimore to scout the Navy–Notre Dame game on the same day and left the coaching to head backfield coach, Andy Gustafson, later the head coach at Miami. Gustafson, an army private at the time, did all he could to keep down the score—Blanchard was kept out of the game because of a sprained knee—but could not as nine different players scored touchdowns and Dick Walterhouse kicked 11 extra points. Davis and 5'7" 170-lb. Johnny Sauer each scored three touchdowns in a game shortened to nine-minute quarters in the second half.

Next up for Army was Notre Dame at Yankee Stadium. As it turned out, the best game of the week preceding the Notre Dame game may have been played at West Point. During a 30-minute scrimmage on Wednesday between the talented A and B teams, both units scored all three times they had the ball in a bruising encounter during which Blaik left the players unrestrained. Describing the scrimmage as "the best football I ever saw," Blaik said neither team was able to stop the other. "The speed, power, coordination, and ferocity were something I have not seen equaled on a gridiron," the coach said later, realizing all the more that his Army team of 1944 was very special indeed and apparently were peaking just before the final and probably most difficult games of the year.

The game would be held four days after President Franklin Roosevelt, who had already won a unprecedented third term in 1940, won a fourth term despite obviously failing health by winning 53.4 percent of the popular vote and 432 electoral votes while the Republican nominee, Thomas Dewey, a former New York City prosecutor, had garnered 46 percent of the popular vote but only 99 electoral votes. It was also to be played less than three weeks since General Douglas MacArthur had fulfilled a pledge to Filipinos that he would return to the Philippines from Australia after having left when Japanese forces invaded in 1942 that led to the infamous 75-mile Bataan Death March during which between 600-700 Americans and more than 5,000 Filipinos died of hunger, illness, and brutal maltreatment by Japanese forces.

But by early November 1944, Japanese troops were still fighting to regain possession of the Philippines despite the success of U.S. forces that had regained control of the American possession and were making substantial advances against the Japanese elsewhere in the Pacific. Indeed, on the day of the 1944 Army–Notre Dame game, American bombers in the Pacific attacked and sank four Japanese transport ships and six destroyers that were carrying 8,000 troops to Leyte in the Philippines. General MacArthur, back in the Philippines, called the Japanese resistance "a supreme effort to crush our liberation of Leyte." That same Saturday, American B-29 bombers—by then known as the Super Flying Fortress—flying from bases in China, hit manufacturing, transporting, and storage facilities in Japan and in China at Shanghai and Nanking with the loss of only one B-29.

Meanwhile, the new and deadly 13½-ton unmanned German V-2 rocket bombers fell on Allied sectors in France and Belgium. With England having joined U.S. forces in the Pacific, British submarines over a period of several weeks had sunk 45 Japanese ships in Far

Eastern waters, according to the British Admiralty. But there was sobering news from the Pacific, too. In the battle for the Japanese-held island of Saipan, 14,000 American Marines had been killed before the island was secured during one of the most bloody battles of the Pacific war.

Thus, in the context of the war, and the tens of thousands of American servicemen who been killed in Europe and in the Pacific, a football game, no matter its significance, paled in comparison. But it had become evident throughout the war that Americans on the home front were able to find succor from the war news and working in defense plants by attending sports events—and in particular big-time college and professional football games, Major League Baseball games, championship fights, hockey games in the then six-team NHL, and horse races. And the Army–Notre Dame game that November had transfixed many sports fans throughout the country and particularly those in the New York metropolitan area. Tickets had been sold out since August, leading scalpers, by then an integral part of New York's sporting scene, to offer tickets for as much as 10 times their face value. In addition, many of Manhattan's best hotels had been booked for weeks. So for at least three hours on a Saturday afternoon in November 1944, the war would largely be overshadowed by a college football game.

If ever Army had a chance in recent years to end a long losing streak to Notre Dame—the Cadets hadn't beaten the Irish since 1931 and hadn't been able to score in the last five games—the 1944 game gave the team its best opportunity. Though Notre Dame had lost most of its V-12 Marine players, along with tackles George Terlep and Chick Maggioli who had been called to duty by the navy, the Irish had an exceptionally strong wartime team that featured halfback Bob Kelly, quarterback and future NFL player Frank Dancewicz, All-American guard Pat Filley, and tackle George Sullivan. However, after winning its first five games while giving up only 20 points, the Fighting Irish had been beaten by a very strong Navy team 32–13 the previous Saturday.

In its favor, the majority of fans in the capacity crowd of 76,000 at Yankee Stadium again would assuredly be pulling for Notre Dame even though the game was ostensibly a home game for the undefeated and favored team from West Point, which resided only 55 miles away.

Because of Blanchard's booming kickoffs, even when it won the coin-toss, Army almost always kicked off, knowing that most of Blanchard's kicks would end up in the end zone and force opponents to start at their 20-yard line or even father back in their own territory. By 1944, Army's defense was better than ever and usually forced fumbles or interceptions deep in its opponent's territory.

Notre Dame won the toss and, as most teams are inclined to do, chose to receive, exactly what Army wanted. Although the Cadets were a slight favorite, the consensus was that it would be a close game. However, it was anything but. Within a span of about three minutes, Army scored three touchdowns, two after interceptions. On its first possession, after Notre Dame had netted only two yards, the Irish punted out of bounds at their 44-yard line. From that point the Cadets drove to their first touchdown, a six-yard run by senior quarterback Doug Kenna behind a fierce block by Blanchard. Less than two minutes later, Kenna intercepted a pass by Dancewicz and ran it back to the Notre Dame 28-yard line. On the next play, Kenna, a superb all-around athlete who had mastered the T formation quickly, faked a handoff to Glenn Davis, then gave it to the other halfback, Max Minor, who shot through tackle and sprinted 26 yards for the second touchdown.

Kenna also figured in the third touchdown. After Blanchard had intercepted another Dancewicz pass at the Irish 35-yard line, Kenna fired a touchdown pass to end Ed Rafalko to make it 20–0 at the end of the first quarter. Next it was Davis' turn to intercept a Dancewicz pass and run it back 47 yards before scoring from the 6-yard line by racing around right end. Several minutes later, Mr. Outside darted around right end again from six yards out after the ubiquitous Kenna had gained 34 yards on a punt return to make it a surprising, even shocking to many fans, 33–0 halftime lead. That point total was more than the Cadets had scored in the last 10 games against the Irish, the last five of which had ended in shutouts. By then the 2,500 cadets gathered in the grandstand were in a veritable uproar, while Notre Dame fans sat in stone silence. Meanwhile, West Point alums and thousands of other GIs in the army, many of them listening to the game abroad via short-wave radio, exulted over Army's first-half performance that seemed to have put the game out of Notre Dame's reach.

During Coach Ed McKeever's halftime oration he tried to assure his charges that with 30 minutes left the Irish still had plenty of time. "This game isn't over," said McKeever, a Notre Dame assistant coach who took over for Frank Leahy who had gone into the navy following the 1943 season. "We haven't done anything yet."

McKeever finally realized it was over early in the third period when Kenna caught a punt, started to his right, and then handed off the ball to Minor going the other way, after which the speedy Minor reversed his field and outraced a half-dozen Irish defenders during a 60-yard sprint down the right sideline. By now the Army rout was in full flower with the Cadets adding another touchdown when, after end Dick Pitzer recovered an errant Notre Dame lateral at the Irish 16-yard line, Kenna found Pitzer in the end zone with a six-yard pass.

Davis then scored his third touchdown early in the final quarter when he intercepted yet another pass and, three plays later, faked a pass and raced 55 yards into the end zone for his 27th touchdown in nine games since he made his debut in Army's opening game against Villanova on September 25 of the previous season. Many in the huge crowd had left by the time Army scored its ninth touchdown when backup Irish quarterback Joe Gasparella, on his own goal line, threw the ball into the hands of tackle Harold Tavzel on the Irish 6-yard line and Tavzel ran it in to make the final score 59–0.

Dominating both the offensive and defense lines, Army netted 226 yards on the ground against only 70 yards by Notre Dame. Both teams gained 100 yards passing, but the difference was that Notre Dame's quarterbacks were intercepted eight times while Kenna, also a basketball and tennis star, had only two of his 22 passes picked off. McKeever, fearing, and rightfully so, that Notre Dame would have trouble running against Army's bigger and better line, had decided to have Dancewicz throw far more than usual—a tactic that proved costly for the Irish. Later, Blaik said that had Notre Dame played more conservatively, Army most likely would not have scored 59 points. "After the first touchdown by Kenna, they went for broke with a passing attack that boomeranged to hand us one touchdown after another," he said. In retrospect, McKeever might well have agreed.

Though he did not score and gained only 25 yards on seven carries, Blanchard was outstanding, throwing several bruising blocks, intercepting two passes, making a number of jarring tackles from his left linebacker position on defense, and consistently booting kickoffs into and even beyond the end zone. One of Blanchard's blocks on 6'7" tackle John Adams was so severe that it also knocked down head linesman Davis Reese, who suffered a dislocated elbow and an injured knee.

Sportswriters had to plumb their vocabularies for words to describe Army's crushing rout of a team it hadn't beaten in 13 years and hadn't scored on during their five previous games. Typical of the accolades heaped on the Cadets in the next day's newspapers, *The New York Times* described the Cadets' performance as "an awesome exhibition of blazing offensive speed and throttling defensive power" in inflicting "the worst disaster the Fighting Irish have suffered on the football field."

Next up was a Pennsylvania team that had yielded only 20 points to Army in their last four games over the last four years, three of which the Quakers had won while the fourth had ended in a 13–13 tie. (The teams previously had met only once, in 1901, when Army beat Penn

24–0 at a time when touchdowns counted for only five points and the forward pass was still not legal.) However, in posting a 4–2 record in 1944, Penn had lost by more than three touchdowns to Navy and Michigan, making Army a prohibitive favorite over the Quakers.

*　*　*

In winning its first seven games so decisively, Army had racked up 419 points for an average of almost 60 points a game while limiting its opponents to 21 points on three touchdowns. But apart from the Coast Guard Academy, those opponents had all been weakened by the loss of players to the military, although a few had actually improved thanks to the navy's V-12 program that brought some outstanding players from other schools to their campuses. The question also arose as to whether Army was playing on a figuratively level playing field since most of its starters, and even a number of good reserves, had already played on the college level before being recruited to West Point.

That plethora of talent was evident by Red Blaik's decision to use two separate and equally skilled units. Almost all of those 27 players (both units had substitutes) most likely would have been starters at any other school. At least some fans and other observers also felt that some of the transfers had willingly accepted appointments to West Point because it made them exempt from the military draft during at least part of the war—certainly no one thought the war would end earlier than expected in 1945—even though the ones who lasted until graduation would have to serve three years in the army or the Army Air Corps. The biggest exception was Glenn Davis, who had gone directly from high school to West Point. Had he not, some skeptics pointed out, he might well have been drafted into the army. Ironically, there did not seem to be any wholesale resentment toward the Army team, but the term "slackers" often was directed at other teams, most notably Notre Dame, perhaps because the Fighting Irish continued to field strong teams throughout the war, albeit with players from other colleges who had been sent to Notre Dame to train as future officers in the navy and Marines under the navy's V-12 programs. Some Notre Dame alumni and fans thought that such taunts came from bigots and were reminiscent of the days in the 1920s and 1930s when calls of harps, hibernians, micks, and papists were directed at Fighting Irish football teams that usually had as many Protestant as Irish starters, including the great George Gipp, and one of the best players in the late 1920s and in 1930, Marchy Schwartz, an All-American halfback in 1930, who was Jewish. Then there was the famed Notre Dame coach of that era, Knute Rockne, who was a Protestant during his playing days and until he converted to Catholicism in 1925, seven years after he became the head coach in 1918.

Despite some critics and skeptics, the 1944 Army team became perhaps the most popular ever to represent the U.S. Military Academy— its overwhelming success seemingly perceived by many Americans as a symbol of the U.S. Army's strength and power throughout the world. Many sportswriters, caught up with Army's overwhelming successes, began to use battlefield terms in their stories about the Cadets' play, such as comparing their drives down field as going into "enemy territory" and calling the team "a swift infantry" and a "juggernaut." No one seemed to object as, week by week, Army added more followers and in due time to many sports fans became "America's team" and link it with the army, navy, Marine, and Air Corps teams fighting abroad. Nor did sportswriters or fans seem to object that Army was loaded with players from other schools who were lured to West Point, some felt, to ensure that Army would be a winning team and perhaps serve as a metaphor for the entire U.S. Army and its rich and glorious history.

4

Racial Divide Even
During War Time

B Y LATE NOVEMBER 1944, THE TIDE HAD TURNED IN THE ALLIES' favor following the D-Day invasion, the bombing of military targets in Germany, and advances, albeit with a great loss of American lives, in the Pacific. That summer, for example, 14,000 American Marines had been killed during the battle for Saipan in the Mariana Islands before the island was secured on July 9, and there were heavy losses, too, during the invasions and battles for Guam and Tinian, also in the Marianas. That meant that the relatively new B-29s, the largest bombers ever built and a sturdier version of the famed B17 fortresses, would then have bases close enough to bomb Japan, which they did.

Sadly, an incident in Philadelphia demonstrated that there was still racial conflict among Americans, even during a war when most of the country was united. It was bad enough that blacks, then usually referred to as Negroes or colored, were forced to serve in separate units until late in the war and faced racial bias while in service, especially at bases in the south. When, out of desperation, blacks were integrated with white units late in the war, they drew heavy praise, and in many cases fought heroically. And the famed Tuskegee Airmen, an all-black unit, distinguished itself by winning a number of high honors, including the Silver Cross.

Yet despite an executive order issued by President Roosevelt in 1941 banning a strike, 10,000 mass transit employees who worked for the Philadelphia Transportation Company went on strike on August 1 when eight of the company's 500 black employees who had been restricted to menial jobs applied for jobs as motormen and finished high enough on the list that they had to be hired. The strike in the city that prided itself on its nickname, the City of Brotherly Love, halted all of the city's buses and streetcars, making it impossible to get to work for most of the 900,000 defense workers in one of the largest war production centers in the country. Three days after the strike virtually immobilized Philadelphia and some surrounding towns, Roosevelt, furious over the strike, issued another executive order authorizing the War Department to take control of the Philadelphia Transportation Company with army troops to operate the buses, streetcars, and subways. The following day, August 5, strike leaders were arrested, and five hours later 5,000 army troops moved into the city. That night the striking workers were warned on Philadelphia radio stations that unless they returned to work the next day, Sunday, by midnight, they would be fired and subjected to the military draft. By then most Philadelphians had turned against the strikers who then capitulated and returned to work and the eight black workers began training to become the city's first black motormen.

At first some of them faced problems. "The first runs were tough," said one of the new motormen, William Barber. "People spit at me, and I almost lost my temper, but I said, 'No, I'll just take it.' And gradually things settled down." Roosevelt's strong-arm tactic worked. By the time the war ended, the total number of blacks working in manufacturing, most of it defense work, had increased by 500,000 to 2 million, and the number of blacks in unions had gone up by 700,000. That progress was not to say that racial harmony was on the rise throughout the country, however, not when a number of violent attacks had occurred against black servicemen in the south.

Integration in sports was still a long way off. There may have been popular black boxers, such as heavyweight champion Joe Louis, but in 1944 there still were no blacks in professional baseball and football, and the professional Basketball Association of America, the precursor of the National Basketball Association, was still two years into the future, and it was an all-white league until 1950. Pro football was the first professional league to integrate when four players signed contracts and played in 1946, the year before Jackie Robinson became the first black player in the major leagues in modern times.

On the college level, the Army football team would not have a black player until 1966 when Gary Steele, then a 19-year-old sophomore (third class in West Point lingo) became a wide receiver. That was five years after Darryl Hill, also a receiver, broke the football color barrier at Annapolis, where he became one of eventual Heisman Trophy–winner Roger Staubach's favorite receivers on the plebe team. By then most colleges had fielded black players since the early 1940s, including Robinson who was a star halfback at UCLA from 1939 through 1941. Steele soon became a starter, was selected to play in the then prestigious Shrine Bowl game for college stars, was drafted by the Detroit Lions, and then served in the army for more than 20 years before retiring as a colonel after which he worked in human resources for the Kansas City school system and later for Pfizer, the pharmaceutical company.

During the summer of 1944, President Roosevelt signed into law what became the GI Bill of Rights, which he regarded as one of the government's proudest achievements. The law entitled servicemen and women who had served at least 90 days in the military and had been honorably discharged up to four years of college, prep, or vocational schools, zero-interest home loans, and low-interest loans to start up businesses along with cash payments of $20 a week (more than $200 by 2014 standards) for a year under what became known as the 52–20 club, and other benefits that entitled several million veterans to attend college and to buy and establish businesses they otherwise would not have been able to afford.

*   *   *

Cadets who graduated from West Point were not eligible for most of those GI benefits, but they would receive sizable pensions if they pursued careers in the army, which a considerable number did. So the GI Bill was hardly on their minds as they prepared for the Penn game. Penn was much on the mind of Red Blaik, who feared a letdown after the impressive victory over Notre Dame. None of Blaik's first three teams had been able to beat the Quakers, and Blaik was well aware that in 1940 Penn had inflicted the worst beating Army ever received when it crushed the Cadets 48–0. That whipping during a season when Army won only one of its nine games—its opener against Williams—was believed to have so disturbed the West Point superintendent, Lieutenant General Robert Eichelberger, who was at the game in Philadelphia, that he eventually convinced the West Point Athletic Board to accede to his request that the Academy make an exception to an unwritten rule of having only regular army officers coach the Cadets and hire Blaik, a former assistant coach at Army, then the head coach at Dartmouth and a 1920 graduate of the Point but no longer an army officer. (Blaik soon thereafter accepted a commission as a colonel, the title by which most of his players referred to him.)

Blaik, hardly known as an optimist, feared that his Army team would be overconfident coming into the Penn game while looking ahead to a much stronger Navy team the following Saturday. Before a crowd of 70,000 at Franklin Field on the Penn campus, his concern was validated early in the opening quarter when Army was kept pinned inside its 15-yard line during the first 10 minutes while the Quakers reached the Army 12 before being repulsed. But on Army's next possession, halfback Max Minor, a member of Army's starting team—the A unit—found a hole through right tackle, cut to the right sideline, and raced 68 yards for the game's first score. Less than three minutes later, Penn end Bill Schuman scooped up a fumble by Dale Hall and followed a covey of blockers 49 yards to tie the score at 7–7. Hall quickly made amends for his fumble late in the opening quarter when he shot through left tackle past the Quakers' star 250-lb. George Savitsky, then dodged several defenders in the Penn secondary while running 45 yards for a touchdown. Army then began an unanswered 49-point scoring burst with touchdowns by Blanchard and Davis in the second period to open up a 27–7 halftime lead.

Thereafter, the flood gates were wide open with the Cadets scoring four touchdowns in the third period, including two more by Davis and another by Blanchard, which exemplified both his talent and versatility. After kicking off, Blanchard raced down the field and hit the receiver, George Opel, so hard that he jarred the ball loose and pounced on it at the Penn 14-yard line. Then, after running to the 10, Blanchard caught a pass from quarterback Tom Lombardo in the end zone for a touchdown. The final touchdown, in the final quarter, came when one of Red Blaik's backup halfbacks, Dean Sensanbaugher, the transfer from Ohio State, recovered a Penn fumble on the Army 10-yard line and sprinted 90 yards for a touchdown to make it 62–7. Army placekicker Dick Walterhouse, who also played halfback, then tied the NCAA record when he booted five extra points to give him 44 points. Walterhouse may well have broken the record had Penn students sitting in the end zones not refused to throw back the balls Walterhouse kicked into the stands (screens to preclude that from happening were still years away). Thereafter, at the officials' request, Army resorted to two runs by

Sensanbaugher and a pass to Hank Foldberg for their final extra points, lest the supply of balls be exhausted.

Although Army had been a prohibitive favorite, the Cadets' offensive onslaught stunned the capacity crowd and some veteran sportswriters who realized they might have been watching the best Army football team of all time. Now, after the worst loss ever inflicted on Penn, only Navy stood between Army and its first undefeated season—and that did not shape up as an easy task since the Midshipmen, despite two defeats, were out-ranked only by No. 1 Army in the national rankings. Because of wartime travel restrictions, the game was scheduled to be played at Thompson Stadium at Annapolis as had the one in 1942, followed by the 1943 game at Michie Stadium in West Point. However, top officials in both the army and navy departments convinced the Roosevelt administration to permit the game to be played in Baltimore where a war-bond drive would be held in conjunction with the game. It proved to be a wise decision as war-bond sales at the game would almost amount to $60 million. Opponents of having the game played in front of a large crowd amid considerable hoopla were led by army secretary Henry Stimson.

Although Army's remarkable run occupied much of the country's attention, news from both the European and Pacific theaters of operation dominated the news, and most of the news was good. While Army was crushing Penn, the new B-29 bombers, now known as Flying Fortresses and flying out of bases in China, had bombed a strategic iron and steel center in the northern Japanese island of Kyushu and dock and warehouse facilities in Japanese-occupied Nanking. Meanwhile, navy ships and planes sank three Japanese transport ships and seven destroyers that were in a 19-ship convoy on their way to landing troops off Leyte in the Philippines.

In the European theater of operations, General George C. Patton's Third Army burst through German defenses outside the French city of Nancy, thereby threatening the key city of Metz and the nearby coal-rich Saar Basin. In that same day, more than 750 American B-17 bombers dropped 40,000 bombs on industrial and communication centers around Frankfurt and Cologne, cities through which troops and supplies were funneled to the western front.

*   *   *

With two weeks to go before the Army-Navy game, sportswriters and sports broadcasters had more than ample time to build up the game as the most significant in the long rivalry and the biggest college game of the year. For years, Harvard and Yale alumni, along with much of the media in New England and the New York metropolitan area, had referred to the annual game between the Crimson and the Bulldogs as "The Game," which it undoubtedly was in the latter part of the nineteenth century and into the 1920s when the outcome often decided the national championship. As had been the case since intercollegiate football became popular in the early part of the twentieth century, Harvard and Yale had been national powers and quite often the best college teams in the country. Indeed, from their first meeting in 1893 through 1909, Army had beaten Yale only once in 17 games (four ties), even though all of those games were played at West Point, with the one victory coming in 1904. Thereafter, Army won only two of the next seven games (one tie) until dominating the series in the 1930s and early 1940s.

In November 1944, "The Game" definitely was the one between Army and Navy. In the two weeks leading up to the meeting of the two military academies, even the dour and pessimistic Blaik called it "the greatest of all Army-Navy games." What made it all the more attractive to many Americans was that it would involve players already in the military who were being trained to be army and navy officers, and during a war, no less. More than a few of those players never would have considered going to West Point or Annapolis during peacetime, while some very likely jumped at the chance to do so since the alternative was to be drafted. Even players like Blanchard and Coulter who were already in the service when they were recruited to play for Army and no doubt realized that they were in effect buying time before they might actually be sent into battle and might even be able to spend the rest of the war at West Point. Certainly no one knew that the war would end in 1945 when most members of the 1944 team would still be at the U.S. Military Academy. Indeed, some of those players told me years later that they looked forward to getting involved in the war and were actually disappointed when it ended while they were still at West Point. Only then, some of them said, did they feel a sense of guilt about having been able to avoid being in harm's way and playing football when young men of their ages were being killed or wounded in Europe or the Pacific.

"I was disappointed that I didn't get to serve," said Roland Catarinella, normally a center but occasionally used in the backfield, who received a medical discharge but no commission because of a severe leg injury suffered in his last game against Duke in 1945 while running the ball. "I wanted very much to be an officer and serve my country."

Some others not only did not get a commission but did not graduate or receive medical discharges, either, which certainly did not look good for West Point or the players, three of whom went on to play in the National Football League. But in the 1944 Army-Navy game, they would still be integral parts of what had become "America's team."

5

★ ★ ★

The Midshipman-Cadet

I T WAS A GORGEOUS LATE OCTOBER AFTERNOON AND THE VERY accomplished six-piece band on stage, along with a talented "girl singer," was making its last performance of the summer-fall season at the Tokeneke Club on the shores of Long Island Sound in Darien, Connecticut, before about 150 members of the high-tone tennis and swim club. The talent of the band was very obvious, and no wonder. One of the musicians, drummer Joe Corsello, once played for the Benny Goodman Orchestra, while another, Johnny Morris, played piano in the Buddy Rich band. Indeed the only "amateur" in the group was the band leader, Bob Woods, a very good trumpet player who held the distinction of being the only player to have played on both sides in the traditional Army-Navy football game.

Perhaps befitting the band leader's seniority, and the fact that Woods selects the numbers to be played, the songs included such old chestnuts as "Don't Get Around Much Any More," "Have You Met Miss Jones," and "The Very Thought of You," some of them sung by Annalise Bryan, who hadn't yet been born when most of the songs in the medley became popular.

In a group of professional musicians, all of whom had been recruited by Woods, who started the band in the 1980s—he was the only club member—Woods more than held his own with his trumpet, which he has been playing for more than 80 years. Even when he wasn't playing with great verve and enthusiasm Woods, wearing an open-neck white shirt, tapped his feet, clapped his hands, and swayed from side to side with the music. Besides being the only founding member of "Bob's Band," as it's called, Woods, who was a halfback at both Annapolis and West Point, then at 93 years old, was far and away the oldest member of the band. Though she had heard him play the trumpet since before they were married in June 1945, Woods' wife, Gerry, watched with obvious pride in her husband's performance and the songs he had selected, some of which they may have danced to when he met her after cutting in on another cadet during a "hop" at West Point in 1945. After the two-hour performance, Woods and other members of the band were surrounded by club members and thanked for their first-class musical efforts, after which the nonagenarian trumpet player and his wife drove to their nearby home in his 1967 Mercedes-Benz with Woods already talking to Gerry about the following year's series of Sunday afternoon pop band concerts.

About as lean and athletic-looking as he was as a football halfback and track star while playing for Navy (after a year at Bucknell) and then for the next two years for Army, Bob Woods was hardy resting on his laurels, either on his days as an all-round athlete (he was also a sprinter and baseball pitcher at Bucknell, Annapolis, and West Point), as the onetime First Captain of Cadets at West Point (the highest honor a cadet can achieve) as an army officer, or as a successful businessman. For one thing, he practiced on the trumpet almost daily, still trying to improve at an age when most musicians have long since retired.

Few if any former players know how big the Army-Navy football game was from a player's point of view as Bob Woods, who played for Navy in 1940 and 1941 and for Army in 1942 and 1943, something that no football player has ever done on the varsity level as of 2013 when the only playing Woods was doing was the trumpet. After a season on the freshman team at Annapolis, Woods was a halfback for Navy the following year and then played the same position for Army during the next two seasons. After his last football season in 1943, when he scored three touchdowns against Princeton at Yankee Stadium, Woods accomplished another unprecedented feat when, as a first-classman (senior year parlance at the U.S. Military Academy), during the 1944–45 academic year, he became one of the few athletes at West Point—and the first former varsity football player at Annapolis—to be selected as the First Captain of Cadets, also known as brigade commander at West Point. Indeed, previous First Captains included eventual generals John Pershing, the commander of U.S. expeditionary forces in Europe during World War I and later army chief of staff; Douglas MacArthur, who after World War I served as superintendant at West Point from 1919 until 1922; and William Westmoreland, who was the commander of American forces in Vietnam from 1964 to 1968.

In that exalted position, a year after he had played in his last Army-Navy game, Woods broke another barrier when, as the First Captain of Cadets, he led the march of about 3,000 cadets from Baltimore Harbor—a distance of almost two miles—into Municipal Stadium on December 2, 1944, as a prelude to what even Red Blaik called the biggest Army-Navy game of all time when Army was ranked first and Navy second in national polls. As First Captain of Cadets, Woods was also in charge of the cadets who, turning sailors for a night, made a 12-hour seagoing trip from the West Point dock to Baltimore on the passenger ship *Uruguay*, which was on leave from its primary work as a troop ship during World War II. During the voyage down the Hudson River and into the Atlantic Ocean, because of German submarines known to be in the area, the *Uruguay* was escorted along the East Coast by several destroyer escorts and a dirigible overhead. While the *Uruguay* never did encounter any Nazi U-boats, it did encounter rough conditions in the Atlantic and, as Robert Woods vividly recalled, more than half of the cadets became seasick. But not Woods, perhaps because he had trained at sea during his two years at Annapolis. Among the cadets on board was Alexander Haig, later to become a four-star general, secretary of state under President Ronald Reagan, chief of staff for presidents Richard Nixon and Gerald Ford, and commander of NATO forces in Europe. Whether or not Haig weathered the trip without getting seasick, Woods did not recall.

But he most definitely recalled being leader of the 3,000 cadets after they arrived in Baltimore on the bitter cold morning of the game. "Leading the cadets into Municipal Stadium that day as the First Captain of Cadets was very special, all the more so since I had played in the Army-Navy game for both academies and knew quite a few of the players on the Navy team," Woods said during an interview at his Fairfield County home in the fall of 2013. It may have even been more special than in 1942 when Woods lined up at halfback for Army at Thompson Stadium on the Naval Academy campus against many players he had played with the year before. "I remember how, when I first lined up for Army, Vince Anania, a teammate of mine at Navy, called out to me, 'Where do you think you're going, Woody?'" Woods said with a laugh while sitting in the living room of his home with his wife. As it was, neither Woods nor any other Army back went very far in that game as the Midshipmen, for the fourth year in a row and the third time by a shutout, beat the Cadets as they would do again in 1943 at West Point during the two home-and-home series ordered by President Roosevelt as a wartime effort to curtail travel.

That Woods would be picked as the First Captain of Cadets at West Point—an honor bestowed on a cadet who had shown leadership skills and done well in classes and as an athlete—was all the more surprising since Woods had in effect flunked out of the Naval Academy because of academic problems. "I didn't study as hard as I probably should have at Annapolis, because of my total concentration on sports, but realized I had to when I got to West Point where conditions were even more severe," he said. "And so I really buckled down academically and wound up graduating on schedule in June 1945."

Woods barely made it to West Point on time. "When I got home after leaving Annapolis in the spring of 1942, I called Coach Blaik to let him know I was available," Woods said. "They showed some interest, and I met with one of the assistant coaches at the Point, and we went to Washington in search of a congressman to get an appointment, but that didn't work out. Then, when I didn't hear back from West Point, and since the war was on, I decided in late July to join the Marines. But when I drove to the nearest recruiting station in Elmira, about 10 miles from my hometown of Corning, I saw a sign on the storefront window saying it was closed because of a death in the family."

For Bob Woods, that turned out to be a fortuitous break.

"Later that day, after I got home, I got a call from Red Blaik, asking me if I was still interested in coming to West Point, but that since I was going to turn 22 the next day, I had better hurry to get up there so that I could get sworn in by midnight," Woods recalled in alluding to the fact that incoming cadets other than Army enlisted men had to be under 22 to be enrolled. "I told Blaik, 'I'll be there.' By then it was already Friday night, and so we didn't have much time since West Point was about 270 miles away from my home in upstate Corning, and the weather was bad, foggy and raining. When my dad and I were only about 10 miles away, we got stopped by a state trooper for going too fast. But when we explained our situation, he understood and led us the rest of the way. We finally arrived about a quarter to midnight, which was my deadline, and went directly to Coach Blaik's house at the Academy.

The coach then hurried us over to the adjutant general's house and he swore me in just minutes before midnight. By then my dad was heading back to Corning. Later I found out that Blaik had gotten an appointment for me from a congressman in Georgia, a somewhat inexplicable chain of events but common in the 1940s when Army was building the strongest teams in its history. Ironically and, so far as I know strictly a coincidence, my roommate during my first year turned out to be the congressman's son," Woods said.

During the following week, Woods had to contend with Beast Barracks, being addressed as "Mr. Dumbjohn," the common term used by upperclassmen while being commanded to "Brace Up!" "Get that smile off your face!" "Suck up your gut!" and others that were at least or even more derogatory during what was still traditionally an acceptable and degrading form of bullying at West Point, even though it had been toned down during the war. Other indignities included being ordered to get supplies for upperclassmen, marching with rifles, and running endlessly while also doing basic training at nearby Pine Camp. Learning that Woods had attended the Naval Academy made matters worse. "It could be rough, but it was bearable once you got used to it and knew it wasn't going to last," Woods said.

★   ★   ★

Fortunately, during early preseason practice sessions in September, Woods, a 170-lb. halfback, did not face any harassment from his new Army teammates, many of whom remembered him from the last Army-Navy game. From the outset of the 1942 season, Woods saw considerable action as a halfback on offense and a cornerback on defense, including his three-touchdown spree against Princeton. However, his playing time diminished the following season, largely because of a leg infection that put him in the West Point infirmary, and also because of the presence of plebe Doc Blanchard who was now in the backfield with Glenn Davis. The following year—his last as a Cadet—Woods helped coach the Army junior varsity football team while serving as the time-consuming First Captain of Cadets. "Things turned out very well for me when Earl Blaik recruited me to West Point," Woods said. Indeed things hardly could have turned out better for Woods since he met his wife during his last year at West Point while the bride was a student at Smith College. They were married in the West Point chapel the day after Woods graduated and was commissioned as second lieutenant in June 1945.

Actually, Woods was the second football player to play at both Army and Navy. The first was James Kelleher, who played on the Navy freshman team but never the varsity before transferring in 1940 to West Point where he spent three seasons as an end, including the 1942 season when he played alongside Woods. However, Kelleher's situation in switching military academies differed from that of Woods. While he was at the Naval Academy, Kelleher's brother, William, who played on the 1938 Army football team and was playing on the Cadets' 1939 baseball team, died of pneumonia in April of that year when he was a 20-year-old cadet. After William's death, their father, a career army officer, asked James Kelleher if he would transfer to West Point to, in effect, take his brother's place. Like his father, Kelleher became a career officer, retiring from the military in 1967, 24 years after his graduation from West Point. In a remarkable series of events, Kelleher was named First Captain of Cadets in 1942, two years before his fellow former Midshipman, Robert Woods, received the same high honor. "Jim was a very handsome and nice guy, and we obviously had a lot in common in having both gone to Annapolis and winding up as captains of cadets at West Point," Woods said.

It is an honor that no one applies for, although firsties (another term for seniors at West Point) become aware—in advance and unofficially—that they're in the running for First Captain of Cadets. "You don't find out until the first day of classes during the fall semester when it's announced while all the cadets are having dinner in Washington Hall," said Woods, who also pitched for the Army baseball team and was a sprinter and threw the shot put on the track team. "When I heard my name called, it seemed like all of the 3,000 cadets threw their hats in the air and cheered. And I was thrilled." Six months later, Woods got another surprise when, while First Captain of Cadets, he was informed by West Point superintendant Francis Wilby that he was going to be on the cover of *Time* magazine. A week after graduation, he appeared in uniform with a group of cadets marching in the background in the June 11, 1945, issue. Along with a photo of Woods and his new bride, *Time* ran a six-page spread that focused mainly on Woods. Not surprisingly, copies of that issue remain a prize possession in his Darien home and later at the Woods' apartment in nearby Stamford.

Unlike the other Midshipman-turned West Point cadet, James Kelleher, Woods did not make the army a career. After serving as an infantry officer and with the Eleventh Airborne Division in the Philippines and Japan, Woods was discharged in 1949 and began a long career as a business executive, mostly in New York, that included 19 years with the Doubleday publishing company before he retired as a vice president in 1989. "That gave me more time to spend with my family and my trumpet," Woods said before beginning a practice session for his last gig of the year at the Tokeneke Club.

Surprisingly, despite his football exploits at Annapolis and West Point, Woods' finest sports memory is from a baseball game in the spring of 1944 between Army and the Montreal Royals, the Triple A farm team of the Brooklyn Dodgers. Both teams did spring training at the nearby Bear Mountain Inn and indoors at West Point and played occasional games against one another. "I was the starting pitcher, and I think because I was so nervous going up against a team with some future big leaguers I walked the first three men I faced," Woods recalled, "but then I settled down and struck out the next three batters. I'll never forget that inning." To Bob Woods, apparently, that accomplishment was even more memorable than the three touchdowns he scored against Princeton in 1942 at Yankee Stadium or playing on both sides in the Army-Navy series during the previous three football seasons.

6

★ ★ ★

A "Story Book" Team

IN THE MEMORY OF MANY LONGTIME SPORTSWRITERS AND
broadcasters (the start of television on a large scale was still about
five years away) no one could recall a sports event that received the publicity buildup leading to the Army-Navy game of 1944. "There never
had been a sports event, perhaps an event of any kind, that received the
attention of so many Americans in so many places around the world,"
wrote Al Laney, a veteran sportswriter for the *New York Herald Tribune*,
a few days before the game. That may have been hyperbole given the
intense media interest in the two heavyweight title fights between Jack
Dempsey and Gene Tunney in 1926 and 1927 that each drew more
than 100,000 spectators while millions more heard the broadcasts on
radio. Almost as much publicity preceded the rematch between Joe
Louis and Max Schmeling at Yankee Stadium in New York on June 22,
1938, when Louis knocked out Schmeling in the first round to retain
his heavyweight title.

But during those years, boxing was as popular as football, both
college and professional, in the U.S. However, it's safe to say that by
1944 college football had expanded in popularity to the point where

games between long-time rivals such as Yale and Harvard and of course Army and Navy received as much if not more national attention than big fights. Also by 1944 the National Football League, with stars such as Sammy Baugh, Sid Luckman, and Don Hutson, was attracting a growing interest that led to a growing popularity where today there is an almost overwhelming amount of hype during the two weeks leading up to the annual Super Bowl game in early February. In 1944, though, no other sports event seized the attention of the American public like the Army-Navy football game, which outshone baseball's World Series between the St. Louis Cardinals and the St. Louis Browns two months earlier and other high-profile sports events.

Fretting over the forthcoming Navy game, Blaik worked his charges harder than he had all season during the week leading up to the game. On Wednesday, during a scrimmage, Doc Blanchard burst up the middle only to be stopped by several teammates who took considerable punishment in doing so, especially center Ug Fuson.

"Run that one again," Blaik called out.

That prompted Fuson, still groggy from helping stop Blanchard, to reply, "Colonel, if we run this play much more, you're not going to have any center left."

Blaik smiled at Fuson's response but still ordered the play run again, much to his center's dismay.

Forever suspicious that an opponent would do most anything to beat his Army teams, especially now that it had become the dominant college team in the country, Blaik was inclined to ensure that he had well-placed observers aware of the opponent's pregame plans. Such information occasionally paid off as it did in the week leading up to the 1944 Army-Navy game when Blaik was informed that Navy was re-sodding the field at Municipal Stadium in Baltimore. To Blaik it was a maneuver to slow down Davis, Blanchard, Dale Hall, and Max Minor among other Army runners. He thereupon dispatched Captain

Jack Buckler, an assistant Army coach and former Cadets halfback, to travel to Baltimore to check out the field. Arriving the Monday before the game, Buckler saw that the field had already been resodded on one side from the 40-yard line to the goal line. Acting on Blaik's order, Buckler demanded that the installation of the new soft and spongy turf be stopped. However, Navy's graduate manager and a retired National Guard general, no less, who was representing the Naval Academy on the project, pointed out that although the game was to be played in Baltimore it was be a "home game" for Navy, the same as Army was the home team at the game it played in New York, and Navy had decided that the resodding was necessary. During a rather heated exchange, Buckler's request was denied. Then, as Blaik had feared, more rain fell during the week, and by the day of the game, the field was soft and uneven at points, which the coach felt might well slow down his outstanding corps of runners.

Summing up the anticipation of the much-heralded contest, Allison Danzig of *The New York Times* wrote, "In all of the history of this service rivalry, there has never been a game that commanded the attention centered in tomorrow's clash. It stands among the sports naturals of all time, and arrangements have been made to broadcast it, not only throughout the nation, but by short-wave to the armed forces all over the world." In all, 143 stations of the Columbia Broadcasting System would carry the broadcast of the game in which Army was a 14-point favorite. Most likely not many GIs cared who won or lost, although most alumni of the military academies no doubt did, especially those on active duty, including famed generals Douglas MacArthur, Dwight Eisenhower, George Patton, and Omar Bradley, all of whom were huge Army football fans, and admirals William "Bull" Halsey, Chester Nimitz, William Leahy, and Ernest King.

Although snow flurries fell in the early afternoon, fortunately for Army, by game time it was clear but still cold. While the playing surface was relatively soft, Blaik did not think it would hinder his outstanding corps of running backs, but he was far from sure. It may have been wartime, but the crowd of almost 70,000 included some of the U.S. military's top brass. Among them were army chief of staff General George C. Marshall; his navy counterpart, Admiral King; General Henry "Hap" Arnold, head of the Army Air Corps; President Roosevelt's chief of staff, Admiral Leahy; and Admiral Jonas Ingram, commander of the Atlantic Fleet. Representing FDR in the presidential box was his daughter (Roosevelt also had five sons), Anna Boettiger, along with some friends, all of whom showed at least public impartiality by cheering for both teams. The president, a Navy fan because of his stint as an assistant secretary of the navy from 1913 to 1920, had planned to attend the game but was at what he called the "little White House," his retreat in Warm Springs, Georgia, on his first vacation since his arduous fourth election campaign.

No other sports event comes close to the panoply of an Army-Navy game, and the 1944 game was particularly special since American military forces had begun to turn the tide in the war against Germany and Japan and because the two academy teams would be playing for the national championship. Spectators, millions of radio listeners, and an untold number of other Americans also knew that while more than ever was at stake in the game between the arch rivals, many of the players would soon be brothers at arms during the war. The game was also unique because it involved perhaps the only major football-playing schools that had not been hurt by the military draft—both cadets and midshipmen were exempt—and thus as strong, if not stronger than ever, with the addition of star players who had been recruited from other colleges. For Army it was particularly special because the Cadets had not beaten Navy since 1938, and in the ensuing five games had scored only six points on a touchdown by Jim Watkins in the 1941 game, Army's first under Red Blaik, while Navy had scored 65 points. Both teams were also motivated because of the bad blood that had developed during the 1943 game at West Point when a number of fights broke out, some of them, in Army's opinion, by Navy's All-American and pugnacious tackle Don Whitmire, who had also been an All-American at Alabama before transferring to Navy, as had the Midshipmen's best runner, All-American Bobby Jenkins, and track star Clyde "Smackover" Scott, who would finish second in the high hurdles at the 1948 Olympics.

How good were these 1944 Army and Navy teams? In the week leading up to the game, seven of the 11 players (only 11 players were named to various All-American teams during the two-way player era) named to the United Press All-American team were from the two academies: Blanchard, Davis, Barney Poole, and guard Joe Stanowicz from Army, and Jenkins, Whitmire, and guard Ben Chase of Navy. Of the seven, four had previously played at other schools—Blanchard, Poole, Jenkins, and Whitmire—before transferring to either West Point or Annapolis. Like Army, Navy was not averse to bringing in players from other schools, which it rarely did during peacetime. Army had done so since just before World War I and in the 1920s, and almost all of them had achieved All-American status before they got to West Point. Even more players were eventually named to the Associated Press and other All-Star teams, either on the first, second, or third teams, or for honorable mention.

* * *

At 1:00 in the afternoon, an hour before the opening kickoff with snow falling lightly, the West Point band marched on to the field, playing "Anchors Aweigh," followed by the approximately 2,500 cadets led by Robert Woods. Shortly thereafter, the Naval Academy band paraded on to the field and, repaying the tribute from the West Point band, played a medley of songs associated with the army, with around 3,000 midshipmen to the rear. Perhaps because of the war, the sight of the cadets and midshipmen parading across the field drew an almost deafening roar from the crowd before what Red Blaik had said was going to be the greatest Army-Navy game of all time.

By the time of the kickoff at 2:00 PM, the snowfall had ended and the sun had broken through while millions of Americans, both throughout the United States, on ships at sea, and at far-flung outposts in war zones in Europe and the Pacific, were tuned in for the broadcast. Among them was Lieutenant General Robert Eichelberger who, while superintendent at West Point, was primarily responsible for bringing Blaik to the Academy from Dartmouth. At his request, an enlisted soldier who was an aide to the general awakened Eichelberger at 2:00 in the morning in Leyte in the Philippines, his headquarters as commander of the Eighth Army, and where he had members of the Army Signal Corps erect an antenna in front of his house and put a powerful radio in his office. A huge Army football fan since his days at West Point, the general sat transfixed in his office with fresh coffee nearby, listening to the short-wave broadcast of the game. At one point during the game an air raid alert sounded, but Eichelberger and some other high-ranking officers closed the blackout curtains in his office and kept on listening without paying attention to the Japanese raid on the base, which, fortunately, did very little damage and did not result in any casualties.

Indeed, never before had an audience for an Army-Navy game been so large over such a far-flung area. But then never before had Army played Navy in a game in which the teams were ranked first and second and that would no doubt decide the national championship. And its timing occurred during the largest world-wide conflagration of all time that would soon involve many of the players on the field. The teams appeared to be strong in two opposing key elements: Army on offense, and Navy on defense. The Midshipmen had lost two games, one by a 21–14 score to a North Carolina Pre-Flight team loaded with prospective pilots who had already starred at other schools, and to Georgia Tech 17–15. Army, of course, was undefeated. Apart from its loss to North Carolina Pre-Flight, Navy had trounced Notre Dame, Penn, Duke, Purdue, Penn State, and Cornell, which was still a national power, as were many of the Ivy League teams at the time. The teams used different offenses with Army utilizing the T formation for the second year and Navy still employing the single-wing. The chief difference was that Army would alternate separate units during most of the game, while Navy would primarily stay with its starting team for all 60 minutes, except for eight substitutes who would also play briefly.

As so often happens in football games, injuries may have played a significant outcome of the 1944 game. As was usually the case when Army won the coin-toss at midfield, Blanchard kicked off. As usual Blanchard boomed his kick into the end zone, and from there it was run back to the Navy 32-yard line by "Smackover" Scott, a halfback who would earn All-American honors during his two years at Annapolis and three at Arkansas.

During Navy's first possession, Jenkins, who was already nursing an infected toe, was following a covey of blockers but Stanowicz brushed past two of them and flattened Jenkins with a high hit, and Army linebacker Bobby Dobbs also crashed into Jenkins as he was on his way down to the moist turf. With stunned midshipmen in the crowd looking on, a groggy Jenkins had to be helped off the field and would not return until late in the game. It was a portent of the brutally hard hitting that would continue throughout what Stanley Woodward, the legendary sports editor of the *New York Herald Tribune*, would call a "savagely fought game."

Neither Army nor Navy got beyond the opponent's 45-yard line in the opening quarter, with each team managing only a single first down, and with only one pass thrown by Navy for a four-yard gain. With Army's second unit that included Blanchard and Davis now in the game, in the second quarter the Cadets began to move. Navy appeared to be on the verge of scoring first early in the period when Clyde "Smackover" Scott returned a punt by Blanchard to the Army 35-yard line and on the next play carried the ball to the 26. But after Navy's 5'9" 160-lb. halfback Hal Hamberg, a transfer from Arkansas, was sacked for an eight-yard loss, he fired a pass that was intercepted by Army linebacker Herschel "Ug" Fuson. Mainly on the strength of running by Blanchard and Davis, the Cadets drove to Navy's 16 before losing the ball on an incomplete pass by quarterback Doug Kenna. However, on its next possession, with Navy's line showing signs of tiring against the fresh Army unit, the Cadets drove 66 yards for a touchdown with right halfback Dale Hall scoring from the Navy 24-yard line after Kenna had flummoxed the Navy defense by faking a handoff to Davis going to his right and then handing off to Hall who ran around the Middies' right side and across the goal line unmolested. Reserve halfback and quarterback Dick Walterhouse then made it 7–0 when he kicked his 45th extra point of the season, a new NCAA record.

Walterhouse, a reserve halfback in the game and a backup quarterback in 1945, said he was unaware that he had broken a record set by Clyde LeForce, a Tulsa quarterback, in 1943. "I had no idea I had set a record," he recalled in the fall of 2013. Walterhouse no doubt would have broken the record in Army's previous game against Penn had game officials not almost run out of balls. Following one of Walterhouse's earlier extra points, Army was asked to use some of its practice balls for his conversion attempts, Walterhouse recalled, because spectators in the end zone were refusing to throw the balls back onto the field. Blaik, apparently not wanting to lose any more of his practice balls, finally decided to run and pass for Army's last three conversions. Walterhouse also might well have scored more points had Red Blaik not once tried for a field goal in 1944. "The closest I came to a field goal was when, after I had kicked the extra point, we were penalized 15 yards and I had to kick it from the 18-yard line instead of from the three, but still made it," he said. "As for field goals, we never tried one." That, of course, could have been because when the Cadets got deep down field, they always either ran or passed on fourth down, and more often than not succeeded without attempting field goals.

★ ★ ★

Navy was at a severe disadvantage during that Army scoring drive since, a short while earlier, the Midshipmen had lost Whitmire, their best lineman, when he was hit hard by Tex Coulter, with whom he had been waging a fierce one-on-one war at the line of scrimmage. Coulter leveled Whitmire with a jarring block that resulted in a knee injury that sent the star Navy tackle to the sideline for the rest of the game. Even before halftime, Navy had lost its best defensive player and best runner in Jenkins, both of whom had been roommates at Alabama, although Jenkins returned late in the second half but was unable to do much because of an ankle injury and grogginess from the hard hit that had knocked him out of the game early in the first quarter.

Given the newfound concern over the apparent increase in concussions on both the college and NFL levels in recent years and the disinclination to let players sustaining conditions return to the same games, Jenkins almost assuredly would not have been allowed to return in the Army game since it is quite likely that he had suffered a concussion. "I don't remember any player getting a concussion when we were playing," Walterhouse said, expressing a recollection shared by most of the other players from the 1940s Army teams. That seems somewhat remarkable since, by then, players were wearing hard plastic helmets, and moreover, most players went both ways—playing on offense and defense—meaning, of course, that they played longer in every game. Many agreed that they felt the lack of concussions in bygone years was because most players tackled low, by the knees and even ankles, compared to the head-to-head and waist-high or even higher tackles so common today among college and professional players.

★　★　★

Army threatened again shortly before the half when end Hank Foldberg intercepted a pass at the Navy 36-yard line. Kenna then passed to Davis for a 15-yard gain before time ran out. It was a brutally played 30 minutes, particularly at the line where Army held its own against its Navy counterparts who were considered superior to the Cadets up front. Nevertheless, neither Davis nor Blanchard were able to break away for long-gaining runs, as either one of them or both had in almost every first half of games against Army's first eight opponents.

At halftime, both locker rooms were quiet. Blaik was no Knute Rockne or Vince Lombardi (later an assistant coach under the colonel), exhorting his players on or reminding them that they hadn't beaten Navy since 1938. "'You know what you have to do,' is about all he'd say at halftime," end Ed Rafalko recalled. "Not much more." Quiet also prevailed in the Navy locker room, though coach and Navy commander Oscar Hagberg, no spellbinding orator either, circled the room encouraging his players and reminding them that they only trailed by a touchdown.

Early in the third quarter, Army scored again when All-American guard Joe Stanowicz blocked a punt by Navy's John Hansen on the Middies' 10-yard line. The ball bounced into the end zone where Hansen pounced on it for a safety to give the Cadets a 9–0 lead. Navy responded after the ensuing kickoff, driving 73 yards with the slightly built Hamberg filling in for the injured Jenkins gaining most of the yardage both running and passing and Smackover Scott powering through left guard for a touchdown from a yard out. Vic Finos converted, and Navy now trailed by only two points at 9–7, which remained the score going into the final quarter.

With Jenkins back in the game for Navy at halfback after having been rendered nearly unconscious by Stanowicz and Dobbs early in the first quarter, Hamberg returned a Blanchard punt 24 yards to the Army 46-yard line as the brigade of midshipmen let out a collective roar in the stands while the Corps of Cadets on the other side of the field went silent. The Middies roared even louder when Jenkins and fellow halfback Bill Barron reached the 39-yard line. By then it appeared that the momentum had shifted in Navy's favor. But then Jenkins, obviously not up to par, threw a wobbly pass that Davis intercepted at the Army 35, and he ran it back to the Cadets' 48-yard line.

It was then that Blanchard, who already had performed well both on offense and defense, took over like a man possessed, smashing through the line and skirting the ends with the speed of a halfback behind superb blocking. With Army totally eschewing the pass, Blanchard proceeded to carry the ball on 7-of-9 plays, starting with a 20-yard sprint around left end during which Davis threw a key block that put the ball on the Navy 32-yard line as the Corps of Cadets erupted in exaltation in the stands. Blanchard, it turned out, was just getting started. From the Navy 20, it was all Blanchard. First he slammed up the middle for three yards, went through left tackle for four more, and then another three yards through the right side to the Navy 10-yard line. The Navy line suspected Blanchard was still coming—and he did, exploding through left tackle behind superb blocks by Barney Poole and Tex Coulter, and streaking into the end zone for a touchdown. When Walterhouse again converted, Army led 16–7 with about five minutes left in the game. In all, Blanchard had gained 48 of the 62 yards during the drive, with Davis and Max Minor picking up the other four yards.

After stopping Navy following the ensuing kickoff, Army put the finishing touches on the Midshipmen after moving from its 31-yard line to midfield, where quarterback Tom Lombardo called a play specifically designed for Davis named the "California Special" in honor of Army's star halfback that Blaik had devised for Davis but had never used. On the play, the other Cadets halfback, Max Minor, playing in his final game, went in motion to the left side while Blanchard was flanked to the right. Davis then took a pitch out from Lombardo and broke to Army's left side, circling Navy's right end and encountering Navy's swift halfback Hal Hamberg. Just when it appeared that Hamberg might bring Davis down, Davis slowed down and faked Hamberg to the Middie safety's left, then, switching to his fifth gear, as Blaik called it, shot to Hamberg's right and raced down the left sideline for a touchdown that covered 50 yards. In a letter to General MacArthur the following week, Blaik called Davis' touchdown run "one of the most beautiful runs in Army-Navy history."

When Walterhouse converted with only a few minutes to play it was 23-7, an insurmountable lead, and Army's first victory over Navy since 1938 and gave Walterhouse a total of 47 extra points during the season, a record that still stood 70 years later. Though Navy was considered to have the stronger line, Army backs rushed for 181 yards while its line held Navy to 71 yards rushing. In the stands, the Army band struck up the team's fight song, "On Brave Old Army Team," while many of the cadets who began to stream onto the sideline near the Army bench threw their hats into the air and erupted into a collective cheer.

Amid the celebratory mood in the Army locker room, perhaps no one was prouder than the line coach, the popular Herman Hickman, who in two years had helped develop the Cadets' strongest line ever with his recruiting of players like Poole and Coulter from other schools. "I expect Blanchard won it for us," the rotund former Tennessee All-American, said graciously. "But then our line didn't do so bad. Why hell, our line outplayed their line." Tackle Bill Webb went even further. "All year long, they've been saying our line was untested. Well, we met the great Navy line, and we're still untested."

★   ★   ★

In Leyte in the Philippines, General Eichelberger, having withstood another Japanese air attack, had to contend with a downpour while listening to the game that created static that made the broadcast almost impossible to hear. By then, though, Davis had scored the touchdown that put the game out of Navy's reach. Later, however, as Eichelberger was to tell Blaik in a letter, he'd been able to hear the closing minutes of the game during a re-broadcast. Anxious to share the news of Army's momentous victory later that morning, the general and several other officers who were West Point graduates got into a jeep and drove to the Ormoc Valley in Leyte to give the glad tidings to Colonel Charles "Monk" Meyer, a star 140-lb. halfback for Army in the mid-1930s. Meyer, who was the leader of an infantry battalion fighting remnants of the Japanese army in the hills at the northern end of the valley, was ecstatic to hear of the victory. By contrast, the news of the defeat was hardly edifying to Naval officers and especially alumni of the Naval Academy, such as the leading admirals in the Pacific Theater of Operations, William "Bull" Halsey, a onetime fullback for Navy, and Chester Nimitz, commander and chief of the Pacific Fleet.

Immediately after the game, MacArthur, who had also listened to the broadcast in the Philippines, sent a wire to Blaik marked urgent that said:

THE GREATEST OF ALL ARMY TEAMS. WE HAVE STOPPED THE
WAR TO CELEBRATE YOUR MAGNIFICENT SUCCESS.

Blaik tended to agree with that assessment of his 1944 team—it was the first Army team to go undefeated and untied and to win a national championship. Although two previous teams, in 1916 and 1922, had also gone unbeaten, the 1922 team had two ties. Asked by sportswriters after the game to describe his unbeaten team, Blaik said, "It is the greatest of all Army teams. And it beat the greatest of all Navy teams." Later, in a souvenir booklet to his players and others connected with the team, Blaik wrote: "From her sons, West Point expects the best—you were the best. In truth you were a story book team."

The question was: could there be another one in 1945 when the war would end in August and many college teams would be strengthened by players returning from military service?

7

★ ★ ★

"There's Good News Tonight"

WHILE OSTENSIBLY STRONG AND HEALTHY YOUNG MEN WERE
playing in one of the most anticipated football games ever, U.S.
military forces continued to risk and lose their lives in Europe and the
Pacific. On the day of the 1944 Army-Navy game, the Third Army, led
by West Point alumnus and high hurdler on the track team General
George Patton, fought fiercely to gain control of the German-held
coal-rich city of Saarlautern in the Saar Basin in Germany, while in the
southern tier of the Western Front, the American Seventh Army elim-
inated the last pocket of resistance in the industrial city of Strasbourg.
More than 200 American soldiers would be killed and almost 1,000
wounded in the battle that lasted almost three weeks.

Meanwhile in the Philippines, while General Robert Eichelberger
took a late-night respite to listen to the Army-Navy game, American
bombers struck at a number of Japanese air bases, which would soon be
over-run by American forces and re-gained as another West Point alumnus, General Douglas MacArthur, was by then back in the Philippines
as he famously predicted. Understandably, war news dominated front
pages on Sunday, December 3, 1944, with stories on the Army-Navy

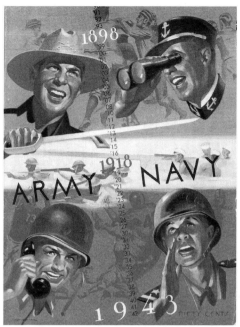

The program for the 1942 Army-Navy game reflects the nation at war.
(U.S. Naval Academy Athletics)

The program for the 1943 Army-Navy game has a wartime motif dating from the Spanish-American War of 1898.
(U.S. Naval Academy Athletics)

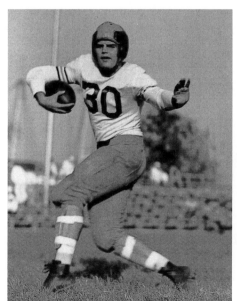

Navy halfback Bobby Jenkins, who previously played at Alabama.
(U.S. Naval Academy Athletics)

Edmund "Rafe" Rafalko, a star end during Army's glory years in the 1940s who rose to the rank of major general in the Air Force after his graduation from West Point.
(U.S. Military Academy)

Hal Hamberg, Navy's 160-lb. halfback in the 1944 Army-Navy game for the national championship. (U.S. Naval Academy Athletics)

War hero and All-American Michigan halfback Bob Chappuis in action against Army at Ann Arbor in 1946. (University of Michigan)

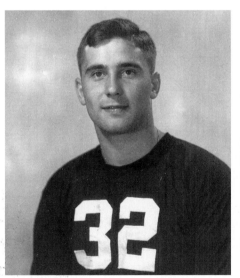

One of Notre Dame's best quarterbacks, Johnny Lujack, whose tackle of Doc Blanchard prevented an Army touchdown in the 1946 game that ended in a scoreless tie. He won the 1947 Heisman Trophy. (Notre Dame Media Relations Office)

All-American Navy tackle Don Whitmire, a thorn in Army's side in two Army-Navy games. (U.S. Naval Academy Athletics)

In this October 13, 1945, photo, Army halfback Felix "Doc" Blanchard (35) weaves away as three Michigan men close in to tackle him after a short first-period gain. His Army teammates Arnold Tucker (17) and Herschel "Ug" Fulson (22) are in the background. (AP Photo)

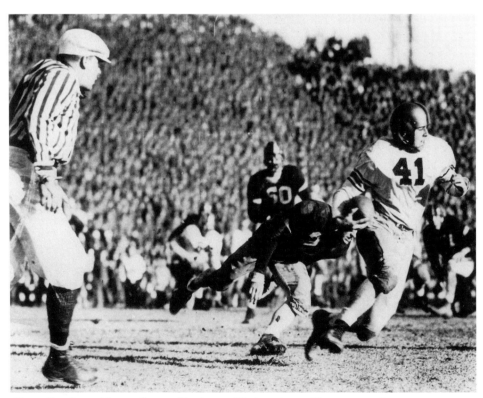

Glenn Davis avoids another tackler in an All-American effort. (U.S. Military Academy)

Actress Elizabeth Taylor with her boyfriend, Lt. Glenn Davis, arriving for the annual Academy Awards ceremony in Hollywood, California, on March 24, 1949. (AP Photo)

Left to right: Arnold Tucker, Doc Blanchard, Red Blaik, and Glenn Davis the day before the 1945 Army-Navy game in Philadelphia. (AP Photo)

Army's 1944 backfield (left to right): Bob Chabot, Glenn Davis, quarterback Tom Lombardo, and Doc Blanchard. (U.S. Military Academy)

Glenn Davis in full dress uniform.
(U.S. Military Academy)

Felix "Doc" Blanchard in full dress uniform. (AP Photo)

Army football team member Felix "Doc" Blanchard Jr. (right) gets an advance look at the 1945 Heisman Memorial Trophy to be presented to him a few hours later at the Downtown Athletic Club of New York. Wilfred Wottrich, then-president of the Downtown Athletic Club, poses beside Blanchard. (AP Photo)

Army's All-American halfback Lt. Glenn Davis (left), Army coach Col. Earl Blaik (center), and Wilfred Wottrich, president of the Downtown Athletic Club, are shown with the 1946 Heisman Memorial Trophy at the Downtown Athletic Club in New York City. The trophy was presented to the Cadet at a dinner reception that evening. (AP Photo)

Glenn "Mr. Outside" Davis and Doc "Mr. Inside" Blanchard formed one of the greatest backfield tandems in college football history. (U.S. Military Academy)

Doc Blanchard and Glenn Davis during a West Point weekend in 1988 when they were greeted royally by cadets and alumni. (AP Photo)

game relegated to the sports pages where, given the continuing loss of American lives, they, of course, belonged.

By Monday Army players were being congratulated by fellow cadets and staff on the West Point campus for the victory while everyone prepared to study for final examinations before the Christmas break. Indeed, Christmas wreaths and other holiday decorations already adorned the lobby and dining room of the elegant and historic Thayer Hotel on the Academy grounds, which was named for West Point's first superintendent, Sylvanus Thayer. Several offers for Army to play on New Year's Day were turned down as the West Point hierarchy had done in the past—an easily understandable decision in 1944 after the Cadets had won Army's first national championship. What had Army to gain by playing in a bowl game?

With the Allies on the offensive in both Europe and in the Pacific, many firsties (seniors) at West Point began to think that they might not get to see any action after graduating, which to many cadets if indeed not all of them, was disappointing, particularly for those planning a career in the military. But then two weeks after the Army-Navy game, a huge German force, believed to have been trapped in the Ardennes in Belgium, caught the Allies by surprise with a massive counter-offensive. During the ensuing week-long confrontation that became known as the Battle of the Bulge, approximately 75,000 Allied troops, most of them American soldiers, faced about 250,000 German troops. Vastly outnumbered in troops and equipment—the Germans had amassed about 2,500 tanks, far more than the Allies—and within a matter of days almost 9,000 Americans were forced to surrender, the second largest mass surrender of U.S. troops in history (Bataan in the Philippines was the largest). The tide finally turned shortly before Christmas when General George Patton's Third Army, drawn from 50 miles away, attacked the Germans from the south. That force, coupled with the superiority of the Army Air Corps, forced the Germans back to where they had begun their offensive. And by mid-January the battle—one of the fiercest of the war—was over. The number of casualties was staggering—about 125,000 Germans had been killed or wounded while almost 20,000 Americas had lost their lives and almost 50,000 had been wounded.

The severity of the German attack and the subsequent American casualties came as stunning news to President Roosevelt, who like many top U.S. officials and military leaders thought the end of the war in Europe had been near. As it developed, the German offensive was in effect its last major attack of the war. But no one at West Point knew that, and the German attack convinced most members of the first class that they would see action after all. And by the Christmas break, not many cadets or anyone else at West Point was reveling in the victory over Navy or Army's best season ever. Indeed, it all seemed very insignificant until the massive German retreat, which still left many cadets with mixed emotions at the good news.

★   ★   ★

In addition to Army having gone undefeated in 1944, Blanchard and Davis were named to the Associated Press first team, while Jack Green and St. Onge were picked for the second and third teams, respectively. Others who received All-American honors by various news services and magazines included Barney Poole, Tex Coulter, Joe Stanowicz, and Doug Kenna. The team's average score for the season, an astonishing 56 points a game, was the largest ever in modern times. (Michigan had averaged 57 points in 1904 before the forward pass was legalized, and what rules existed were radically different.) Overall, Army had scored 504 points while holding the opposition to 35. Among those who set new NCAA records were Glenn Davis, who averaged almost 12 yards per carry in 58 rushing attempts and scored 20 touchdowns, 14 of them rushing, and Dick Walterhouse whose 47 extra points was still an Army record in 2014. Blanchard, who like Davis rarely played more than 30 minutes under Blaik's two-unit system, carried the ball 61 times for a 5.5 yards per carry average and scored nine touchdowns, three of them on passes. Meanwhile, the defense, which of course included Blanchard and Davis when their unit was on the field, gave up only 35 points in nine games.

That winter, Davis was a sprinter on the indoor track team while Dale Hall, who had been an All-American on Army's undefeated basketball team during the 1943–44 season, captained the Cadet cagers, who also included Doug Kenna. Davis, though a good basketball player, was not in the class of Hall and Kenna, but he would be a guard a year later. In addition, he starred as an outfielder on the baseball team and was a standout sprinter on the outdoor track team. These accomplishments made him a four-sport letterman, a rarity at any school, especially one like West Point with its rigorous academic grind.

In addition to Kenna and Hall, others who had played their final year of football for Army were Stanowicz, St. Onge, tackles Bill Webb and Archie Arnold, backs Max Minor and Dean Sensanbaugher, and fullback Bobby Dobbs, who played for Army's first unit and could legitimately claim that he started ahead of Blanchard at fullback and often finished in the position because of Blaik's tendency to take Blanchard and Davis out for good as early as the third quarter when the Cadets were far out in front, which was usually the case during the 1944 season. Minor and Sensanbaugher actually had another year left but were declared ineligible for the 1945 season by the West Point Athletic Board since they had already played four seasons of college football—Minor two years at Texas while in the navy's V-5 pre-flight training program, and Sensanbaugher two seasons at Ohio State. However, Army's outlook for 1945 was hardly gloomy since 21 lettermen, most of them starters in Blaik's two-team system, would be back, barring academic problems for the remainder of the 1944–45 school year. Because of academic difficulties, particularly in math, two of the returning starters, Tex Coulter and guard Arthur Gerometta, would be repeating their plebe years.

During the summer of 1945, and even during the past academic year, Hickman, Andy Gustafson, and a few other assistant Army coaches—Army had about a half dozen at the time compared with the 12 it had during the 2013 season—again went after players to fill positions vacated by the graduated members of the 1944 team, some of whom they were attracted to when they watched them on film while some others had been recommended by former Army players and coaches. Hickman and the other Army recruiters had some strong lures to dangle in front of prospective recruits: the Cadets had won the national championship, Blanchard and Davis had become household names in many homes, even those where there was scant attention paid to college sports, and West Point offered a haven from the military draft.

Thus it was not particularly difficult to sign up exactly whomever Hickman and the other Army coaches were after. A good example was Tom McWilliams, incongruously called "Shorty" in spite of his height—6'3", which at the time was especially tall for a halfback. Hickman's eyes brightened when he saw McWilliams star as an 18-year-old freshman halfback for Mississippi State during the 1944 season after he had emerged from high school as one of the most sought-after players in the country, and what he saw was more than enough to put him at the top of Army's recruiting list. Understandably so, since as a freshman starter, McWilliams led the Bulldogs in rushing despite missing two games because of a knee injury (the only games Mississippi State would lose during a 6–2 season) and was named to the Associated Press second All-American team and finished 10th in the Heisman Trophy voting, which was highly unusual for a freshman. Davis, in his second year in 1944, had finished second in the voting to Les Horvath, who had played quarterback and halfback at Ohio State, while Blanchard, in his first season, had finished third in the voting, which, of course, was even more remarkable, while Doug Kenna was eighth in the voting. Remarkably, Army had placed three players in the top 10 of the Heisman Trophy voting, and two of them, Blanchard and Davis, still had two seasons remaining.

Hickman didn't even wait until McWilliams had finished playing his first college season until he went after him.

"They sent Herman Hickman down to see me during the fall of my freshman year at Mississippi State, and he asked if I was interested in going to West Point," McWilliams said, "and that I already had a congressional appointment, which I understand came from New York."

McWilliams playfully responded, "Coach Hickman, I can go to West Point anytime. I'm only 35 miles from there." McWilliams' home was indeed at West Point—West Point, Mississippi, that is.

"No, I don't mean West Point, Mississippi," the fun-loving Hickman responded with a laugh while appreciating McWilliams' sense of humor. "I mean West Point Military Academy." McWilliams, of course, knew that Hickman wasn't talking about the West Point in Mississippi.

"Well, I never really have thought about it," McWilliams said, adding that he wanted to discuss the offer with his father, who, it turned out, was against the idea. Hickman thereupon returned to West Point unsure whether McWilliams' father might change his mind. By the time he did, in early 1945, he was nearly on his death bed. "He was kind of against it until he got real sick that summer," McWilliams recalled. "Right before he died, he called me and he said, 'I think you ought to go ahead and go to West Point.' That's when I decided to go."

What had changed McWilliams' father's mind?

"I guess he saw World War II escalating and figured I'd be better off going there to become an officer than I would be to just get drafted. So I decided to go," McWilliams recalled.

His stay at West Point was to be short, spectacular, and ultimately controversial.

When McWilliams arrived at the military academy in July 1945, the war in Europe was over—Germany surrendered on May 7—and he was part of another recruiting bonanza. The newcomers included eventual starters such as tackle Goble Bryant, who had played at Texas A&M and then while in the army; end Clyde Grimenstein, fresh from the Virginia Military Institute; Elwyn "Rip" Rowan, recruited from Louisiana State; Bobby Stuart from Tulsa; and LeRoy Martin, another southerner and highly touted guard who had spent the previous academic year prepping for Army at Cornell after having been recruited by Hickman. Starting on July 1, the newcomers had to take part in six weeks of basic training at nearby Camp Bruckner that was so intensive it corresponded to what draftees did over a 13-week period. In doing so, they got their first taste of hazing during Beast Barracks, which by then had been toned down because of the war. Still, the new plebes had to endure wake-ups during the middle of the night and being ordered by upperclassmen to do push-ups, run sprints, and other grueling tasks during the daylight hours. Meanwhile, returning players who had finished their first and second years underwent training camp at nearby Lake Popolopen, a 10,000-square-yard area of land acquired by West Point in 1942. By then the summer curriculum included the building of bridges with pontoons, along with amphibious, motorized, and mechanized training, more extensive use of marksmanship ranges, running obstacle courses, and performing other chores that some West Point graduates were primarily supervising in Europe and the Pacific.

Proving he was as good a recruiter as he was a line coach, the extremely personable Hickman had recruited almost all of the new players. But he was particularly ingenious in recruiting Steffy, who was brought to his attention while playing at the Baylor Prep School in Tennessee, which Hickman also had attended, by the school's athletic director, J.B. Reich, who had been Hickman's football coach at the school more than two decades before. Watching Steffy play once convinced Hickman that the teenager from Knoxville was a star in the making. However, Tennessee, whose head coach, John Barnhill, was his best friend, also wanted Steffy. For Hickman, that was no problem, especially since Steffy's first choice was West Point. Aware of that preference, Barnhill said he was willing to have Steffy play one season at Tennessee and then transfer to the Point. "Barnhill said [to Hickman], 'Let him come there for a year where he could take the courses he will have to take at West Point, and then let him go to West Point,'" Steffy said he was told. Hickman agreed, feeling that he could help Barnhill, at least for one season, and that Steffy could get some additional seasoning and yet be eligible to play for three seasons at West Point.

"At Tennessee, I took exactly what I was going to be taking at West Point," recalled Steffy, who obviously had been informed by Hickman of a plebe's curriculum at the Point. He also became a starter on an undefeated Volunteers team that went on to play in the Rose Bowl where the Volunteers lost to Southern California. Like almost all of the players that Army recruited from other schools, Steffy knew that by going to West Point he would be immune to the draft. But the rationale of almost all of the players interviewed was that they were not avoiding military service since they would be committed to serve in the army after graduation, although not all of them did, and as officers instead of as enlisted men, which they knew would be the case if they had remained at "civilian" colleges and been drafted.

* * *

Most of the news during the early part of 1945 centered on the war, of course, and almost all of it was good, except for the fierce battle for Iwo Jima that began on February 19 when American Marines landed on the island. That prompted Gabriel Heatter, probably the best-known newscaster in the country, to lead most of his early evening newscasts that year with what had become his signature greeting, "There's good news tonight." Night after night, Heatter described the intensified bombing of major German cities and the Allies' march toward Berlin and, ultimately, the German surrender. It was much the same in the Pacific as American forces, during fierce island-to-island invasions, drew closer to Japan and by mid-summer made a Japanese surrender inevitable.

It's safe to say that Heatter's familiar voice and almost nightly delivery of good tidings gave millions of listeners a lift, especially those with family members or other close ones in service. As it developed, Japan's surrender on August 14 came earlier than expected after American bombers dropped the first atomic bombs on Hiroshima on August 6 and Nagasaki on August 9, approximately two months after the last wartime graduation. By then Bob Woods, the first football player to have played on both sides in the Army-Navy game, and the other graduates had begun advanced training before being sent on their assignments—in Woods' case after a brief honeymoon on Cape Cod in Massachusetts. Now a second lieutenant, Woods' first postings took him to the Philippines, where the infamous Bataan Death March had taken place after the Japanese invasion in 1942, and then to Japan, by then under the command of General MacArthur.

"When we graduated, I felt sure many of us would see action before the war ended, and the sudden end caught me by surprise," Woods said. That was also true of most of the other graduates who no doubt looked forward to becoming involved in the war that had taken the lives of 487 West Point graduates. It was a natural response given the extensive coursework, military training, and the paramilitary lifestyle they had lived through at West Point.

When preseason practice began in late August, Blaik and his staff knew that many of Army's opponents would be strengthened by the return of players who had left to serve in the military, although due to the tens of thousands of GIs who were being discharged, most teams would not be at full force again until the 1946 season. Once again, neither

Army nor Navy would have to wait that long. Though the Cadets had lost quarterbacks Doug Kenna and Tom Lombardo and running backs Max Minor, Dean Sensanbaugher, and Bobby Dobbs (whose varsity eligibility had expired), it soon became evident that the backfield would be as strong as ever with the addition of McWilliams at halfback and Arnold Tucker at quarterback.

McWilliams was a better runner and definitely much faster than Minor, Sensanbaugher, and Dobbs, and Tucker would be a far better passer than either Kenna or Lombardo, for whom he had backed up and thus saw very little action in 1944. And then, too, both Blanchard and Davis would return for two more seasons. Meanwhile, the line, mainly because of the addition of Steffy and Goble Bryant, would be as strong as—and perhaps stronger than—the one the previous season, so long as Coulter and Poole, who had struggled academically during their first year, could cut it in the classroom. At any rate, going into the 1945 season, Army was the consensus and prohibitive choice to repeat as national champions.

8

★ ★ ★

Sky-High Expectations

FOLLOWING SUMMER TRAINING FOR PLEBES AT CAMP BRUCKNER, situated on property that the army had acquired in the early 1940s for upperclassmen and at Army bases around the country for cadets in their second and final years, preseason practice at the Academy began in late August with the highest expectations of any Army team even as Red Blaik was lamenting the loss of so many players from the alternating units of 1944.

Worried that his returning players might be affected by what Blaik called "a tidal wave of publicity," the coach found it necessary to appeal to their pride. "'You are the champions,' I told them many times. 'From you, people expect only perfect performances,'" Blaik said years later.

With Japan having surrendered on August 15 via a radio broadcast by the Emperor and on the battleship *Missouri* on September 2, it would be the first peacetime football season played since 1941, Blaik's first year at West Point. While many opponents would benefit from players returning from military service, Blaik knew that, for the most part, teams would not be at full strength until the 1946 season, by which time most World War II veterans would have returned home and, in the case of former players, to school. If anything, the schedule for the reigning champions appeared lighter than in 1944, with the addition of two service teams that had lost many of their players along with Wake Forest and Michigan.

★   ★   ★

Though the war had ended, peace had come at a price. With no need for the production of planes, tanks, or other military weaponry, tens of thousands of Americans lost their jobs by late September after the Pentagon canceled billions of dollars in war contracts. Boeing Aircraft, where hundreds of bombers and other planes had been manufactured during the war, laid off more than 20,000 workers. And Ford, which had produced several thousand B-24 Liberator bombers along with jeeps, tanks, and various other weaponry, had let go about 50,000 employees, most of who had been hired during the war. In addition, thousands of other "war workers" lost their jobs at a time when the first wave of around 12 million American servicemen and servicewomen were returning home with the hope of finding either their old jobs or new ones waiting for them. All of this occurred after the U.S. had prospered during the war years when more people had been employed than at any time in U.S. history, most of them making double of what their income had been before the war and with unemployment at a record low of 2 percent. By the end of 1945, thousands of former GIs not only found themselves unable to get jobs, but they were also homeless. Adding to the country's economic woes, automobile, oil, and lumber workers— and in New York even elevator operators—went on strike after declining to do so during the war. The biggest strike involved about 175,000 employees at General Motors and lasted three months.

Many Americans assumed, after undergoing rationing and being unable to buy cars and other peacetime products for more than three years, that things would return to normal. Alluding to the reluctance of a Republican-controlled Congress that had done little to prepare for a resumption of peacetime or embark on demobilization despite President Truman's urging that it do so. In a letter to his mother, Truman said, "Congress is balking, labor has gone crazy, and management isn't far from insane in selfishness." Things would eventually get better, but not for quite a while. Rising to the occasion, Truman came up with a 21-point domestic program that among other things, provided for increased unemployment compensation, an increase in the minimum wage, tax reform, and a GI Bill of Rights that would enable millions of veterans to go to college and for other vets to collect $20 a week (the equivalent of about $250 in 2014) in what the recently discharged veterans called "The 52–20 Club."

In addition, Truman called for national compulsory health insurance that would be funded by payroll deductions. But with so many Americans out of work, Truman's radical proposal—which would not be implemented until passage of President Barack Obama's Affordable Health Care Act by Congress in 2010—had no chance of passage, and neither did his call for universal military training for one year for young men from 18 to 20 years old. In 1945, Truman was eventually successful in another effort, though, when he proposed unifying all of the armed forces under a secretary of defense, rather than have them headed by individual secretaries, as was the case during World War II and had been for decades. However, it wasn't until 1947 that Congress approved the Truman plan and not until 1949 that the titular head became known as the secretary of defense. Meanwhile, First Lady and syndicated newspaper columnist Eleanor Roosevelt was in the forefront of a move to ensure that those women who had been recruited to work in defense plants, shipyards, and in other war-related work and who had lost their jobs but wanted to continue working be treated equally with male counterparts who were also in search of employment, a proposal endorsed by most unions.

★ ★ ★

Given their heavy schedules, both during the summer and the academic year, few Army football players spent much time, if any, keeping up with postwar developments in the country, almost none of which would affect those who would graduate from the Academy. Indeed, if anything, the U.S. Military Academy was literally a gated haven and sanctuary from the outside world during the war. Yet there were ample reminders of the war since tanks, jeeps, and other military vehicles had been brought to the Academy early in the war for training purposes.

While most of the players brought in from other schools had never expressed any prior interest in going to West Point, at least two of them did—running back Bob Richmond of Lyndon, Kentucky, and guard Al Joy, both of whom would be firsties (seniors) during the 1945 season. "I wanted a military career and always wanted to go to West Point," Richmond said. However, Richmond was unable to get an appointment after finishing his secondary education at the Kentucky Military Institute and enrolled at Hampden-Sydney College in Virginia, where he played one year of football until an appointment came through. Un-recruited and at 5′9″ and 150 lbs. considered too light for the varsity, Richmond went out for the junior varsity team and led it in scoring for two years in a row. Then during a preseason scrimmage between the jayvees and a team of Army varsity reserves, Richmond scored the game's only two touchdowns as Red Blaik looked on.

"When the game was over, Colonel Blaik called me over to the sideline and said, 'Richmond, I want you on the varsity.' I said, 'Colonel Blaik, I don't want to be on the varsity because I won't play any football over there.'

"'Oh yes, you will,' Blaik told me. So I said 'Okay.'"

As it developed, Richmond did play, but with Davis, Blanchard, and Shorty McWilliams in the backfield, he didn't play enough to earn a letter. Still, years later, he had no regrets about accepting Blaik's offer to join the varsity.

Neither did Joy, a 180-lb. guard who also spent two seasons on the junior varsity before making it to the varsity in 1945. "I became interested in going to the Academy because I grew up near it and had gone there to see football games," Joy said. "My parents liked the idea, and after getting an appointment I spent a year at the New York Military Academy prep school." Like Richmond, Joy also played for the varsity, but not much and thus did not get a letter, either. He did not regret persevering hard enough to make it to the varsity in 1945, not even after Tex Coulter, who out-weighted Joy by about 40 lbs., had kicked and dislocated Joy's hand after Joy had successfully blocked Coulter all three times on a play that Blaik had called three times in a row when Joy was playing on the "scout" team that was emulating Navy during a scrimmage in advance of the 1945 Army-Navy game. "I knew that I could get Tex by getting to him a little quicker," said Joy, whose hand had still not "popped back in" more than four decades later.

With McWilliams, the transplant from Tennessee, at right halfback and Arnold Tucker at quarterback, it soon became apparent in preseason scrimmages that Army would be even stronger in the backfield even though it had lost Max Minor and Doug Kenna, an honorable mention All-American quarterback. McWilliams was faster and more elusive than Minor and although Kenna was the better runner, Tucker was a more accurate passer, which meant that Army no doubt would throw more often, making its three outstanding running backs more effective. The line, meanwhile, appeared to be strong despite losing Stanowicz, St. Onge, Webb, and Arnold.

As was common in the 1940s, Army's opening game wasn't until September 29, on a warm humid afternoon before a crowd of about 10,000 at Michie Stadium. The opponent was an unusual one, a team from the Third Air Force (the Army Air Corps had been renamed the Army Air Forces) Personnel Distribution Command, which included both officers and enlisted men and was bigger, heavier, and most certainly older than the Cadets and included several former National Football League players, such as 31-year-old Dick Plasman, who had already spent six seasons as an end with the great Chicago Bears team of the late 1930s and early 1940s and was the last player in the NFL to play without a helmet; Jim Castiglia, a fullback and linebacker with the Baltimore Colts and Philadelphia Eagles who was celebrating his 27th birthday; another former Eagle, 35-year-old linebacker Maurice Harper; former Pittsburgh Steelers end Tom Brown; along with center and linebacker Bill Remington, who would be playing for the San Francisco 49ers the next season.

Like other service teams, the Comets, as they were called, had only been put together that summer before the Japanese surrender to entertain Army Air Force personnel while playing in a league of military teams and some college squads. In its first game the week before against another Third Air Force team called the Gremlins, who, led by eventual All-American halfback and NFL star Charley Trippi, beat the Comets and their former Army All-American center Casimir Myslinski 27–9 in Tampa. Still, given the former NFL players on its squad, along with a number of former college stars, it would seem that the Comets would be a very strong test for Army, especially on the line where the Air Force team vastly outweighed Army. "I remember that team because they were huge people," Doc Blanchard recalled. All the more so because the Cadets would be without Tucker, who was sidelined with a shoulder injury, and at least early in the game, without the team's best end, Barney Poole, who did not start any of Army's games in 1945, apparently because of Blaik's pique over Poole's having tried to resign from the Academy following the 1944 season, a request that was turned down and soured the colonel on his star end. "But I was usually in the game shortly after it started," Poole said some time later.

In his place at left end was plebe Dick Pitzer, who was to turn into an outstanding player but was hardly on par with Poole. Despite the

Comets former NFL players and far greater experience collectively, Tucker was not missed. Nor was Poole at the start of what turned out to be a one-sided affair as the far more disciplined, organized, and younger Cadets, who had won 5-of-9 games, were much too quick and fast for an Air Force squad that also included former Stanford quarterback Frank Forbes, a recent bomber pilot who had spent two tours of duty in the Mediterranean. Plasman, for one, felt out of place playing against what was essentially a college team composed of players as much as 15 years younger. Looking around at the small crowd, he couldn't help but remember playing before a crowd of up to 40,000 at Wrigley Field in Chicago, the Bears home field at the time. On the other hand, he had heard that this Army team was probably as good if not better than some NFL teams of the World War II era, which they probably were.

Though Army completed only 6-of-17 passes, thrown by the reserve quarterback and placekicker Dick Walterhouse and Glenn Davis, for 113 yards, the Cadets overpowered and out-ran the slower and far less cohesive Air Force team on offense and throttled it on defense, with Poole clearly demonstrating that he was one of Army's best-ever ends by catching several passes and making a half-dozen tackles. What became obvious from the start of the game was that the Army backfield undoubtedly was its fastest ever. In Blanchard, Davis, and McWilliams, it had three runners who could all run 100 yards in less than 10 seconds. Because of his power as a fullback, and the opposing defenses' focus on his running up the middle, Blanchard's ability to take off around end like a halfback or catching a pass and out-running most defensive backs made him an all-around offensive weapon. Making the Cadets' running game all the more effective was McWilliams, who was almost as fast as Davis.

Despite the NFL players in its lineup, the Air Force team was unable to contain Army's running game. Davis scored two touchdowns, the first on an 85-yard burst through left tackle and down the sideline in the first quarter, and the second in the second period on a 45-yard pass.

On that play Davis, though covered by two defenders, snared the pass from Walterhouse on the Comets' 25-yard line and, aided by a jarring block by plebe end Scott Grimenstein, sprinted into the end zone. In between those two scores, Williams bolted through the visitors' line from five yards out to give Army a 19–0 halftime lead. With the Comets unable to generate any offense, Army scored twice more in the second half, on a five-yard run by McWilliams and a 21-yard pass from Davis to Blanchard, who had already proven that he was as good a receiver as he was a runner and would have made a first-rate tight end if he wasn't the best fullback in college football. Blanchard gave the small crowd even more to rave about when he twice kicked off into the Comets' end zone and raced down the field fast enough to tackle the receiver before he got beyond the Air Force 25-yard line.

The Air Force team never got closer than the Army 32-yard line and was only able to gain 45 yards rushing, while the Cadets amassed 257 yards on the ground. "They eventually started huffing and puffing and got worn out," Blanchard said. Looking back at the game years later, Davis had an even stronger assessment. "They were in lousy shape and were dead when the game was over," the great Army halfback was to recall. Indeed, the game against a largely unconditioned and inadequate team of active duty army personnel whose thoughts—understandably—were more on their imminent discharges than on football was hardly a good test for what obviously was going to be a very good Army team, even against far stronger opponents in games that lie ahead.

Overshadowed by Army's opening-game victory that late September weekend was a grand slam home run in the ninth inning against the St. Louis Browns on the last day of the Major League Baseball season by Hank Greenberg that earned the Detroit Tigers a berth in the World Series, which the Tigers would win in seven games. Notable about the game, and indeed their entire season, was that the Browns' lineup included the remarkable one-armed outfielder Pete Gray, who batted .218 while playing 77 games and striking out only 11 times in 234 at-bats for a team that had won the American League pennant the year before.

* * *

Wake Forest, Army's opponent a week later at Michie Stadium on a rainy afternoon, would not be one of the stronger foes even though the Demon Deacons, coached by Herman Hickman's close friend under whom he had served as an assistant in the late 1930s, the highly regarded Peahead Walker, had won 8-of-9 games in 1944. But the outlook was not too good for 1945. For one thing, Wake Forest had only a dozen returning lettermen and lacked both depth and size, although halfback and captain Nick Sacrinty—his brother, Otis, was the other halfback—was one of the best backs in the strong Southern Conference and good enough to play a season with the Chicago Bears. Like Red Blaik, Coach Walker was eternally pessimistic. "We just don't have the kind of ball club that can beat Duke or Tennessee or Army," he said before the season started. "They'll take us to the cleaners." Not quite, at least in the case of Tennessee that had edged Wake Forest 7–6 the previous Saturday. Against a strong Duke team that would finish the season ranked 13th, the Demon Deacons lost by a touchdown. Regarding the meeting with Army, reserve Wake Forest halfback Herbert Appenzeller later quoted Walker as saying, "We aren't going to win this game, but you can tell your grandchildren that you played against the best football team in history." Hardly inspiring, but then the Wake Forest players were accustomed to Walker's bleak predictions, which they felt would actually inspire them and perhaps make Walker eat his pessimistic words.

However, they couldn't do so against the home team. An ominous sign confronted the Deacons the day before the game—on the way to a practice session at Michie Stadium, they stopped to watch the Army junior varsity playing a team from the Maxwell Army Air Base. Incredulously they saw Max Minor, a starting halfback on Army's 1944 team, and Bobby Dobbs, a productive running back on the same squad, playing for the Cadet jayvees. Somewhat stunned, Appenzeller and some of his teammates felt that if players like Minor and Dobbs were playing on the Army junior varsity, what in the world could they expect against the varsity the next day. Unbeknownst to Appenzeller and his Wake Forest teammates, Minor and Dobbs had used up their varsity eligibility but could still play for the jayvees and did so because of their love of the game. Nevertheless, it was a bad omen for Wake Forest.

One intriguing aspect of the game was that it pitted brother against brother on the line—plebe guard LeRoy Martin against his younger brother, Sidney, a tackle for the Demon Deacons. Another interesting connection was the fact that Army tackles Al Nemetz and Bill Webb had played for Wake Forest before transferring to West Point. Otherwise, the teams had nothing in common. That especially applied to the teams' head wear, since Army by now wore the revolutionary new and hard-plastic helmets that had become popular in the early 1940s, while Wake Forest looked like a team out of the past with its old-fashioned, soft-leather helmets. The one exception for Army was Webb, who wore a leather helmet, apparently because the plastic one-size-fits-all helmets were too small for him.

On a bleak rainy afternoon before a crowd of around 8,000, helmets made no difference in the outcome of the game that was broadcast nationally by the ABC network and overseas via short-wave radio. In a portent of the eventual outcome, Army scored on its first possession when Herschel "Ug" Fuson, a 215-lb. guard who occasionally was used as a running back, took a pitchout from Tucker, circled left end, and behind a jarring block by Davis (the man could do it all) raced 51 yards for a touchdown. Blaik never did say why Fuson started at right halfback when Shorty McWilliams was available, but Blaik had no regrets as Fuson also scored again in the second half when he bolted through left tackle and scored from 12 yards out.

In a devastating display of running on a muddy field no less, Army scored six more touchdowns, including two by McWilliams, who would be Army's starting right halfback for the rest of the season, on runs of 78 and 12 yards. In all, four of the Cadets' touchdowns were on runs of more than 50 yards, including a 65-yard sprint by Davis who, after Tucker had faked a hand-off to Fuson going left, handed off to Davis who burst through a huge hole opened on the right side of the line, straight-armed a Wake Forest linebacker, broke loose from a defensive back, and head-faked Nick Sacrinty, playing safety, before crossing the goal line. Blanchard, held to only 13 yards rushing on three attempts while, like Davis, playing less than half of the game, scored the fourth 50-plus-yard touchdown when he intercepted a pass and ran 65 yards for another Army six points.

By game's end, Army had not only won 54–0 but had amassed 443 yards on the eight touchdowns and runs from scrimmage as opposed to 78 by the Demon Deacons, while throwing only six passes, five of which were completed. With Army leading 48–0 after three quarters, Blaik and Walker, who had removed their front-line players by then, agreed to shorten the final quarter from 15 to eight minutes. Better, Walker felt, to spare his best players from injury with the game so far out of hand and save them for the following week's Southern Conference game against Duke.

★ ★ ★

After the game, Walker, hardly surprised by the outcome, said, "Army, and I guess Navy, too, is completely out of the college class. They've had the pick of the football players in the country during the war because the boys wanted to go to West Point and Annapolis." Walker knew that an awful lot of them did just that because of the war. Nick Sacrinty,

Wake Forest's best runner, who missed the second half because of an injury, said many years later while a physician in North Carolina, "It was almost impossible to think of winning against them," an opinion no doubt shared by his teammates on their long train ride back to their Winston-Salem, North Carolina, campus.

Next up at Yankee Stadium, a much larger venue than Army's home field, was Michigan—a team that Army had never played and would enter the game a four-touchdown underdog. At the time, teams usually were not favored by points but by odds, much like a race horse or a prize fighter, or by touchdowns, as was the case in the upcoming Army-Michigan game, even though the Wolverines had won three of their first four games under the legendary Coach Fritz Crisler.

Despite the odds and the team's relative inexperience, the Wolverines would lose only one more game in 1945 and finish the season with seven victories and three losses, and two of those would come against teams ranked in the top five in the nation in 1945. Just maybe Michigan would be a far stronger opponent than the four-touchdown odds against them.

9

★ ★ ★

Changing the Game

A LTHOUGH IT WAS EXPECTED TO BE A ONE-SIDED MATCH-UP, given the inexperience of the Michigan team—nine starters were freshmen—a near-capacity crowd of around 70,000 turned out for the Army-Michigan game on a cloudy and 60-degree afternoon at Yankee Stadium on Saturday, October 13. Many no doubt were drawn by the superlative Army team and probably as many to see the indomitable backfield pair of Mr. Inside Doc Blanchard and Mr. Outside Glenn Davis, although there was a large contingent of Wolverines, including the student band, fans from Ann Arbor, and a considerable number of alumni, particularly since many Michigan graduates were from the New York metropolitan area. Among the Army fans was General Maxwell Taylor, the new West Point superintendent who had distinguished himself as the commander of the army's 101st Airborne Division and was the first Allied general to land in Normandy on D-Day June 6, 1944, when he parachuted to earth with his men.

Unbeknownst to the vast crowd, it would also see a precursor of what would come to be known as the "two-platoon" system that would revolutionize football. At the time, players played both offense and defense, even though most of them were at their best at running, passing, and blocking or tackling and defending against passes unlike great runners like Blanchard and Davis who also excelled on defense. That traditional system was necessary because until 1941, if a player left the game in a quarter, he could not return in the same period. But under the relatively new rule, which had largely been devised by Crisler and Southern Methodist Coach Matty Bell, there could be unlimited substitution whereby a player could be taken out of a game and return during the same period.

The rule change, as Crisler explained it, was attributable to World War II. Although the United States had not yet entered the war, and would not until December 8, 1941, the military draft that was put into effect in 1940 had resulted in the conscription of thousands of college students, including many varsity football players. Thus the draft had, in Crisler's words, "created a tremendous drain on manpower" that had drastically reduced the number of eligible football players and would create an even larger drain once the U.S. entered the war. As Crisler put it, "If a team had a limited number of players and you had to make substitutions for reasons of injury or one thing or another, you might well run out of men altogether. But if a player—with a minor injury or the wind knocked out of him—could be taken out and returned as soon as he was able to play again, that would be most helpful." The Association's rule committee then approved the rule that permitted a player to enter a game at any time. But even as Crisler was to say, "I don't think anybody at the 1941 meeting visualized platooning as it was later developed." But the transformational and ingenious Crisler, who had been an assistant coach under the legendary Amos Alonzo Stagg at Chicago and then head coach at Minnesota and Princeton before coming to Michigan in 1938, was a coach ahead of his time, in addition to being a mover and shaker. Ranked as one of the greatest football coaches of all time, Crisler was also the first coach to recommend that teams have the option of place-kicking for one point after a touchdown or running or passing for two and widening the goal posts to encourage more field goal attempts. Both of those ideas were adopted years later in the late 1950s, first for college play and later by the NFL.

Like many college coaches who did not benefit from the navy's V-5 or V-12 programs, Crisler found himself with a very young and inexperienced team in 1945, albeit two players would eventually play in the NFL and some freshmen would be part of Michigan's unbeaten 1948 squad that would win the mythical national championship. But Crisler said that he decided to implement a two-platoon system against Army in 1945 out of "sheer necessity."

"By comparison with Michigan, Army had a team of mature men," Crisler said. "So I asked myself how our poor spindly legged freshmen were going to stand up against these West Pointers all afternoon. I knew I would have to spell them off during the game, so I picked our best defensive men and said, 'When we lose the ball, you fellows automatically go in.' As it turned out, I only platooned the lines and the linebackers on defense." Crisler has good reason to be concerned about his outweighed line. Its center, Harold Watts, weighed only 175 lbs., and it contained only two starters who weighed more than 200 lbs. Its job was to face the likes of Barney Poole, Tex Coulter, Al Nemetz, and John Green, all of whom would be first-team All-Americans in 1945. However, one of the Michigan freshman was Joe Sobeleski, who would go on to play with the Chicago Hornets of the All-America Football Conference and then with four teams in the NFL. The backfield was also relatively light with none of the players weighing more than 190 lbs., and it included 17-year-old freshman Walter Teninga and senior Bob Nussbaumer, who after serving in the Marines would play for three teams in the NFL and then spend 13 years as an assistant coach in the league. Nevertheless, Crisler told the entire team before the game that they might actually have fun playing the Cadets.

"On paper, we don't stand a chance," the veteran coach said, "but as the old saw goes, we're not playing this one on paper. And you might actually have some fun playing."

For a while they did. While his semi-platooning scheme didn't spare Michigan from defeat, it certainly kept the game relatively close during the first three quarters as its defense held Army to its lowest scoring total yet. As noted college football writer Allison Danzig of *The New York Times* wrote, "So full of fight and so resourcefully clever was the Big Nine [it became the Big Ten several years later] that it was not until almost the end of the third period that Army ended any doubt about the outcome to score its twelfth successive victory over a two-year period. Despite their tender youth in the line and the disparity in weight and experience, they tore into the dreaded West Pointers with a savageness and disrespect that amounted to *lese-majeste* [Danzig, a Cornell graduate, might well have been the only sportswriter of the era to utilize in a game story a French expression that denoted in effect an offense to a supreme power] and had the 2,500 cadets in the stands genuinely concerned over the challenge to their idols."

Indeed, the freshmen-laden Wolverines threw a scare into the Cadets in the stands and on the field when Michigan reached the Army 10-yard line in the first quarter and the 7-yard line in the second period before being stopped on both occasions. While holding Army scoreless in the first quarter, the young Wolverines defense could contain Blanchard and Davis for just so long. From the outset, Crisler employed a strategy of using his heaviest linemen on defense and his lighter and quicker linemen on offense. And it seemed to work—for a while. But then early in the second quarter, right halfback Shorty McWilliams scored from five yards out after Blanchard had run for 19 yards on three carries. Actually, Davis had combined with Arnold Tucker on a 65-yard touchdown play on Army's first possession of the game, but the touchdown was nullified by a holding penalty. On Army's next possession after McWilliams' touchdown, Blanchard took a handoff from Tucker, exploded through a huge hole on the right, and eluded two defenders in the secondary who collided with one another during a deft fake by the big fullback who covered 68 yards on his touchdown run, which made it 14–0 at halftime.

Years later, Blanchard said the Michigan game of 1945 stood in his mind because the Wolverines played a defense that Army had never seen before, which was not surprising given Fritz Crisler's ingenuity. "It was kind of a stacked eight-man line with four down linemen [defensive players who play up front] and four linebackers playing behind the linemen And they were stunting every time," he said. "That's very difficult for an offensive line to pick up on, and they're filling all the holes every time. It wasn't easy to block up front, and a lot of people were coming into our backfield unblocked. I remember being very tired and sore after that game."

By the second half—no doubt because of suggestions by Red Blaik and Herman Hickman—Army began to figure out that seeming impenetrable defense, but not before the young Wolverines cut Army's lead to seven points. From the opening kickoff of the half, Michigan drove 70 yards to the Cadets' 8-yard line without throwing a single pass. But at that point, 17-year-old tailback Walt Teninga threw a bullet pass that bounced off tackle Tex Coulter's helmet and over the heads of defensive backs Arnold Tucker and Shorty McWilliams and into the arms of end Art Renner for the touchdown. Quarterback and captain Joe Ponsetto kicked the extra point to make it 14–7 Army, as Michigan adherents in the packed stadium roared their approval of the long drive and the touchdown.

But that was as close as the Wolverines would get in this bruising battle. After receiving the ensuing kickoff, Army drove to Michigan's 3-yard line with Davis accounting for 53 yards on an 18-yard run and a 35-yard pass to end Dick Pitzer only to lose the ball on a fumble.

Army also fumbled the ball away on its next possession, but Blanchard got it back on Michigan's first play when he recovered a fumble on the Wolverines' 31-yard line. After Davis and McWilliams each had swept around Michigan's ends, Blanchard smashed over from one yard out to give Army a 21–7 lead at the end of the third quarter. Michigan still had one more scoring chance when the Wolverines drove to the Army 30 early in the final period before being stopped. On the very next play, Davis knifed through right tackle and outraced five defensive backs as he ran down the right sideline to put the game out of reach. Dick Walterhouse, the backup quarterback who had grown up in Ann Arbor and played on the Michigan freshman team before his appointment to West Point, added his fourth extra point to end the scoring. Appropriately enough, his Army teammates then gave Walterhouse the game ball.

Following the game Crisler, then in his 15th year as a college coach, said that Blanchard and Davis were the best college backfield combination of all time, that he had never seen a back faster than Davis, and that Blanchard had, "tremendous power and more speed than Bronko Nagurski," in referring to the former All-American and Chicago Bears star regarded as one of the best football players in the game's history. So fast was he that Crisler said, no doubt in jest, that he had told his players "not to chase him but to save themselves for the next play." Presumably he had told them the same thing about Davis who was even faster than Blanchard.

In all Blanchard and Davis had accounted for more than 300 yards, in addition to making several tackles, intercepting a pass from the left linebacker's spot, throwing several key blocks, punting, and kicking off. Overall, Davis averaged slightly better than 10 yards on 19 carries and Blanchard 8½ yards on 21 rushes. Davis also completed both passes he threw while Arnold Tucker connected on three of his six throws as Army once again concentrated its attack on the ground with little need to pass.

If Crisler was impressed with Blanchard and Davis, Red Blaik was greatly influenced by the Michigan coaching legend's use of separate offensive and defensive players. "What I saw that day in Michigan's separate units for offense and defense stayed with me and was to exert a salutary effect on Army football soon after the Blanchard-Davis era," Blaik said while in effect saying there was no point in adopting the two-platoon system when he had such good two-way players as his celebrated backfield tandem, along with Coulter, Poole, Green, Nemetz, and Tucker. "It's very helpful to the team to be able to concentrate one way. So many who play offense are not very good at defense." Coming from an essentially old-school coach, that appraisal was somewhat surprising, but while Blaik was a traditionalist coach in many ways, he was prescient enough to know that the platoon system was the wave of the future in football. The innovative Crisler, even in a losing effort by his Michigan team, had opened Blaik's eyes to that eventuality, which, of course, became a reality to most college teams by the late 1940s and then the 1950s when Blaik decided to adopt the platoon system. About two decades earlier, when asked where Notre Dame's "box" formation had come from, the legendary coach Knute Rockne said it had come from Yale "where everything in football comes from," with an allusion to Yale's highly imaginative coach of the 1880s, Walter Camp, who has been called "the father of college football."

From 1945 on, that was no longer true, thanks to Fritz Crisler.

10

★ ★ ★

Better Than Ever?

MIKE HOLOVAK WOULD HAVE BEEN QUICK TO ADMIT THAT AS
a coach he was no Fritz Crisler, although he posted a winning
record during his eight years as a coach in the AFL after having been
an All-American fullback and linebacker at Boston College and playing
with the Los Angeles Rams and the Chicago Bears. But Crisler never
had to undertake the task that Holovak did after serving as the commander of a PT boat in the Pacific that sank 18 Japanese ships during
World War II.

On relatively short notice, the then 26-year-old Holovak was asked in
the summer of 1945 to form a football team consisting of veterans of the
Pacific Theater at the navy's Torpedo Boat Squadron Training Center in
Narragansett Bay near Newport, where John F. Kennedy had trained in
late 1942 before becoming a PT boat commander in the Pacific. Recruiting was no problem since the players who turned out were assured that
they would spend the rest of the war at the base and not have to return to
the Pacific Theater of Operations. Almost 40 players took advantage of
that opportunity, most of whom had played in college along with two who
had already played in the NFL—27-year-old fullback and linebacker Joe

Hoague and 29-year-old lineman and halfback Elmer Kolberg, who had been teammates on the Pittsburgh Steelers in 1941 during brief professional careers. Because of a shortage of offensive backs, Holovak, though almost 50 lbs. beyond his playing weight at Boston College, also dressed for games and saw occasional action both at fullback and quarterback. Like Holovak, many of the players were still recovering from malaria contracted in the Pacific and were hardly in very good shape for football. The Melville station soon became one of the few remaining servicemen's football teams after the war ended in mid-August, shortly after the team began practice, the powerful pre-flight teams had been disbanded at the University of North Carolina and at Iowa.

Despite their relatively late start, the veterans of the Pacific fighting acquitted themselves well at the start of their first season, winning four straight games against lower-level collegiate teams from New England while essentially doing nothing more than practicing, playing, and relaxing at the officers' club on the Melville base while awaiting discharges now that the war was over. But on Saturday, October 20, the torpedo boat squadron team found itself arrayed against an Army team that was ranked first in the country ahead of longtime rivals Notre Dame and Navy, before a small crowd of about 10,000 on a sunny and mild afternoon at Michie Stadium. Army originally had been scheduled to play the North Carolina Pre-Flight Cloudbusters, as they were called, but Melville was invited to fill in for the Cloudbusters who had been disbanded shortly after the war ended. "Most of our players had played in college, and we heard about was Blanchard and Davis," Holovak said. "We were looking forward to it." Had there been a betting line, younger and far better conditioned Army most likely would have been favored by about five touchdowns in what appeared to be a one-sided mismatch.

Obviously convinced that Army would prevail easily, Red Blaik decided to start his second team, which consisted of five plebes and was hardly on par with the second unit of a year before when it was so good that it alternated with the first unit. It was not long before Blaik regretted his decision and rushed his first stringers onto the field midway through the first quarter. By then, shockingly, Melville had opened up a 13–0 lead on two long touchdown runs by 150-lb. lieutenant commander and speedy halfback Jackie Welsh, recently returned from combat in the Pacific, who had starred in Penn's victory over Army in 1942. Those 13 points were the most scored on Army since Navy scored the same amount in 1943. At that early juncture of the game, Holovak said later, "I was wishing that it was third quarter."

Unfortunately for Holovak and Melville, it wasn't, and Army unloaded its heavy-duty ground game arsenal in the second when Davis and Blanchard each scored touchdowns, Davis on runs of 43 and 71 yards and Blanchard on plunges from the one-yard line. Both scored once more in the third period on 23-yard runs by which time the torpedo squadron team had trouble keeping Army's offense in check while failing to mount any offense of its own as the Cadets went on to win 55–13 in a rout.

Referring to the slow start by Army's second team, 5′7″ 170-lb. quarterback Johnny Sauer, whose father had played with Blaik in high school in Dayton, Ohio, had a logical explanation. "I would have to say that a bunch of youngsters were overwhelmed by a lot of experience, and I believe they found out they could intimidate some of the youngsters at West Point. There was a lot of flutter in the heart and stomach by us who had never started a game."

However, that intimidation ended as soon as Blanchard, Davis, and the rest of Army's first team took over before handing over the reins to the second and third teams in the final quarter. "I think that what happened was that they had the stamina and the experience for the first 10 or 15 minutes of the game," plebe tackle Goble Bryant said. "But we were so strong and so good that they weren't even in the game by the end of the third quarter. They were worn out."

Holovak agreed. "It was a good game for a period," the Melville coach said. "But training at the officers club was not the ideal situation for playing football." Also, he might have added was the realization by the Melville players that they would soon by civilians again.

The statistics reflected what happened in the game. Army's offense gained a whopping 570 yards, almost all of it on the ground, while Melville managed only 196, most of it by Jackie Welsh in the first quarter. No one knew it at the time, but the game was the last one for the short-lived torpedo squadron team. Like other servicemen's teams, the Melville team became a casualty of the war's end as most of its players faced imminent discharge and had little interest in continuing to play football, especially against teams like Army.

★ ★ ★

By mid-season of 1945, Army was ranked first, followed by Notre Dame and Navy. The team also had a new nickname, the Black Knights, pinned on the Cadets by *New York Sun* sportswriter Will Wedge, and which was based on the team's attire—dark jerseys with golden numbers and arm bands, and golden helmets with a black band up the middle. Until Wedge's appellation, still in use today, the team had been known as "the Cadets." By any name, the Black Knights were far and away the best college football team in the country.

Next up on October 27 was Duke, a team that had held Army to 27 points in a losing effort in 1944 and was ranked 19th after winning three games. Duke lost to Navy but would win the Southeastern Conference title and finish with a commendable 6–2 record. But even Coach Eddie Cameron was pessimistic about the Blue Devils' chances against Army. "We are trying to get ready to give Army a good game, but we don't have any illusions about beating them," Cameron said of his team, which included about 15 V-5 and V-12 players and one, tackle Jake Poole, who was actually in an army training program at Duke. The roster was relatively young—about half the 52 players were freshmen—but it had a fairly good nucleus from the 1944 team that went on to beat Alabama 29–26 in the Sugar Bowl on New Year's Day, along with backs who recently had been discharged from military service. Among the starters was navy ensign and halfback George Clark who was married two days before the game and spent his honeymoon night on a train headed for New York. Also in the starting lineup was 235-lb. (heavy for a lineman at the time) tackle Al DeRogatis, who had grown up in Newark, New Jersey, about an hour's ride from West Point and who would go on to play four seasons with the New York Giants.

The game was vastly overshadowed by President Harry Truman's first visit to New York as the nation's chief executive. That morning the President christened the new aircraft carrier *Franklin D. Roosevelt* at the Brooklyn Navy Yard. Then after a brief stop with New York Mayor Fiorello La Guardia at City Hall, Truman spoke to a crowd estimated at 1 million at Central Park and a nationwide radio audience. The highlight of his whirlwind visit was a review of a line of 50 navy warships in the Hudson River from the deck of the battleship *Missouri* on which Japan had surrendered two months earlier while 1,200 navy planes flew overhead. It was one of the most spectacular military displays ever held in the country and it attracted a huge throng, both on land in New York and New Jersey and on boats on the Hudson. All of that made getting to the Army-Duke game difficult, especially by ground transportation. Nevertheless, a crowd of around 45,000 turned out for the game that was played on a relatively cold, cloudy, and windy day.

As always, Red Blaik was hardly optimistic as he focused on Duke's three victories and hardly mentioned the loss to Navy. As it turned out, he had little to be worried about. On the first play of its first possession, less than five minutes into the game, Army scored when Shorty McWilliams took a handoff from Arnold Tucker and, following Tucker, Davis, and Blanchard burst through the left side of the line and raced 54 yards

for a touchdown, shaking off two would-be Duke tackles at the Blue
Devils' 25-yard line. It was a bad omen for Duke as Army proceeded to
open up a 28–0 lead at halftime then scored three more touchdowns in
the second half to win 48–13. In all, five Cadets crossed the goal line,
including Blanchard, who scored twice on a pass from Davis that covered 59-yards and on a 36-yard run behind great blocking, and Davis,
who scored on a bolt through the center of the Duke line from seven
yards out. Nineteen-year-old plebe Bob Stuart, a reserve halfback, also
scored two touchdowns on a 20-yard run after receiving a lateral from
end Hank Foldberg who had caught a pass from Tucker, and on a pass
from Dick Walterhouse that covered 52 yards.

Duke was not able to score until late in the game by which time
Army's third team was on the field. Both of the Duke touchdowns
came on passes from the new bridegroom, George Clark, who completed seven passes in a row on both touchdown drives. Army again
netted better than 500 yards, amassing 594 yards running and passing
against 190 yards, most of it earned late in the game, for Duke. Sadly
for Army, Roland Catarinella, who Blaik had converted from a fullback,
a position that he had played for one year at Pittsburgh, to a guard and
center, broke a leg while playing fullback late in the game. "Because of
Navy Day in New York, the traffic was so bad that it took three hours
to get me to a military hospital on Governors Island," Catarinella said
in referring to the Revolutionary War–era fort in New York Harbor. "I
was in the Fort Jay Hospital for six weeks, and although I graduated the
following June I didn't get a commission and was discharged from the
army because of my injury and returned home to Pennsylvania to work
with my father's home building business. I was disappointed, but I like
to think that by me not getting a commission, it was the army's loss."

Disappointed, to a far less degree during Army's lopsided win over
Duke, was plebe end Bob Wayne, a New Yorker playing in his hometown before friends, relatives, and his girlfriend. Wayne recalled Dick

Walterhouse hitting him, literally, with a pass on the 1-yard line late in the game. "The pass was absolutely right to me, and I thought, *Wow, I'm going to make a touchdown,*" Wayne said. "But the ball hit me on the shoulder pad, bounced up, and they intercepted it. After the game, Colonel Blaik said to me, 'What happened, Bob? Did the sun get in your eyes?' Of course there was no sun." The tongue-in-cheek comment by Blaik showed a rarely seen part of the coach—a sense of humor. Perhaps all of Army's impressive victories were making good impressions on the usually dour coach, who might even have more to smile about in the coming weeks.

11

★ ★ ★

The Colonel as Coach

AYS LIKE NAVY DAY WERE AN ELIXIR OF SORTS, ENABLING President Truman to enjoy his unexpected role as president. He hardly could do so at the White House. While the cost of living had risen by 30 percent, the incomes of average workers had doubled and unemployment was at a remarkably low 2 percent even though millions of American servicemen and servicewomen were being discharged. Moreover, with Americans clamoring for new cars and other products unavailable during the war, the production of goods and services was almost double of what it had been in 1939 when World War II broke out and the country was still in the grip of the Great Depression, which would not really abate until 1940 and 1941 when war production increased dramatically, creating millions of jobs.

But there were still ample problems.

By October, Boeing Aircraft had laid off about 20,000 workers, and Ford had let go of more than twice that many despite its conversion to peacetime production of cars and trucks. In addition, a flurry of strikes were called by those unions that had kept their pledges not to strike during the war. The biggest strike was at General Motors where

175,000 workers walked off their jobs at plants in 19 states and would remain out for three months. By fall, the country also faced a housing shortage that was the largest in U.S. history. Deeply affected were returning veterans hoping to resume a normal prewar lifestyle. That was hardly the case in Chicago where about 100,000 veterans found themselves homeless. Conditions in other big cities like New York and Los Angeles also faced serious housing shortages. In some cities old streetcars were converted into living quarters. Despite all of those problems, in 1945 President Truman appeared to be more popular than ever and had an approval rating of 80 percent.

Meanwhile, Truman was calling for universal military service for men from 18 to 20 on the grounds that the country would be better prepared if another war broke out and could turn to young men who already had military training unlike what happened at the outset of America's entry into World War II when the country was desperate for manpower and had to rely to a large degree on untrained civilians who for the most part did remarkably well. But his proposal for what was called UMT found little support in Congress—nor did his call for compulsory national health insurance to be funded by payroll deductions.

★ ★ ★

In an era of high-profile coaches, Red Blaik was attracting more attention than any of his coaching counterparts despite his low-key manner. Neither as innovative as contemporary coaches Clark Shaughnessy. Amos Alonzo Stagg, and Fritz Crisler, nor as inspirational and colorful as Knute Rockne and Vince Lombardi, Blaik seemed to be a perfect fit for the Army football team thanks to his no-nonsense military bearing, his discipline, and his organizational skills. Like most good coaches, he was consumed by football all year long, putting aside that passion only to spend time with his wife and two sons or to play a round of golf, usually with his assistant coaches, where the conversation invariably turned to football. "I seldom took a vacation from the job, and then only when my doctor warned me that some relaxation was necessary," Blaik once said. "I would arrive at my desk on the top floor of the South Gym around 8:00. Our staff meetings began at 9:00 and lasted, except for a very brief lunch period, until mid-afternoon when it was time to go on the field. During fall and spring practice, we [the Army coaches] worked far into every night. Our families saw little of us—part of the price of our mission, and the steepest part of all. I always drove my assistants as hard as I drove myself, and I never found one who couldn't or wouldn't take it."

Even holidays were work days for West Point coaches, including some New Year's Days when Blaik would ring in the New Year with a staff meeting at 8:00 in the morning, no matter how much his assistants had celebrated the night before. That was the case on New Year's Day 1944 while Andy Gustafson was a backfield coach at West Point. "Years after, when he was head coach at Miami of Florida, Gus never failed to phone me long distance to West Point on New Year's morning, usually before 8:00, to inquire whether I was in the office, and if not, why not," Blaik wrote in his autobiography.

12

★ ★ ★

"Say a Little Prayer for Us"

BY 1945, EARL BLAIK HAD BEEN PROMOTED FROM LIEUTENANT colonel to colonel, a quantum leap from the rank of second lieutenant he had held when he resigned from the army in 1922. By 1944 he was addressed by most of his players as "Colonel" rather than coach. At any rate, he could hardly be more content as the head coach of what certainly appeared to be the best college team in the country and with the accolades his team was getting. He also took pride in the fact that his youngest of two sons, 16-year-old Bob Blaik, was the star quarterback and a top-tier college prospect at Highland Falls high school. Blaik and his wife also savored their life of living on the Academy grounds and socializing with other regular army officers and their wives and other members of the West Point staff.

One of Blaik's most distinctive traits was his habitually calm demeanor, both during practices and games, which endeared him to his assistants and his players. Another was his dire warnings to his troops about upcoming opponents. Once, after Blaik had done just that in advance of a game against an over-matched team, Glenn Davis, usually not prone to question the colonel's judgment, said, "Hey Colonel, why are you building them up like that? You know they're not that good."

"Listen, Glenn," Blaik snapped back at his star halfback, "our scouts say they've got a very dangerous passing attack. If we're not on our toes, they'll pass us dizzy."

To which Davis replied, "And while they're throwing all those passes, what are we going to be doing?" Davis, of course, knew, as did Blaik, that the Army pass defense, led by Davis and Blanchard, was outstanding. That response drew a laugh from Davis' teammates and a scowl from Blaik.

As it was, though, the players rarely questioned the coach. The consensus of his former players interviewed for this title was that Blaik was a very good coach who kept his distance from his players and certainly did not play any favorites. "He was a super coach and a very nice person," All-American guard Joe Steffy said of his coach. "He never, ever, raised his voice." Other members of his 1945 team voiced similar encomiums about their coach. "Colonel Blaik was very reserved and kind of aloof," said Arnold Tucker, an All-American quarterback in 1946. "But he was an excellent communicator." However, Tucker also learned that you had to execute a play his way and weren't supposed to deviate from what Blaik wanted you to do. "During one practice in 1945, Blaik quietly chided Tucker for his execution of a play during a scrimmage and took him aside to correct him. "I told him, 'Gee, Colonel, I thought we did that just right,'" Tucker recalled. Blaik, somewhat surprised by Tucker's comeuppance, responded by saying firmly, "There are coaches here who have been around longer than you have. Now get in there and do it the way I want it done." Laughing at the recollection of that conversation 59 year later, Tucker said that from then on, he executed plays exactly the way Blaik wanted them done.

End Ed "Rafe" Rafalko, who would wind up as a major general in the Air Force and then as athletic director at the Air Force Academy, said, "Coach Blaik had a no-nonsense approach to what he did. He was detailed as to individuals but was also innovative in game preparation. But he didn't say a helluva lot, and he wasn't big on halftime speeches." Bob Woods, the midshipman who became a cadet, said he had a great deal of respect for Blaik. "But I felt closer to Herman Hickman, even though Hickman was the line coach," Woods said.

* * *

Though it still had a number of V-5 and V-12 aspiring naval officers along with some returning war veterans, including halfback Romeo Capriotti, who had received a Silver Star for heroism while in the army, Villanova had no illusions about beating Army in the Cadets' sixth game at Michie Stadium. Among other reasons, Capriotti and a number of other starters were out with injuries, leaving a team with little depth even more short-handed. "They ran plays with the precision that the Corps of Cadets marched," Villanova captain Charley Welde said years later, alluding to the pregame march of Cadets. Though the Wildcats had won three games, they had been soundly beaten by Navy 49–0 and also by Holy Cross but would later stun a favored Boston College team 41–0.

Convinced that the Cadets would have little trouble with Villanova, Red Blaik left the coaching to backfield coach Andy Gustafson, while he, Herman Hickman, and three other assistant coaches traveled to Cleveland to scout future opponents Notre Dame and Navy. Blaik's decision could hardly be questioned as Army scored four touchdowns in the first quarter—two by Blanchard. On Army's first possession, Blanchard grabbed a 20-yard pass from Davis and raced 35 yards for a touchdown, and shortly thereafter broke through a huge hole opened by Army blockers and ran 60 yards for his second touchdown. Davis, meanwhile, gaining yardage with ease, twice crossed the goal line, from the 2- and 6-yard lines. Gustafson replaced both Mr. Inside and Mr. Outside 11:00 into the game and saw no need to put them or the remaining Cadets starters back in for the rest of the way. Two more touchdowns gave the newly named Black Knights a 42–0 halftime lead. By the intermission, rain was falling and about half of the crowd of around 10,000 had departed.

Although by mutual agreement the second half was shortened from 30 to 20 minutes, as was the case with three games during the 1945 season, Army, by now using second- and third-stringers, still added two more touchdowns to give the Cadets a 54–0 victory over the totally outclassed and undermanned Wildcats. The statistics reflected the one-sided nature of the game, with Army gaining 402 yards on the ground as against only 20 by Villanova. The home team gained 104 yards in the air on 17 passes, while Villanova was able to net five yards in completing only 1-of-9 passes.

Plebes Rip Rowan and Bobby Stuart scored two of Army's four touchdowns after Gustafson had pulled out the Cadet starters. There is no doubt that Rowan and Stuart could have been starters at most other colleges, but they saw considerable action for the Cadets because of Blaik's penchant of removing Blanchard and Davis early in the second half if not earlier, as was the case in the Villanova game. That irked Davis, who once went over to Blaik when he was on the sideline of a lopsided game and said, as Blaik was to recollect, "Colonel, why can't I go back in the game?" Blaik tried to pacify Davis by telling him he wasn't needed because Army was leading by about four touchdowns in the second half. "But I want to play football," Davis said, imploring the coach to put him back in the game. This time, Blaik merely shook his head and walked away, well aware of the intensity of Davis' competitive spirit.

Bob Chabot, who also scored a touchdown in the game and no doubt could have been a starting back at other schools that had recruited him, said there were no rivalries or jealousies on the outstanding 1945 team despite all the publicity about Blanchard and Davis. "The team had everything," said the professorial-looking Chabot who, after completing his military commitment, became a high school coach and science teacher and director and part owner of a summer camp in West Stockbridge, Massachusetts. "It had stability, it had an untold desire, it had character, and it had integrity," he said years later. "And playing for West Point was great fun."

Once again in 1945, the Army–Notre Dame game was one of the biggest sports events of he year, with Cadets ranked first and the Fighting Irish second. Both teams were unbeaten, although Notre Dame had been tied by Navy the week before in Cleveland which Blaik, Hickman, and three other Army coaches had watched from the press box to scout their two toughest rivals. The game was not only especially important to Red Blaik because Army had only beaten Notre Dame six times in 30 meetings since the series began in 1913, but because most of the spectators—almost 75,000 on November 10, 1945—rooted for the Fighting Irish, even though it was ostensibly a home game for Army since the stadium was only about 50 miles from West Point. That, of course, was because of Notre Dame's Subway Alumni, which in the 1940s not only consisted of thousands of subway-riding Irish-Americans from New York, heavily Irish at the time, to the game but encompassed thousands if not millions of Irish fans throughout the country. Somehow, Blaik failed to understand the link, and it most definitely gnawed at him.

With Frank Leahy still in the navy, Notre Dame's first interim coach, backfield coach Ed McKeever, left South Bend after one season as head coach to accept the head coaching job at Cornell. Filling in until Leahy returned in 1946 was Hugh Devore, a onetime Notre Dame end who had coached the Irish freshman team and had been an assistant at Fordham, Providence (yes, the Friars once had a football team), and Holy Cross and would return to coach at his alma mater again in 1963 after being an assistant coach in the National Football

League. As was customary when Notre Dame played in New York, on Friday the 40-member squad was bussed from West Point to the Knollwood Country Club in White Plains in Westchester County, about 20 miles from Yankee Stadium, and then had a light workout at the Stadium that afternoon before returning to the country club to have dinner and spend the night. Notre Dame, meanwhile, spent Friday night at the Bear Mountain Inn, a picturesque hotel and restaurant overlooking the Hudson River and only 15 miles from West Point. The Irish also had a light practice session at the Stadium before returning to Bear Mountain for a team meeting, dinner, and then to bed.

Notre Dame was still smarting from the 59–0 defeat inflicted by Army in 1944, the Cadets' first victory over the Irish since 1931. Although Notre Dame had a few players back from military service, it was primarily a young team centered around veteran quarterback Frank "Boley" Dancewicz and All-American guard John Mastrangelo, both of whom would be second team All-Americans in 1945 and later play in the NFL. Essentially, though, it was a young team with about 25 freshmen on the 50-man squad, and five in the starting lineup, including starting center 18-year-old Bill Walsh, who would go on to play six seasons with the Pittsburgh Steelers, and tackle Bill Fischer, also 18, who would spend five years with the Chicago Cardinals, the precursor of the St. Louis and Arizona Cardinals.

Other future NFL players on the squad were fullback Elmer Angsman, end Bob Skoglund, and backup quarterbacks George Ratterman and Frank Tripucka, who would have distinguished professional careers. The best runner on the team, also an 18-year-old freshman, was Phil Colella, a 5′10″ speedster who could run as fast as Davis and was good enough to start in the backfield with another freshman, Terry Brennan, then only 17, who would be a star on the 1946 and 1947 teams and eventually the head coach at Notre Dame. After one year at Notre Dame, Colella decided to follow Devore to St. Bonaventure, where he was a starting halfback for three years. "I think Phil left because he wasn't too happy with the way things were going in spring practice under Leahy" (who had returned from the navy), said Ernie Virok, a backup center on the 1945 team, who also wound up at St. Bonaventure in 1947 after spending a year in the army.

The game was virtually a replica of the 1944 game when Army ended a 13-year winless drought against Notre Dame with the Cadets crushing the young Fighting Irish 48–0. Davis and Blanchard both had spectacular games, with Davis scoring touchdowns on runs of 26 and 21 yards and on a 15-yard pass from Arnold Tucker followed by a 16-yard run through the Notre Dame secondary. Actually, the Irish kept the game close at the outset, holding the Black Knights to a single touchdown in the opening quarter that came on their first possession when Davis, by now also a very good passer, faked a pass and raced 26 yards down the left side behind fierce blocks by Tex Coulter and end Dick Pitzer. With Army's defense overpowering Notre Dame's young and inexperienced line, that turned out to be the only scoring the Cadets needed. Notre Dame, meanwhile, reached the Cadets' 25-yard line in the first period, primarily on the running of the speedy Colella and Angsman.

Davis gave the big crowd a demonstration of both his versatility and running early in the second quarter when he snared a short pass over the middle from Tucker, faked out one linebacker, and after picking up speed juked three defenders with quick shifty moves and eluded Ratterman with another deft move at the 5-yard line for his second touchdown. Before leaving at the end of the third quarter, Davis scored once more on a dazzling 21-yard touchdown sprint after bolting through the left side of the Army line, veering to his right and out-running the Irish secondary again. Blanchard, after scoring on a one-yard plunge, scored again from his linebacker's position when he intercepted a Ratterman pass and raced 37 yards for a touchdown. With Davis and Blanchard watching from the sideline, Army substitutes registered the team's final touchdowns in the last quarter on a five-yard run by Shorty McWilliams and on a 10-yard pass from Dick Walterhouse to Clyde Grimenstein.

Irish coach Hugh Devore conceded that he was in awe of his alma mater's team. "That's one of the greatest teams ever to represent a college," said Devore, who, as a head coach at St. Bonaventure, New York University (also a big-time football school in the 1940s), and Dayton, would never have to worry about facing Army again and who eventually returned to South Bend as head coach of the Irish for one season in 1963. "What convinced me was that Army players were still driving as hard in the fourth quarter when the game was won as they did at the start." That, no doubt, was because after playing in the shadows of Davis, Blanchard, Tucker, and linemen like All-Americans Barney Poole, Tex Coulter, and John Green, the reserves wanted to show Red Blaik they could more than hold their own.

★ ★ ★

Next up was the traditional game against Pennsylvania at Franklin Field in Philadelphia. "That's going to be a tough one," Red Blaik said in advance of the game against the seventh-ranked Quakers who had won five of their first six games, losing only to Navy and then only by a touchdown. "We never have played well against Penn." Blaik obviously had forgotten, or chose to forget, that the Black Knights had crushed Penn 62–7 the year before. So famous had the Cadets' team become that the issue of *Life* magazine the week of the game carried a spread about Army that included a photo of the backfield that the article said was "the most spectacular backfield since Notre Dame's backfield of 1924." In truth, most football historians and sportswriters who had seen the famed Irish backfield in action disagreed, feeling that Blanchard, Davis, Tucker, and right halfbacks Shortly McWilliams and Bob Stuart comprised a better backfield and may have been the best one of all time.

What made the 1945 Penn team different than Army's other opponents was that about half of its starters were veterans—not of previous seasons as players for the Quakers, but as veterans of World War II. Of the roughly 20 former GIs on the team were the captain, tailback Bob Evans who had been decorated for heroism as a member of the Army Air Corps in Europe; 245-lb. tackle and former Marine George Savitsky, an All-American in 1945 who later spent two years with the Philadelphia Eagles; army veteran Chuck Bednarik, who became the last NFL player to play offense and defense (as a center and linebacker) with the Eagles and whose swashbuckling play earned him All-American honors and later election to the Professional Football Hall of Fame in Canton, Ohio; and halfback Don Schneider, who spent one season with the Buffalo Bills of the All-America Football Conference. Indeed, overall, about a third of the 50-member squad were war veterans who played alongside a number of 18-year-old freshmen and about two dozen players who had returned from the 1944 squad. At any rate, even though Army was a four-touchdown favorite, the 1945 Quakers team appeared to be much stronger than the 1944 version that had gone 5–3 without the benefit of any returning war veterans.

But even outstanding players like Bednarik and Savitsky, who later were both inducted into the College Football Hall of Fame, could not do much against the Army juggernaut before a crowd of about 70,000 at 50-year-old Franklin Field, the first double-decked stadium in the United States and, 50 years after it opened, still the home of Penn football teams and the Philadelphia Eagles. Once again, Blanchard and Davis put on a scintillating display during which each of them scored three touchdowns—Blanchard had two others called back and Davis one in the first quarter because of illegal motion—as the Cadets inflicted an even greater rout than they did a year before in winning 61–0 while amassing 525 yards rushing and passing. Once again, the Army defense was virtually impregnable in recording its third straight shutout, even though Davis, Blanchard, and the rest of the starters sat out most of the second half. That again gave Army's reserves opportunities to shine, including backup halfback Bob Chabot, who on a day that he later said, "I could do no wrong," ran 62 yards for a touchdown and returned a punt 45 yards. Nor could his teammates do anything wrong in Army's most awesome display of running, blocking, and tackling of the season.

Four of the six Army touchdowns scored by Blanchard and Davis covered more than 25 yards, with Blanchard scoring on runs of 27 and 38 yards and on a pass play with quarterback Arnold Tucker that covered 72 yards, and Davis crossing the Penn goal line on two one-yard runs and one fleet zig-zag dash from 32 yards out. They did all that with Davis also passing and catching passes and Blanchard repeatedly breaking away for substantial gains.

Army tackle Tex Coulter, matched up against a fellow All-American in the huge George Savitsky, more than held his own. "I was making tackles all over the place in what was probably the best football game I ever played," said Coulter, who also marginalized Savitsky with his outstanding blocking. In his story in the next day's *New York Times*, one of the country's most respected sportswriters Allison Danzig wrote, "Here was one of the most devastating exhibitions of aggression and bolting speed the gridiron has known."

Only an undefeated Navy team two weeks later (neither team had a game the following Saturday) stood between another unbeaten season for Army and its second straight national championship. A comparison between the teams showed they had fared about equal against common opponents. For example, Army had beaten Michigan by three touchdowns, one less than Navy had. But both had beaten other common rivals by about the same number of touchdowns—except for Notre Dame, which the Cadets had trounced 48–0, while the Irish had held the Middies to a 6–6 tie; and Penn, which Army had thrashed 61–0 in its last previous game, while Navy needed a late touchdown to beat the Quakers. Still, even Navy coaches had trouble being optimistic against the high-scoring Cadets and their ferocious defense. Leaving the press box after the game, one of Navy's assistant coaches, Ray Swartz, never known to be a pessimist, said, "That's the best football team I ever saw. Say a little prayer for us on December first."

No one at West Point was saying any prayers for Navy, which for the second year in a row came into the season's climactic game ranked second in the nation behind Army. For years, Yale and Harvard, and much of the media, had referred to their annual last game of the season as "The Game." But Army and Navy alumni, along with their legions of fans, certainly begged to differ in the 1940s, and even later. In fact The Game in 1945 as in 1944 was the one in Philadelphia between the two service academies. Even after the subsequent turn of the century, when all four teams had fallen in stature and rarely ranked in the top 20, the Army-Navy game was televised nationally every year, while the Yale-Harvard game was rarely even telecast on a regional basis. But in 1945, when both Yale and Harvard still fielded strong teams—in 1941, Red Blaik's first year as the Army coach, Harvard beat Army 20–6 after the Cadets had defeated a good Yale team 20–7—Army did not play either school and would not until 1948 when the unbeaten Cadets beat the Crimson 20–7 at Michie Stadium. In 1945, even the most avid Yale and Harvard alumni would agree that The Game that year was between Army and Navy.

How big was the game? In addition to the huge media interest in newspapers and radio, the game and much of its panoply, including the pregame march by the cadets and midshipmen and the arrival of President Truman's limousine, became the first Army-Navy game to be televised, albeit on a limited basis on stations in Philadelphia, New York City, and Schenectady in upstate New York. By far the largest audience was on radio, with Red Barber—one of the country's most renowned sports announcers and best known as the announcer of Brooklyn Dodgers baseball games—describing the game to millions of listeners in the United States and via short-wave radio to American military bases abroad.

In the days leading up to the climactic game, both General Dwight Eisenhower and Admiral William "Bull" Halsey, two of the most prominent military figures during World War II, addressed pep rallies at West Point and Annapolis, respectively, by telephone and loud speaker. Eisenhower went so far as to equate football with war during his address to almost the entire corps of 2,500 during suppertime in Washington Hall (lunch was dinner and the evening meal was supper, not uncommon terms for those two meals in the 1940s). "Each contest requires guts, brains, physical power, skillful teamwork, and heart," said Eisenhower, who became an Army cheerleader after an injury ended his football career. "But there is a vital difference. In war victory is everything, and anything to gain it is fair. In football, the game is the thing—the good clean fight with everything we've got." After saying that Army and Navy had a close relationship during the rest of the year, Eisenhower added, "But on this one half day next Saturday afternoon, we reserve the right, the sweet privilege of rocking them and socking them into respectful recognition of West Point's superiority."

In his suppertime address to the Midshipmen at Annapolis, Halsey urged the Middies' team "to fight like hell and win that game." Then Army superintendent Major General Francis Wilby, who had been replaced by General Maxwell Taylor three months before the 1945 game, had gone even further when, in a letter to Red Blaik before the 1944 Army-Navy game, he said that he didn't care whether or not Army lost every other game so long as they beat Navy, since to him it was "the only thing that counts." Presumably, Wilby, who retired three months after leaving West Point, felt the same way before the 1945 game, even though he knew that Army hardly was going to lose every game in the mid-1940s with the talent it had. Red Blaik, hardly a cheerleading type of coach, even went so far as to say that the 1945 game was "the main objective of the whole season." For Blaik, that was downright hyperbolic.

Advance publicity for the game seemed to have drawn as much attention, if not more, as that given by Americans to the Nuremberg war crimes trials that had begun in Germany and a series of strikes across the country that bedeviled President Harry Truman and the Labor Department, along with a congressional hearing into possible culpability on the part of top American military commanders that may have been at least partially to blame for the country's unpreparedness at Pearl Harbor four years earlier.

Never before have so many military leaders gathered at a sporting event in the country than did on Saturday, December 2. Along with the president, the Washington entourage included Secretary of State James Byrnes, Attorney General Tom Clark, Secretary of the Navy James Forrestal, Secretary of War Robert Patterson; a half-dozen other cabinet members, around a dozen senators, numerous congressmen, and Postmaster General Robert Hannegan. Among the high-ranking military leaders were Army Chief of Staff General George C. Marshall, author of the post-war Marshall Plan who had just been named ambassador to China; General Henry "Hap" Arnold, commander of the U.S. Army Air Forces; General Maxwell Taylor; Lieutenant General Jimmy Doolittle, who had led the first American air raid on Japan; and admirals William Halsey, Chester Nimitz, and Ernest King. It was a dazzling display of ribbons, brass, and medals that literally glittered in the afternoon sun on a cold and windy day before a crowd of slightly more than 100,000 spectators at U-shaped Philadelphia Municipal Stadium.

Army appeared to have the edge in coaching. While Red Blaik had been a coach since 1927 and a head coach since 1934, 36-year-old Swede Hagberg, a career Naval officer, was in his second year as Navy's head coach after serving as a submarine commander during the war after playing at Annapolis and would be replaced following the 1945 season. Hagberg hardly inspired any confidence in his team before the Army game when he said, "To me, it's just another game, and I think it isn't impossible for us to beat Army."

With the team Hagberg had, that actually seemed possible. With a strong line that averaged better than 200 lbs. and a backfield that was so good that Bob Kelly, a second team All-American at Notre Dame the year before, was a backup halfback. As at Army, although not to the same degree, Navy continued to use a number of transfers from other schools, such as Bob Jenkins, who had starred at Alabama and then became an All-American at Navy in 1944; Skip Minisi, who had been a star running back at Penn the previous season; Bob Hoernschemeyer, who had played two seasons at Indiana; and Clyde "Smackover" Scott, so called because he came from Smackover, Arkansas, and had spent two years at the University of Arkansas. Of the seven linemen, five had played elsewhere before transferring, or more correctly, been recruited by Navy, which obviously had a lot to do with the Middies' record and its ranking in 1945. But at game time, Army had been established as a four-touchdown favorite.

Before the game, the entire brigade of 2,700 midshipmen that had traveled to Philadelphia by ship, paraded onto the field, followed by the 2,500 cadets from West Point, who had arrived that same morning by train. Also on the field were the two teams' mascots—the Army mule and Navy's goat. President Truman had traveled to Philadelphia by train with his wife, Bess, and other family members and friends, along with five servicemen who had been wounded during the war. A private who had worked his way up to captain during World War I, Truman, accompanied by his entourage, sat on the Army side during the first half and then at halftime was escorted over to the Navy side by Forrestal and a detail of Secret Service men, where he would remain for the second half. As much as he appeared to remain neutral, it became evident that

Truman's sympathies were with Army, no doubt because of his army service.

Earlier in the week, Blaik had cause for concern when Arnold Tucker, Barney Poole (still not a starter because of Blaik's ire over Poole's effort to transfer after the previous season), and reserve lineman Al Joy came down with heavy colds. In Tucker's case, his cold was bad enough for the starting quarterback to check into the Academy hospital. It wasn't until just before the Cadets left for Philadelphia that Tucker was discharged from the hospital, although it seemed possible that Blaik would have to go with backup quarterback and ace place-kicker Dick Walterhouse. However, by Saturday Tucker was well enough to start.

By the time President Truman changed sides at halftime to a loud cheer from the crowd, the outcome had already been determined after Army scored three touchdowns in the opening quarter, all of them by the Cadets' dynamic duo of Blanchard, who scored two, and Davis, who made the third.

Army captain and All-America guard Jack Green won the toss and elected to have the Cadets take the side with the wind at their backs for the first half. Navy, given the choice of kicking off or receiving, elected to kick off, which turned out to be the Middies' first mistake of the day. Navy guard Jim Carrington's kickoff into the wind only reached the Army 35-yard line, from where the Cadets launched a 65-yard drive that ended when Blanchard burst through the Navy line from the 2-yard line for a touchdown. Two possessions later, Army took advantage of a poor 11-yard Navy punt that gave the Cadets the ball on the Middies' 37-yard line. After a 24-yard run by Tucker, Davis was tackled for a rare loss, but then Blanchard again broke through the Navy line, knocking over Navy guard John Coppedge when they collided head-on, and then bowling over Smackover Scott in the open field as he raced 17 yards for the second Army score. Army also scored on its next possession when Davis shot through left tackle and out-ran three defensive backs in racing 48 yards to give the Cadets a 20–0 lead at the end of the first period.

Navy managed to hold Army scoreless in the second quarter and reached the 20- and 34-yard lines on two drives, once on a rare shanked 10-yard punt by Blanchard, but was unable to score. Finally, with less than a minute left in the half, Navy quarterback Bruce Smith connected with Scott who out-leaped Davis to catch a 21-yard pass at the Army 40 and then, in a dramatic foot-race between the two speedsters, Scott, who went on to win the silver medal in the high hurdles at the 1948 Summer Olympics, barely out-ran Davis before the Cadets star tackled him by the ankles as Scott crossed the goal line for a touchdown. Following guard Dick Currence's conversion, Navy was back in the game, trailing 20–7 at halftime.

Army quickly extended its lead, though, one minute into the third quarter when Blanchard, playing linebacker, picked off a hurried pass by Smith at midfield and sprinted down the left sideline untouched for his third touchdown. After Dick Walterhouse missed his second of four extra-point tries—extremely rare for Army's normally dead-eye place-kicker and talented backup quarterback—the Black Knights led 26–7, a score that stood through the remainder of the period.

Again, Army appeared to have put away its arch rival, but the Middies battled back to draw within 13 points again early in the final quarter after Smith intercepted a pass by Davis, who usually passed on option plays and was rarely intercepted, and ran it back to the Cadets' 26-yard line. Five plays later, fullback Joe Bartos crashed through from the 1-yard line to make it 26–13 Army, as the brigade of midshipmen in the stands, along with the crew of admirals and other high-ranking Navy brass, erupted into cheers.

But then Davis ran back the ensuing kickoff 25 yards to the Army 29-yard line. From there, the Cadets, aided by two penalties that cost Navy 30 yards, drove to the Middies' 27-yard line. Davis then sealed the victory for Army midway through the final quarter by following crisp blocking by plebe guard Art Gerometta and first-classman and All-American tackle Al Nemetz through the line, and then out-ran three Navy secondary players for his second touchdown. Walterhouse, again battling the strong crosswind that swept across the field throughout the game, missed his third of five extra-point attempts, but no matter as Army held Navy scoreless for the rest of the game to win 32–13 for its 18th consecutive victory and a second unbeaten season during which it had yielded only 46 points while scoring a staggering 412 points. Navy had outgained Army by completing 5-of-15 passes for 106 yards to only seven yards by the Cadets who completed only 2-of-7 passes. But then Army actually never had to throw the ball at all, not when it gained 249 yards rushing compared with 110 yards by Navy. Of those yards, Davis ran 13 times for 97 yards, while Blanchard gained 77 yards on 17 carries. At the game's end, Navy players, in accord with a pregame bet, surrendered their jerseys to their Army counterparts then hurried into their locker room to escape the cold. Amid the celebration and levity in the Army locker room, Davis was, according to Red Blaik, "feeling terrible because he thinks he didn't play a good game." Ever the perfectionist, Army's All-American halfback lamented the pass interception he threw and for allowing Navy's Smackover Scott to out-jump him to catch a pass and then out-run him for the Middies' first touchdown.

Blaik hardly sounded like a winner, either, after the game. "We never had an opportunity to roll, never had a chance to open our attack," the Army coach said while sportswriters and others around him looked at one another incredulously. "We could do very little against the wind. Navy knew it, and they tightened up their defense against our running plays. But I'm very thankful for what we got."

By contrast, Hagberg, the Navy coach, had no alibis for losing. "Army is a magnificent team," he said. "We were physically outmatched in the line, but you can't block a tiger."

In a surprisingly candid assessment of his unbeaten team, Blaik said, "This is the finest team we ever had at West Point, a least in my time," the five-year Army coach said. "We've got a whale of a football team." That was clearly demonstrated by the team's statistics and honors. Army had scored 412 points with an average of 46 points a game, figures that would have been higher if Red Blaik had not usually replaced his starters early in the second half of most games and, by mutual consent with some badly outclassed opponents, not reduced the second half to 20 rather than 30 minutes. The Cadets also led the country in total offense with an average of an astonishing 459 yards per game, while giving up only 172 yards a game. Army also established a national record by averaging 7.9 yards per play, both running and passing, although it was mostly by rushing since the Cadets did not throw very often. Davis, who scored 18 touchdowns, set a rushing record average of a near-incredible 11.5 yards per carry, a mark that still stood in 2014. Blanchard, who scored 19 touchdowns, averaged 7.3 yards rushing, which tied him for second place in the nation with Bob Fenimore of Oklahoma A&M. The team's other halfback, Shorty McWilliams, averaged 8.9 yards per rush while scoring eight touchdowns. Even quarterback Arnold Tucker, who rarely threw more than a dozen passes a game—Army threw only 101 passes during the season—but, like his three fellow halfbacks, was an outstanding runner, ran far fewer times than Davis, Blanchard, and McWilliams, but still averaged 5.6 yards when he did. Army, of course, finished first in the Associated Press rankings, followed by Alabama and Navy. Some critics attributed the Cadets' success to being able to field a team of draft-exempt players and because of the quality of its opponents, even though five of those opponents were listed in the top 20.

★ ★ ★

As for individual honors, Army out-shone every other college team in the country. Blanchard won the highly coveted Heisman Trophy, which is awarded annually to the nation's best college player, with Davis finishing second as he had behind Les Horvath of Ohio State the year before, and Fenimore was third. Blanchard also became the first college football player to win the Sullivan Award as the best amateur athlete. Both Blanchard and Davis were also consensus All-Americans along with teammate linemen Tex Coulter, Jack Green, Al Nemetz, and Hank Foldberg, all of whom made life easier for Blanchard and Davis. That meant that at a time when All-American teams consisted of only 11 players, since they played both offense and defense, Army placed six players on the first team. To the surprise of many, Red Blaik finished second to Bo McMillan of Indiana in Coach of the Year voting, perhaps because Blaik had to do little coaching with so many outstanding players and an array of assistants who would all become head coaches.

Some years later, Blaik, asked to compare his undefeated 1944 squad with the unbeaten 1945 team, said, "The '45 team did not enjoy quite the qualitative depth of '44. The second team [in 1945] was in reality a second team, and not an alternate unit." There, Blaik was referring to the two separate units he used in 1944, which were almost as good as one another, although the one with Blanchard and Davis obviously had an edge. The colonel-coach then went on to say, "The '45 team was smoother in execution, more diversified, and even more explosive than either of the '44 alternate units."

Army had never fielded a better team than either the 1944 or 1945 teams, and it remained to be seen if the team could be even better in 1946 when Blanchard, Davis, Tucker, and most of the other starters would be back. But then so would many good players on most of Army's opposing teams who by then would have been joined by players returned from military service, making their teams much more formidable.

13

★ ★ ★

The Future Dictator
and the Army Halfback

OR PRESIDENT TRUMAN, GIVEN A GROWING NUMBER OF strikes across the country, including what would be a three-month-long walkout by the United Auto Workers starting in November and involving more than 200,000 General Motors employees in 20 states, attending the 1945 Army-Navy game was a welcome respite. Other strikes in the fall of 1945 involved petroleum and lumber workers, and machinists. In all, at one point more than 1 million workers had gone on strike within a few months after the bombing and shooting had ended in the Pacific and following pledges by union leaders not to strike during the war.

Although the war had ended in August 1945, most of the 16 million men and women who had served in the military did not return home until 1946. When they did, thousands found themselves homeless, and many found themselves unable to find work after discovering that their old jobs had been taken while they were at war, some of them by women who had gone to work in defense plants and shipyards, and, after enjoying the sociability and conviviality of other workers, had no desire to return to the kitchen and the life of a housewife.

The veterans' plight in particular was a serious concern to army veteran Truman. But he was finding that the transformation from a wartime to a peacetime country was more difficult than he had anticipated and that one of his most important tasks was to try to find jobs and housing for the returning veterans. In addition, he was concerned about the intransigence of Russian leader Joseph Stalin who obviously was not going to grant autonomy to Poland, Romania, Czechoslovakia, Hungary, Lithuania, Bulgaria, and other Eastern European countries that the Russians had taken over after the war and that Winston Churchill, during a speech at Westminster College in Missouri in April 1946, had termed an "Iron Curtain."

Making matters worse, Stalin, whom Truman had met for the first time in July at the Potsdam conference in Germany along with Churchill, and then Clement Atlee after he had inexplicably defeated Churchill in a stunning upset during the conference, said in February 1946 that another war was inevitable because capitalism and communism could not co-exist. Stalin's comment shocked Truman, who came to like Stalin at the Potsdam conference that had been held to determine how to punish the defeated Axis powers. On the home front, Truman found it virtually impossible to get his national health care plan and his proposal to unify the military services approved by Congress, along with his call for a year's—later reduced by its supporters in Congress to six months—universal military training (UMT) for young men from 18 to 20 years of age.

As 1946—the first full peacetime year since 1940—wore on, things on the labor front got worse with strikes by 350,000 coal miners, 50,000 railroad workers, along with walkouts by electrical workers at General Electric, meatpackers, and about 750,000 steelworkers, the biggest strike in American history. There were also strikes by truck drivers and elevator operators in New York and by longshoremen on the West Coast. Only a threat by the president to draft the railroad workers in May to keep the trains running during a speech to Congress—which some of Truman's closest advisors and his attorney general, Tom Clark, thought would probably be unconstitutional—sent the railroad workers back to work after a one-day walkout.

After having been derided by critics as being indecisive and confused, Truman's hard line against the railroad workers drew raves from all quarters, since he had demonstrated that he could be firm and decisive when an action like the railroad strike threatened to disrupt much of the nation. Still, during a speech in the spring of 1946, an exasperated Truman paraphrased Union General William Tecumseh Sherman's famous statement by saying, half jokingly, "I think peace is hell." Nevertheless, his popularity, which had dropped from a high of 87 percent in the summer of 1945, a few months after President Roosevelt had died, to 63 percent in the fall, plummeted to a low of 40 percent by October 1946.

Though the war was over, shortages continued through much of 1946. Truman refused in early September to remove price controls on meat, but then he agreed to do so a month later. Price controls on margarine, mayonnaise, and salad dressing were also ended in October. But shortages of some clothing and other items continued through 1946.

In view of the labor strikes, the shortage of housing, and the difficulty of many veterans to resume normal lives again, sports would appear to have been insignificant during the first postwar year. However, as was the case during the war, big-time college football, Major League Baseball, hockey, boxing, horse-racing, and to a lesser degree the National Football League afforded many Americans a break from reality. What made it all the better was that star athletes such as Ted Williams, Joe DiMaggio, Bob Feller, and Joe Louis were back from service, and most sports teams were again at full strength. That included college football teams; some of whose players had been in service for as long as four years and still had several years of eligibility left. It also meant that practically all of Army's opponents, some of whom had been severely weakened by the draft and enlistments during the war, would be stronger than they had in years.

Indeed, with its recruitment of players from other colleges, Army had a decided advantage, as did Navy. Now, that would no longer be the case, raising the question of whether the Cadets could still remain the dominant college team, even with such starters as Doc Blanchard, Glenn Davis, Hank Foldberg, Barney Poole, Arnold Tucker, Art Gerometta, and Joe Steffy, returning. Even Red Blaik conceded that most of the teams Army had played during their three straight unbeaten seasons had been weakened by the war, and thus the Cadets had a lot to prove during the 1946 season. Referring to what he called "career carpers," Blaik said, "'The war had been over for more than a year,' they argued, 'and Army was going to meet much tougher competition from civilian college opponents. Now let's see,' they concluded, 'just how good these Blanchard-Davis teams really are.'"

It would indeed be a challenging year, with schools such as Oklahoma, Cornell, and West Virginia on a schedule that was stronger than the one in 1945. Missing, too, would be All-Americans Tex Coulter, who had been "found deficient" in mathematics and would sign with the New York Giants of the NFL, and fellow linemen Jack Green and Al Nemetz. "I would have loved to have graduated from West Point," Coulter said years later after working as a sports columnist and cartoonist for newspapers in Dallas and Montreal, where he and his family lived for 25 years after he had finished his football career in the Canadian Football League before returning to his native Texas. Two other players, end Clyde Grimenstein and guard LeRoy Martin, both plebes who saw considerable action in 1945, resigned before the start of the 1946 season.

Also gone in 1946 was Shorty McWilliams, who after one season as a starting halfback, had resigned from the Academy and returned to Mississippi State, where he already had played for one season and would play two more years, become an All-American, and play in the NFL. At first, McWilliams' request to resign was denied by West Point superintendent General Maxwell Taylor who charged that McWilliams had received a lucrative financial offer to return to Mississippi State. University officials, including football coach Allyn McKeen, challenged Taylor to produce proof that such an offer was made while denying the general's allegation and maintain that Taylor would not permit McWilliams to resign because he was "a star football player."

The West Point superintendent eventually relented and allowed McWilliams to resign but not until after charging that a number of colleges were trying to "hire" star football players from other schools, especially Army. "The financial offers involved were often fantastic and show an apparent decay in the amateur spirit of college athletics which is most regrettable," Taylor said. To more than a few sports observers of the West Point football scene, Taylor's charge was somewhat ironic since Army had lured more than a score of talented football players from other schools to play at West Point and thus avoid the draft, including stars such as Blanchard, Tucker, Poole, and most of the players on Army's 1944 an 1945 national championship teams.

McWilliams, meanwhile, said one of the reasons he resigned was because a future dictator of Nicaragua and fellow cadet had harassed him mercilessly. According to McWilliams, Anastasio Somoza Debayle, whose father was then the president and dictator of Nicaragua, and who would be succeeded by Anastasio Somoza Debayle and his older brother, Luis Anastasio Somoza Debayle, "He was one of the main reasons I left West Point," McWilliams said 40 years after the harassment supposedly took place. "He made my life pretty miserable." He never did figure out Somoza's hostility toward him, although he suspected it was because he was a football player and they lived in the same barracks, McWilliams said. "When I went into the dining room, he would say, 'What did *The New York Times* say about the great McWilliams today?' And if they mentioned my name in those long articles they wrote about West Point football, I had to memorize that article [for Somoza]. And if I didn't know it, I didn't eat any more."

McWilliams said he eventually told Red Blaik about the harassment, which seemed to be more severe than that directed at plebes by most upperclassmen. "I said, 'Colonel Blaik, please don't let them put my name in the paper, I have to memorize that thing, and I'm having a hard time remembering my own name.'" If Blaik did anything to stop Somoza's harassment, McWilliams was not aware of it, and he said it continued. Not surprisingly, Army's "one and done" halfback said, "I had a terrible dislike for him." Still, McWilliams conceded that he did try to get back at Somoza in a physical way. Running late to get into formation one day, McWilliams hurried down the stairs from his fourth floor room. "He [Somoza] heard me coming and intentionally stepped out of his [second floor] doorway, which was right at the bottom of the steps, and I ran slap over him," McWilliams said. "I said to myself that my only chance [to avoid punishment] is that if I hit him hard enough, he won't recognize who did it." But Somoza, a first classmate who would graduate from West Point in June, did. "From then on he made life miserable," McWilliams said. "I reported to his [Somoza's] room every morning for six straight weeks in full field equipment with my mattress in a horseshoe roll. I really came to despise him."

Somoza, who had gone to St. Leo College Prep school in Florida and LaSalle Military Academy on Long Island before being accepted at West Point, succeeded his older brother, Luis, as president and dictator of Nicaragua, regarded as the most corrupt country in South America, in 1967, after their father had been assassinated in 1956 and was replaced by his oldest of two sons, Luis Anastasio Somoza Debayle.

He also became the head of the country's National Guard, which made him the head of the country's armed forces, but he was forced to flee to Paraguay in 1979 as Sandinista rebels were moving towards the capital of Managua. Like his father, Somoza was also assassinated, in his case by seven Sandinistas in 1980 when he was 54 years old. During the reign of the Somozas, which lasted 43 years, Nicaragua was supported by the United States because of its anti-Communist stance despite its brutal and dictatorial regime.

"My regret is that I didn't get to pull that trigger," McWilliams said years later with a laugh, alluding to the youngest Somoza and McWilliams' former tormentor. "Of course I'm kidding, but he did make life miserable for me."

* * *

Whether or not the harassment by the future Nicaraguan dictator had anything to do with McWilliams' departure after only one season at West Point, it was a big loss for the Cadets, even though they would still have Blanchard, Davis, and Tucker, along with Rick Rowan, who had been a backup halfback the previous two seasons, and Ug Fuson, a rarity in that he played both center and halfback in 1945. Also returning was quarterback Bill Gustafson, a nephew of the Army backfield coach, Andy Gustafson, who had seen some, but not much, action in 1945. Among the newcomers was plebe Arnold Galiffa, who would eventually develop into one of Army's best quarterbacks and a starter in 1948 and 1949. Gone, too, was placekicker and backup quarterback Dick Walterhouse who had set an Army record that still stands when he attempted 114 extra points from 1944–1945, converting on 90 of those attempts. As a further testament to Army's high-powered offense, Walterhouse was never called on to attempt a field goal, mainly, as he recalled, because whenever the Cadets, or Black Knights, got within field-goal distance, they almost always scored a touchdown.

Despite the loss of Green and Nemetz, Army's line still looked formidable at the beginning of the 1946 season with the return of starters Barney Poole, Hank Foldberg, Bill Yeoman, Goble Bryant, Joe Steffy, and Ug Fuson, who at 215 lbs. was the heaviest player on the team, and although primarily a center during the previous two seasons, he would spend most of his time alongside Glenn Davis at right halfback. Jack Ray, a senior guard, would replace Walterhouse as the team's placekicker. (Linemen as placekickers was not unusual at the time. For example, eventual Hall of Famer Lou Groza would begin a 21-year career with the Cleveland Browns in 1946 as a tackle and one of the NFL's best placekickers who led the league in field-goal percentage five times.)

As it developed, Army would be bogged down by injuries to two of its best players, Blanchard and Tucker. As Blaik was to say, "The nature of the schedule, the loss of so many 1945 aces, the lack of qualitative depth, and the injuries added up to plenty of pressure." Blaik went on to say that his players in 1946 "knew they were the number one objectives of some dedicated and loaded teams. That was their challenge, and they never forgot it."

Army opened its season on September 21 before a crowd of about 15,000 in rain-swept Michie Stadium against Villanova, which it had held scoreless in three previous meetings, including a 54–0 rout in 1945. With both sides having trouble holding on to a slippery football, Army scored three touchdowns by capitalizing on Villanova fumbles within its own 30-yard line, with Blanchard and Davis both scoring from 10 yards out. However, Blanchard was escorted off the field late in the first quarter after he broke into the open field but was brought down by Villanova end Frank Kane. As Blanchard went down, his right heel sank into the spongy turf, bending his knee back and tearing the anterior cruciate ligament in the knee, which both ended his afternoon and raised fears that he might be lost for the rest of the season.

After being held scoreless in the second period, Army took advantage of another fumble by the Wildcats, this one at the Villanova 27-yard line early in the third quarter. With Davis, Tucker, and Fuson, the one-time center, alternating in carrying the ball to the Villanova 3-yard line, Fuson swept around right end to make it 21-0. Army, which outgained Villanova on the ground 280 to 60 yards, added another touchdown in the third quarter and its final one in the last period on passes from Tucker and Davis to Barney Poole as the Cadets rolled to a 35-0 victory.

Blanchard's injury, serious as it was, only kept him out of Army's next two games, against Oklahoma and Cornell. That surprised doctors, who during X-rays taken after Blanchard's injury, revealed a calcification in the knee, which had resulted after he was hurt playing football in prep school and had to be hospitalized for more than two months. That he had recovered to continue playing football the following year, and then later at Army, surprised doctors who treated him following his knee injury in the Villanova game, but still left them dubious of him playing again in 1946, which of course was his last season at West Point.

To their amazement, Blanchard was in uniform and walked out to the center of the field for the coin toss with co-captain Glenn Davis before a crowd of around 25,000 that included President Harry Truman, believed to be the first president to watch a game at Michie Stadium, sitting alongside West Point's highly decorated superintendent, Major General Maxwell Taylor. That led Oklahoma coach Jim Tatum, a cousin of Blanchard who had installed the winged-T formation for the 1946 season, to believe that the star Army fullback was prepared to play only a week after suffering his knee injury. On the face of it, that was surprisingly bad news for the Sooners, and, if Blanchard did indeed play, an almost impossible feat given the severity of an injury that normally sidelined a player for the rest of the year even that early in the season. In fact, it was a ruse by Red Blaik to convince Oklahoma that Blanchard would indeed play—which Blaik had no intention of letting him do, no matter how close the game turned out to be. It was the first meeting between Army and Oklahoma, which would win 8-of-11 games in 1946, including a victory over North Carolina State in the Gator Bowl and a No. 14 ranking in the Associated Press poll.

As it turned out, a physically fit Blanchard almost assuredly would have helped the Cadets in what turned out be Army's toughest test during its 19-game winning streak. In addition to keeping the Cadets scoreless in the first quarter, the Sooners scored first early in the second period when plebe kicker Joe Green's punt from the end zone was blocked by Stanley West and recovered in the end zone for a touchdown by Norman McNabb. With less than a minute remaining and Army on the verge of being held scoreless for an entire half for the first time since 1943, Arnold Tucker connected with Glenn Davis on a 46-yard pass play followed by a four-yard touchdown pass to end Hank Foldberg to tie the score 7–7 at halftime. By then, Oklahoma had the upper hand, outgaining Army on the ground and in first downs.

But early in the third quarter, Barney Poole, whose play throughout the game demonstrated why he would be an All-American end, blocked an Oklahoma punt. After Tucker had completed another pass to Davis, Fuson burst through the Sooners' line for his second touchdown to put Army ahead 14–7. Tucker, like Blanchard and Davis as outstanding on defense as he was on offense, enabled Army to retain its lead after Oklahoma had driven 74 yards to Army's 3-yard line when he intercepted a pass. First, the third-year quarterback blitzed through the Oklahoma line to nail Darrell Royal, one of five eventual college coaches on the Sooners' roster, for a three-yard loss, and then out-leaped Royal's target in the end zone for another interception that ended the drive.

Late in the third period, Oklahoma again came close to scoring when the Sooners recovered an Army fumble on the Black Knights'

18-yard line near the end of the third period. And again it was Tucker who squelched a scoring attempt when he intercepted a pass intended for Royal and ran it back 86 yards to increase Army's lead to 21–7, the final score. No doubt frustrated by two golden scoring opportunities, Oklahoma never threatened again.

Army's close call was reflected in the statistics, which showed that Oklahoma had gained more yardage rushing than the Cadets, something that had never happened during what was now a 20-game winning streak—129 to 83 yards and a 9–7 edge on first downs, as Davis and the rest of the Army backs were held in check during most of the game. The game also demonstrated clearly that Tucker would be a force to be reckoned with as a passer, runner, and defensive player (who also ran back punts), to complement Blanchard and Davis in what was beginning to look like a backfield that could turn out to be even better than the outstanding one from the 1945 season. But that would depend on how Blanchard's injured knee would stand up if indeed he played again during the 1946 season. In upstaging Glenn Davis, Tucker drew rave reviews, including one in *The New York Times* by Allison Danzig that said the Army quarterback "was a flaming figure with only brief moments of respite."

Red Blaik later recalled a cocktail party given after the game by West Point superintendent Major General Maxwell Taylor for President Truman. "During the party, the president took me aside and said, 'Red, what do you think about your chances with Navy are?'" Blaik said.

"'Reasonably good,' I replied.

"'They've got to be better than that,' the president said. 'I have twenty bucks riding on that game, and I don't want to lose to any Navy so and so.'"

Truman apparently didn't tell Blaik whether or not he had to give any points on his bet, which would be entirely reasonable since Navy had a far weaker team in 1946 than it had the previous year.

* * *

Blanchard also remained on the sideline during the game against Cornell a week later at Michie Stadium, where the Black Knights, as they now were principally known, would play four of their first five games. Even in the forties, unless you were a top-ranked widely known team, you almost had to oblige Army and play at West Point. At that, Cornell had been a national powerhouse in the 1930s when the Big Red went unbeaten for 16 straight games and won its fifth national championship in 1939. One of Cornell's victories during that streak was a 45–0 victory over Army in 1940, the year before Blaik became the head coach. For Blaik it would be the first time he coached against Cornell since the famous, or infamous for Cornell "fifth down" game in 1940, which Dartmouth belatedly won when Blaik was the head coach of the Big Green (then nicknamed the Indians). Cornell had only a few starters back from 1945 but did have a number of players who returned from military service, including fullback Joe Martin and quarterback Walter Kretz, who had last played for Cornell in 1941. Though the team was pleased with the return of war veterans like Martin and Kretz, who were in the service for four years, they were far from being in tip-top shape for football but would improve as the season wore on.

For Coach Ed McKeever, in his second year as the Cornell coach, it was an opportunity to avenge a 59–0 drubbing he had endured while filling in for Frank Leahy, then in the navy, at Notre Dame in 1944. McKeever soon realized that that was an impossible task as Glenn Davis scored four touchdowns as Army beat Cornell 46–21, while giving up the most points since a 26–0 loss to Notre Dame in 1943. Indeed, as against Michigan the week before, Army found the Big Red a tough foe at the outset, as Cornell tied the score at 7–7 in the first quarter after Davis had raced 64 yards around left end for a touchdown less than a minute into the game. Following the Cornell touchdown, Arnold Tucker returned the ensuing kickoff and, behind some devastating blocking, sprinted 79 yards to Cornell's 16-yard line, after which Davis scored again, once more by darting around left end from eight yards out to give Army a 14–7 lead that it would never relinquish. Davis' third touchdown came late in the second quarter after Tucker had run back a Cornell punt 78 yards in another Davis-like dazzling piece of open-field running. On the scoring play, Tucker threw a short pass to Barney Poole who promptly tossed a lateral to Davis who then sped the remaining 18 yards that made it 27–7 at the half.

Army widened its lead to 39–7 early in the third period when Davis culminated a 60-yard drive by scoring from the 1-yard line for his fourth touchdown. With most of Army's starters on the bench, the Cadets scored their final touchdown in the fourth quarter when backup quarterback Bill Gustafson scored on a 65-yard run after Cornell had drawn to 39–21 on a pass from quarterback John Burns to halfback Hillary Chollet. Burns essentially kept Cornell in the game as he completed 13-of-24 passes for 134 yards. But Burns' accuracy could not overcome Army's superiority on the ground as the Cadets out-gained the Big Red 372 to 92 yards.

Whether Army could do as well, particularly on the ground, was doubtful in its first road game the following Saturday in Ann Arbor against a Michigan team that would finish the season ranked sixth in the country and most of its players would be members of the 1947 Wolverine team that would win the national championship and then beat the University of Southern California in the Rose Bowl. Doc Blanchard had been cleared to play after a remarkably swift recovery, which West Point doctors attributed to an unusually strong quadricep muscle group. Still, the Black Knights would have to contend with the legendary and innovative coach, Fritz Crisler, and his single-wing offense and two-platoon defense before a crowd of almost 86,000 under clear blue skies at Michigan Stadium.

The Wolverines' offense would be led by junior tailback Bob Chappuis, who would be an All-American and runner-up for the Heisman

Trophy in 1947, and who had returned to Michigan after joining the American Air Corps following his sophomore season in 1943, as had hundreds of players at other schools. Playing before such huge crowds would hardly phase Chappuis after his experiences as an aerial gunner and radioman who went on 21 missions aboard a B-25 bomber in Europe in 1944 and 1945. On his last mission, Chappuis and two other crewmen were the only two survivors when their plane was shot down over German-occupied northern Italy in February 1945 and they parachuted to safety into an olive field. Shortly thereafter, they were taken in by an Italian family named Ugolini, in the town of Asola in Lombardy province, who lived only a few doors away from the local German military headquarters in the town.

The family then kept the three airmen hidden for three months until the town was liberated by the Allies. "One day the family took us into town to alleviate our boredom dressed as peasants and spoke Italian to us as a ruse, even though we had no idea what they were saying," Chappuis said after his discharge. "Just to play it safe, Mrs. Ugolini called me Roberto while we were walking around." Chappuis stayed in touch with the family and visited them with his college-sweetheart wife in 1974 and received a warm welcome in the town. "I would have hoped that given the same circumstances, I would do what they did," Chappuis said after his discharge. "But to be honest, I'm not sure I'd be that brave."

Though he had missed two seasons and had not been hurt during his parachute jump behind enemy lines, Chappuis already had emerged as the star of the single-wing Michigan backfield in victories over Indiana and Iowa. He would demonstrate why in the Army game. After Army punter Jim Rawers shanked a punt that carried only four yards before going out of bounds at the Army 41-yard line, Michigan, led by the running and passing of Chappuis, took a 7–0 lead on a 13-yard pass from Chappuis to quarterback Howard Yerges, which marked the second time in its last three games that an Army opponent—Oklahoma was the first—scored the game's first touchdown. However, Army responded late in the quarter from its own 16-yard line to tie the score. After Tucker scooted around right end on a bootleg play, Davis showed the big crowd why he had been attracting so much media attention when he cut through right tackle and broke away on a 58-yard touchdown run. Michigan had been alternating the size of its lines from four to seven men, and in this instance the Wolverines had only four men up front, and they paid dearly for doing so as Davis bolted through his left side, eluded three linebackers, and he blazed past three more defenders in the secondary, leaving only safety Paul White between him and the goal line as he sprinted down the left sideline. White appeared to have a good chance of at least forcing the Army speedster out of bounds, if not tackling him, at the Michigan 10-yard line. As usual, without slowing down, Davis feinted inward, faking White out of his shoes, and then shot past him for the tying touchdown.

Blanchard had difficulty breaking loose in the first half, but he compensated for it by his pass-catching ability. Early in the second quarter, Tucker had incurred a shoulder separation and a sprained elbow, both on his passing right side, making it extremely difficult for him to throw the ball, but he remained in the game because of the close score and his running and ball-faking prowess. That left most of Army's passing up to Davis, who by 1946 had become an excellent passer, particularly on option plays when defenses expected him to run. One of Mr. Outside's favorite targets was Mr. Inside. Late in the second period, that combination worked to perfection when Blanchard out-jumped two defenders to catch a 45-yard pass from Davis, who had been doing most of the Army passing since Tucker was hurt but remained in the game, primarily for his defensive play at safety. Then on a fourth-and-18, Tucker called a pass play, took the snap from center, and handed off to Davis. But the ball came loose and bounced away as three Michigan linemen closed in on Davis. Davis, however, was able to grab the bouncing ball, straight-arm a

Wolverine lineman, and fire a pass to end Bob Folsom who made a leaping catch in the back of the end zone to give Army a 13–7 lead. Jack Ray had missed his extra-point attempt. Blaik later was to call the play "one of the best and maddest pass plays" that he had ever seen.

Michigan came out strong in the second quarter following the kickoff. Using a dazzling array of plays that included buck laterals, traps, fake reverses, and end-around runs, the Wolverines drove 83 yards in 13 plays with Chappius doing most of the damage before White cut through left tackle from six yards out for a touchdown. With Michigan within a point of taking a 14–13 lead, center Jim Brieske's conversion attempt was blocked by Army tackle Joe Steffy to make it a 13–13 tie. With the Wolverines playing so well on both sides of the ball before the frenzied pro-Michigan crowd, Army's 22-game winning streak was indeed in danger of being snapped.

When both teams failed to score for the remainder of the third quarter, the likelihood of an upset became even more pronounced, especially when Army reached the Michigan 13-yard line but the Wolverines held, eliciting a huge roar from the crowd. However, on its next possession early in the final period, the Black Knights finally drove 76 yards on 11 plays to score. The high point of the scoring drive was another spectacular catch of a Davis pass by a surrounded Blanchard that put the ball on the Michigan 24-yard line. Four plays later, Blanchard, now running as well as ever despite the still-injured knee, crashed through left tackle from the 7-yard line for a touchdown while literally carrying White over the goal line from three yards out. Jack Ray then converted to give Army a 20–13 lead.

Michigan was hardly done. On its next possession, the Wolverines reached the Army 45, but then Davis, again demonstrating his superb all-round ability, intercepted a pass to end the drive.

With only minutes to play, the Wolverines again drove into Army territory, reaching the 10-yard line, and sending the huge throng into a frenzy. But then with less than a minute to play, two Michigan passes fell incomplete, leaving time for only one more play, another pass that was intercepted in the end zone by Tucker as the final gun sounded.

In addition to his 58-yard touchdown run, Davis, Army's primary passer because of Tucker's injury, completed 7-of-8 passes for 168 yards, while Tucker connected on five throws for 43 yards as Army gained a highly unusual 211 yards passing without a single interception. Michigan, by contrast, made good on only 8-of-17 passes for 95 yards and had three passes intercepted.

Later, Red Blaik said the game had taken a toll, at least for a while, on the Cadets. "The effort of our players was so transcendent, emotional as well as a physical outpouring, that they took a long time to unwind and get to sleep that night on our special train," the coach, himself drained at the end of the game, said. "There wasn't much sleeping by coaches and newspapermen, either. It was a game to be played over and over again until the small hours, to the accompaniment of tinkling glasses. I even had a glass of sherry myself."

Next up was Columbia which, like most of the Ivy League schools at the time, still played top-10 football schools but had beaten Army only three times in 10 games with two of the games ending in ties in a series that dated from 1899. During that early period, Columbia had upset Stanford 7–0 in the Rose Bowl in 1934, a high point in the Lions' football history. However, in their last three meetings, Army had outscored Columbia 99–6. Going into the Army game, though, Columbia had one of its best teams in years and was undefeated after beating Rutgers, Navy, and Yale while featuring an outstanding passing combination of quarterback Gene Rossides and end Bill Swiacki, who would go on to a five-year career in the National Football League.

14

★ ★ ★

Three-Peat Champions?

W HAT ADVANCE PUBLICITY THERE WAS IN THE NEW YORK media about the Army-Columbia game was vastly overshadowed by the hangings on Wednesday, October 16, of 10 top Nazis in the Nuremberg, Germany, prison gym after being convicted of war crimes during the Nuremberg trials of Nazi leaders. Hermann Goering, the No. 2 man after Adolf Hitler in the Third Reich hierarchy, was also to have been hanged, but died after poisoning himself in his cell two hours before he was to be sent to the gallows. Prison officials said that most of the hanged Nazis spent the hours leading up to their hangings reading the Bible, and were calm and unemotional before they were executed.

In sports, the most dominant story was how the St. Louis Cardinals, after trailing the Boston Red Sox 3–2, won the last two games in St. Louis to win the World Series, 4–3. In one of the most memorable episodes in World Series history, the so-called "mad dash" by Cardinals outfielder Enos "Country" Slaughter scored what turned out to be the winning run in the eighth inning of the seventh game when Slaughter raced all the way home from first base on a double by Harry Walker. Slaughter's "mad dash" became the climactic run after

Harry Brecheen, who had limited the Red Sox to only one run in two complete games, won his third game when he came on to pitch the last two innings of the climactic game.

During the same week, American consumers got some bad news when margarine, mayonnaise, and salad dressing were removed from price controls, meaning stores could raise the prices of those items. Some other items and products, however, still remained price-controlled.

With the World Series over, the attention of sports fans was directed at college football, which was still far more popular at the time than the professional game. Much of that focus was on powerhouse Army's 22-game winning streak, which hardly seemed in jeopardy when Columbia, despite its unbeaten record, traveled 50 miles to West Point to play the four-touchdown-favored Black Knights before a standing-room crowd of 26,000 at Michie Stadium. Despite its heavily favored status, Red Blaik worried that his team might suffer a let-down after the difficult victory over Michigan and could be thinking of far tougher rivals than Columbia that lie ahead.

Army took no time in demonstrating that the game was no-contest, with Columbia unable to cope with Doc Blanchard and Glenn Davis. Blanchard, fully recovered from his severe injury four weeks earlier, scored one touchdown in the first quarter, two in the second, and one in the third while running over, through, and around the Lions' defense. The first three came from close up, as the Cadets fullback bulled his way across the goal line from eight, one, and three yards as Army took a 28–0 halftime lead, and then Blanchard showed he could be as swift and elusive in the open field when he ran back a kickoff 92 yards straight up the middle without a hand being laid on him in the third period.

Davis scored only once, on a 66-yard dash in the second quarter when he ripped through a big hole opened in the Columbia line by the outstanding Army line, and then he faked out three defenders in the Lions' secondary, including Lou Kusserow who seemed to have a clear shot at the swift halfback at the Columbia 25-yard line until Davis deftly shifted direction without changing speeds. Like Blanchard, Davis gave the Lions fits during the less-than-half of the game they played, consistently breaking away for long gains, including one for 59 yards, and also completing both passes he threw.

Army reserves came on to play most of the second half on a day when the Cadets' brilliant but still banged-up quarterback, Arnold Tucker, played only a few minutes in the second period while backups Bill Gustafson and Arnold Galiffa played most of the one-sided game in which Columbia scored twice—against Army's backup defenders—in the third and fourth quarters. Forever an alarmist, Blaik became so concerned following Columbia's first touchdown in the third quarter that cut Army' lead to 34–7, that he immediately sent Blanchard, Davis, and his other starters back into the game. Blaik hardly had reason to worry since on the Cadets' next possession Blanchard scored his fourth touchdown to put the game out of reach and enable the Army coach to go with his reserves the rest of the way.

Indicative of how one-sided the game was, Columbia had to punt 10 times. The team was outgained in rushing by 315 to 182 yards, and the Lions also had trouble penetrating Army's pass defense, managing to complete only 5-of-15 passes, while the Cadets connected on 5-of-10, including a 36-yard pass from Galiffa to substitute end Jim Rawers for Army's final touchdown in the fourth quarter.

Duke and West Virginia turned out to be more formidable foes during Army' next two games, but the Cadets shut out both teams by 19–0 scores, Duke first before a crowd of almost 60,000 at the Polo Grounds and then West Virginia at Michie Stadium. Against the Blue Devils, Davis again demonstrated his versatility by scoring his 54th and 55th touchdowns on passes from Arnold Tucker, who, in accounting for all three of Army's scores, also threw a 13-yard pass to Barney Poole. Blaik, who usually eschewed the pass, decided to use it far more than usual because Duke used a strong eight-man line that throttled both Davis and Blanchard during most of the game and held Army scoreless during the first 13 minutes, as Davis gained an uncharacteristically low 70 yards on 16 carries and Blanchard ran 21 times for only 22 yards. However, Army's line, always overshadowed by the heroics of Blanchard and Davis was even more effective, limiting the Blue Devils to only one yard rushing in the first half and 39 yards overall during a game in which both Mr. Inside and Mr. Outside each played 57 minutes—far more than usual.

The following week, before a capacity crowd of 25,500 at Michie Stadium that included General Dwight Eisenhower, Tucker overshadowed Blanchard and Davis again, throwing two touchdown passes, to end Hank Foldberg and Davis, who caught five passes in all while gaining 66 yards on 11 rushes against the Mountaineers who had won four of their first six games. Blanchard, like Davis again playing most of the game, scored the third touchdown on a 59-yard run went he cut through a big hole on the right side and scampered down the right sideline behind some devastating blocking, with Foldberg leveling the final would-be tackler on the 10-yard line.

Convinced that his presence was not needed, Blaik, as he had done in the past, left backfield coach Andy Gustafson to handle the Cadets against the Mountaineers while he, Herman Hickman, and several other assistant coaches went to Baltimore to scout the Notre Dame–Navy game. Gustafson did have some anxious moments, though, as West Virginia crossed into Army territory six times before the Cadets' defense repulsed those threats and held the Mountaineers to only 80 yards running the ball and 76 yards passing.

The build-up to the following week's game between Army and Notre Dame may have been the biggest ever for a college football game, and it was most certainly the biggest since the two heavyweight championship fights between Jack Dempsey and Gene Tunney in the late

1930s. Notre Dame, badly beaten by Army in 1944 and 1945, was a far stronger team thanks to the return from military service of a number of former star players, such as quarterback Johnny Lujack, along with Coach Frank Leahy, who, like Lujack, had spent the previous two years in the navy. With a half-dozen players who would eventually play in the NFL, including Lujack, halfback Emil Sitko, guard George Strohmeyer, tackle George Connor, a transfer from Holy Cross, and quarterback Frank "Boley" Dancewicz, who had filled in for Lujack as the starting quarterback the previous two seasons, Notre Dame had one of its strongest, if indeed not the strongest, teams it had ever fielded. Among them were eventual All-Americans Lujack, Connor, guard Bill Fischer, and three players who would earn second-team All-American status—guard Strohmeyer, guard John Mastrangelo, and tackle Ziggy Czarobski. Also on the squad were freshman end Leon Hart, who would become Notre Dame's third Heisman Trophy winner in 1949 after being named an All-American in 1948 and 1949, although he saw little action in 1946, and sophomore halfback Terry Brennan who would coach the Fighting Irish from 1954 through 1958.

Coming into the 1946 game against Army, Notre Dame had won all five of its games while scoring at least four touchdowns per game and giving up only three touchdowns to their opponents. Notre Dame also would be trying to avenge having been trounced by Army in their last two games by scores of 59–0 and 48–0 after having won 10-of-12 games with two ties against the Cadets since 1931. Overall, since the series had begun in 1913, when an undersized end named Knute Rockne scored a touchdown and led little-known Notre Dame to an upset victory over Army at West Point, the Irish had beaten the Cadets 22 times while losing only seven games and playing three ties.

Unbeknownst, and still unannounced, the long series would end, at least temporarily, after Army played Notre Dame in 1947 in South Bend for the first time after 16 consecutive meetings at Yankee Stadium, which was regarded as a home game for the Cadets. The decision to end the rivalry was Army's, which felt that the game had grown out of proportion. Army's only two victories since 1931 had occurred the previous two years when Cadet players were draft-exempt once they enrolled at West Point, while Notre Dame had lost many of its best players to the military during World War II. Blaik and the others involved in Army's schedule felt that with the war over and parity restored in big-time college football, Notre Dame would again dominate the rivalry as it had before the war. A stronger reason perhaps was Blaik's belief that "an unhealthy atmosphere that had grown up around our game with Notre Dame." Blaik went on to say that Notre Dame authorities were also aware of that atmosphere, "yet they were as helpless as we were to combat it."

"What Army did find sharply distasteful was that segment of Notre Dame's 'Subway Alumni', neither small not quiet, which had in the early thirties and early forties came to regard the game in Yankee Stadium as a sporting event only so long as Notre Dame continued to win it," Blaik said. "With the healthy and unhealthy segments of the Subway Alumni added together, we appeared to have 90 percent of the Yankee Stadium crowd against us. To these people, apparently, our winning two years in a row by big scores after a 12-year drought constituted an unpardonable sin."

The Army coach said that during the long stretch of Notre Dame victories, Army had accepted defeat, which he said was not always easy considering the atmosphere during the games at Yankee Stadium. "In contrast, our 1944 and 1945 teams, leaving the field after victory, heard themselves referred to by people as 'slackers.'" By "slackers," Blaik was referring to a derogatory term directed against men believed to have avoided being drafted during the war. "The shouts of 'slackers' was not confined to those who yelled at Yankee Stadium from a safe distance," the Army coach said. At any rate, the long series would end, at least temporarily, after the 1945 game.

15

★ ★ ★

"Game of the Century"

O N AN OVERCAST AND CHILLY AFTERNOON WITH THE
temperature in the low 40s, all 2,500 cadets marched onto the
Yankee Stadium turf an hour before the kickoff, followed by the Army
and Notre Dame bands, to the cheers of the capacity crowd of 75,000
that included nine generals and scores of lower ranking officers. Among
them were such famous World War II generals as Dwight Eisenhower
and Omar Bradley, both of whom had played football while at West
Point, along with "Hap" Arnold, the commanding general of the
Army Air Corps during World War II, the West Point superintendent,
Major General Maxwell Taylor, and another Major General, Anthony
McAuliffe, whose one-word response of "Nuts" to a German ultima-
tum in Bastogne, Belgium, during the Battle of the Bulge while he was
acting commander of the 101st Airborne in late December 1944 made
him a national hero. Also in the grandstand of "the House that Ruth
Built"—where such great players as Babe Ruth, Lou Gehrig, and Joe
DiMaggio, still an active player in 1946, performed—were Secretary
of War Robert Patterson, Navy Secretary James Forrestal, Attorney
General Tom Clark, and about 100 veterans from the metropolitan

New York area who had been wounded during the war and were guests of the military academy. Down on the field near the Army bench were the team's mascots, the famed Army mules, with two bareback-riding cadets astride them.

The pregame atmosphere was electric, akin to that before a big title fight of the era such as the one in June 1938 when Joe Louis knocked out Max Schmeling in the first round to avenge a knockout by Schmeling in 1936 and to retain his world championship before a crowd of 70,000 at Yankee Stadium in one of boxing's most famous bouts. Given the amount of points scored by both teams in previous games, the expectation was for a wide-open high-scoring contest. After co-captains Blanchard and Davis had shaken hands with their Notre Dame counterparts, Lujack and halfback Gerry Cowhig, Army won the toss and surprisingly elected to receive, which was contrary to Red Blaik's normal choice of kicking off.

From the outset, it became clear that both teams might have trouble moving the ball in light of the bruising defensive play by the linemen who once again played both offense and defense, as did Blanchard, Davis, Lujack, and the rest of the backs. Two outstanding defensive stands exemplified the play of the two lines. In the opening quarter, Notre Dame halfback Emil Sitko fumbled, and Army tackle Goble Bryant recovered the ball on the Irish 24-yard line. A pass from Tucker to Davis advanced the Cadets to the 16, but neither Blanchard nor Davis could go anywhere, and on fourth-and-2 to go for a first down at the 15, Blanchard hit left the tackle only to run into a stone wall, enabling the Irish to take over on downs.

Thereafter, neither team threatened until midway through the second quarter when Notre Dame, led by the running of Cowhig and a 25-yard pass by Lujack, drove 88 yards to the Army 4-yard line. Now it was Army's turn to shine, and the Cadets did, ending the drive at their 4-yard line, as the Irish line had done to Army in the first period and in similar fashion when, in a fourth-and-2 situation, halfback Bill Gompers faked going up the middle and bolted around his left end but was brought down by Hank Foldberg and Bryant a yard short of a first down. The only other scoring opportunities in the half—both by Army—occurred in the second quarter. First, end Tom Hayes recovered the second of what would be five Notre Dame fumbles on the Irish 35-yard line. But then, after Blanchard picked up two yards, three straight passes by Tucker were batted down in the Notre Dame secondary. The second opportunity came on the last play of the half when Tucker intercepted a Lujack pass and raced 30 yards to the Irish 30.

Following that surprising scoreless first half, Notre Dame threatened again early in the third quarter when John Mastrangelo recovered Army's first of three fumbles at the Black Knights' 34-yard line. After two running plays netted only two yards, Lujack went to the air again only to have his pass picked off by Tucker at the Army 10-yard line and run back to the Cadets' 32-yard line. From that point, Blanchard, who had been held in check up to then, broke through a hole opened up by his line on Notre Dame's right side and raced down the left sideline, eluding both Irish halfbacks and leaving only Lujack to beat in order to score. As Tucker approached, Blanchard cut inside, whereupon Lujack hit him around the knees to bring down Army's All-American fullback at the Irish 37-yard line to end a 21-yard run, something that virtually no safety had been able to do in three years. The play elicited roars from supporters of both teams—from the West Point cadets and other Army fans for Blanchard's run, and from Notre Dame rooters for Lujack's dramatic tackle, which had definitely averted a touchdown.

Army fans still had more to cheer about, since the Cadets were on the Notre Dame 37-yard line. Runs by Blanchard and Davis, and a 13-yard pass from Tucker to Foldberg then gave Army a first down at the Irish 20, as Army supporters went into a virtual uproar. But then Tucker, so effective running, passing, and on defense, aimed another pass at Foldberg only to have halfback Terry Brennan step in front of Foldberg and intercept the pass at the 8-yard line to squelch the Army drive.

Early in the fourth quarter, Army threatened yet again, reaching the Notre Dame 33-yard line, but Sitko intercepted a pass by Tucker—his second errant throw—at the Irish 10-yard line. Sitko promptly fumbled, but the ball was recovered at the Notre Dame 5-yard line by Lujack, who, punting from his end zone, got off a gorgeous 55-yard punt to get the Irish out of a precarious position.

Notre Dame had one last chance to score late in the final period after Tucker made his third interception at midfield. With 48 seconds left in the game, Tucker then connected with Blanchard, who made a glittering catch over two Irish defenders who then brought him down near the sideline at the Notre Dame 20 as Army supporters again erupted with cheers. However, officials ruled that Blanchard had caught the ball out of bounds and nullified the play. Notre Dame then took over with less than a half minute left but could do nothing as time expired with the score 0–0 and neither Army nor Notre Dame supporters happy at the outcome.

How could two high-scoring offenses, with stars like Blanchard, Davis, and Lujack, possibly be held scoreless after each team had scored at least three touchdowns in their previous games? That was the reaction of media members and fans throughout the country. The answer seemed to be threefold. First, the surprising conservative play of both teams. Second, the 10 turnovers on fumbles and interceptions. And third, the outstanding defensive play by both the Cadets and the Irish, who, though most players played both offense and defense, used only 10 and 13 substitutes, respectively. Even though Notre Dame came into the contest with a No. 2 ranking while Army was first, the outcome could be construed as a moral victory for the Irish following the two trouncings they had incurred the previous years, even though Notre Dame now had been held scoreless by Army in three consecutive games. If anyone had an edge it appeared to be Army as it penetrated Notre Dame territory nine times, while the Irish crossed midfield only three times. However, the statistics were more reflective of the final score with Notre Dame recording 11 first downs to nine for Army and out-gaining the Cadets 173 to 138 yards. Meanwhile, Army had a slight edge in passing, gaining 57 yards in the air to 52 yards by Notre Dame. The Cadets had also intercepted three of Lujack's 17 passes, while the Irish had picked off two of Tucker's throws. And Notre Dame had fumbled five times, losing the ball on three of those occasions, while Army had lost the ball twice after three fumbles.

Most noteworthy, perhaps, was Glenn Davis being held to 30 yards on 17 rushes, an astonishingly low average of less than two yards per carry—more than six yards less than the 8.3 average he would have over a four-year period. Doc Blanchard, still slowed by his injured knee, had gained only 50 yards on 18 rushing attempts. Perhaps summing up Army's frustration on offense, Tucker said, "I would call for a play for Blanchard to run off tackle, which, when he did, he'd usually rip right through, but he kept getting thrown for losses. They smeared our run, and we had to fight hard for every yard. It was obvious that they were ready for us." So, apparently, was the Army line and its secondary for Notre Dame's offense in a game NBC televised to what it said was an audience of 150,000 viewers at a time when not many people had television sets. Army linemen Joe Steffy and Barney Poole, and Notre Dame's All-American George Connor and Jim Martin particularly stood out on defense.

If there was an offensive standout, it was the ubiquitous Tucker who had outshone both Blanchard and Davis, running for 37 yards on nine carries, most of them spontaneously when he was unable to find a receiver open, and intercepting three of Lujack's 17 passes. Brennan, a rising star for the Irish, led Notre Dame in rushing, gaining 69 yards in 14 attempts. "They called it the game of the century," Brennan said

much later. "But it turned out to be one of the dullest games of the century." In truth, that was hardly the case since it had ample excitement,
albeit without any scoring.

Still, in retrospect, both Blaik and Leahy conceded that they might
have been too conservative on offense. "In our intent on not losing,
Leahy and I may have played it too close to the vest," Blaik said. Leahy
agreed with so-called "Monday Morning quarterbacks" who were
inclined to criticize both coaches for, in effect, failing to take advantage of their offensive weapons. "It was a terrific battle of defenses,"
Leahy said in classic coach-speak. The problem was that not many in
the crowd of almost 75,000 had come to see—or appreciated—a battle
of defenses, especially when it included two high-scoring teams.

Some, like Lujack, also thought that it would have been prudent
for Notre Dame to have attempted a field goal on a fourth-and-2 situation at the Army 4-yard line in the first quarter. "I think that when we
neared their goal in the first quarter, maybe we should have gone for
a field goal," the junior quarterback said. However, Lujack knew that
field-goal attempts by Leahy were anathema to Leahy's style, as they
were to Blaik, who hadn't tried for one since 1943 and whose team was
within field-goal range several times during the game only to have Blaik
eschew a field-goal attempt. Tucker's spontaneity at times drew the ire
of the colonel-coach, who was averse to freelancing by his quarterbacks.
But Tucker thought that Army may have been too restrained on offense.
"I think it's safe to say that we may have been too conservative."

Red Blaik apparently agreed. "While having lunch with Red Blaik and
columnist Red Smith years later, we talked about the game, and Red said,
'Leahy and I both choked,'" Terry Brennan recalled in 2014. Without a
victor in what many regarded as a battle for the national championship,
it remained to be seen which team, if either one, might win the national
title. That would depend almost entirely on which one was most impressive in their remaining games. Army had two, against Pennsylvania the

following week and then the traditional seasonal windup against Navy two weeks later. Notre Dame had an even tougher road to hoe, having to play Northwestern, Tulane, and Southern California.

★ ★ ★

Army had crushed its next opponent, Pennsylvania, 62–7 and 61–0 in their last two seasons, but the Quakers were now far more experienced, with the return of All-American linemen Chuck Bednarik, who starred at both center on offense and linebacker on defense, massive tackle George Savitsky, and a half dozen players who had retuned from military service, including All-American halfback Skip Minisi. While in the navy he was eligible to play for the Naval Academy, which he did in 1945 when he scored the winning touchdown against Penn in a 14–7 victory by the Middies. This season, the Quakers had won five of their first six games—including a victory over Navy—while scoring at least five touchdowns in each one and losing to Princeton by three points.

A crowd comparable to the one that witnessed the Army–Notre Dame game the previous Saturday—78,000—packed Franklin Field on the Penn campus for the Army-Penn game. What they saw in the first quarter stunned Penn fans as the Quakers outplayed the Cadets, holding them without a first down while registering six of their own and getting inside the 20-yard line twice. However, the Quakers were unable to take advantage of those opportunities, fumbling away the ball at the Army 8-yard line and, after recovering an Army fumble early in the second quarter, moving to the Cadets' 4-yard line before their place-kicker missed a field goal from 12 yards out.

After a sluggish first quarter, possibly having suffered a let-down following the Notre Dame game, Army came alive in the second period, largely on Tucker's passing and the running of Blanchard and Davis, who had been held in check throughout the first quarter, along with a stiffened defense. The Cadets scored twice in the quarter on touchdown passes from the versatile and slick quarterback—who wound up completing 6-of-8 passes—to Davis to climax drives of 80 and 73 yards to take a 13–0 lead. A 43-yard pass from the even more versatile Davis to a leaping Blanchard was the key play on the latter march, during which Davis took a knee to the head. Shortly afterward, backup quarterback Bill Gustafson, who had replaced Tucker after he had sustained a knee injury, called timeout and hurried toward the Cadets' bench. Approaching Blaik, Gustafson said, "Coach, you'd better get Glenn out of there. He got hit in the head and he doesn't know what he's doing. He doesn't even remember that second touchdown." Blaik, of course, did, which prompted a dazed Davis to say to Blaik, "What are you taking me out for, Colonel? What did I do?"

During the halftime intermission, Blaik and Tucker asked Davis questions, which, after a while, the great halfback was able to answer coherently. At a time when players were not tested to see whether they had suffered concussions, Davis' correct answers were good enough for Blaik to send him out for the second half, where he was spectacular, leading the way during a 75-yard march to make it 20–0 when Blanchard plunged in for a touchdown from the 1-yard line. Shortly thereafter Davis ran back a punt for 35 yards, and as three tacklers zeroed in on him, he quickly lateraled to reserve tackle Harold Tavzel, who rumbled the remaining 45 yards for the touchdown to make it 27–0, thus silencing the Penn crowd, many of whom began to leave.

Davis, obviously no longer dazed, wasn't done yet as he threw a 35-yard pass to substitute end Tom Hayes early in the last quarter. What had started well for Penn had by now turned into a rout, prompting Blaik to empty his bench. The Quakers, who had not recorded a first down from their sixth possession in the opening quarter until late in the game, finally scored on a blocked punt that made the end result 34–7. Once again, following an early scare, Army had outgained an opponent, both rushing and passing. At Franklin Field, the Black

Knights had gained almost 60 more yards on the ground, and Tucker, Davis, and Gustafson had combined to complete 11-of-22 passes for 148 yards, 64 yards more than Penn. Significant, too, was how Army had gained 106 yards on nine punt returns as against only 16 yards by the Quakers in returning six Cadet punts, which was a tribute to the Army defense.

All that now stood between Army and a third straight undefeated season that so far included 26 victories and one tie was a victory over Navy, which had beaten Villanova 7–0 in its opener but then had lost seven games in a row. That made Army an overwhelming four-touchdown favorite, but the Cadets players, along with football fans throughout the country, were reminded that, as the saying went, anything could happen in an Army-Navy game. Seemingly in this one, the only thing that could happen would be a decisive victory by Blanchard and Davis, playing in their farewell game, and the rest of yet another outstanding Army team.

Leading up to the game, Blaik, fearing that his charges might be overconfident, exhorted them to prepare for the worst, citing Army's poor first-half performance against Penn. The coach was also concerned about Tucker's latest injury, which had kept him out of the second half of the Penn game. Blaik was also worried about Blanchard, who Blaik said had only been around 40 percent of the player in 1946 than he had been during the past two seasons because of the knee injury he had incurred in Army's opening game against Villanova two months ago, and he had also been "drained down to 198 lbs. from his normal playing weight of around 210." Indeed, the day before the game Blaik pointed to a photograph in a Philadelphia paper that the coach said, showed "how Doc's sunken cheeks made him look thinner than Davis, Tucker, and myself." That, sportswriters noted, appeared to be something of a stretch. So did a comment from a Navy official who had remarked "that we looked washed out, peaked, and strained, and we were," Blaik said.

That might well have explained why Blaik did not have a pregame practice after the team's arrival on Friday. Instead, Blaik merely had the team walk up and down the field in their cadet uniforms and topcoats.

"It would just be hell, I thought, to have this gang come this far with the effort they've made and then have the three-year record spoiled in the last game, and by Navy," Blaik said. "We sure would never hear the end of that." Fortunately, as was always the case before Army-Navy games, players on both teams had more time to prepare and, in cases like that of Tucker and Blanchard, to heal, although the colonel-coach would never be sanguine enough to point that out.

Despite Navy's poor record, and what was expected to be a lopsided game, the typical Army-Navy crowd of approximately 100,000 jammed into Municipal Stadium in Philadelphia for the game on an unseasonably warm and humid Saturday, November 30. Like the Yale-Harvard game and other games involving traditional rivals at the time, capacity crowds were the norm and upsets were common because of the fierceness of the competitions and the pageantry surrounding the game that attracted presidents, cabinet members, senators, and scores of high-ranking military leaders. That was the case at Municipal Stadium, the traditional site of the game, with President Harry Truman again in the grandstand along with his wife, Bess, and about a half-dozen cabinet members.

The president certainly was entitled to forget about affairs of state following a grueling and disappointing fall during which Republicans had gained control of the Senate and the House of Representatives for the first time since before Franklin Roosevelt took office in 1933, and a series of strikes—most notably by coal miners and railroad workers—tested the president's mettle and sent his popularity ranking to a low-point of 32 percent. Nevertheless, he was buoyant and smiling when he emerged with the First Lady from their limousine about a half hour before the kickoff. Despite the setbacks he, his administration, and the

Democratic Party had sustained over the last few months and the sharp criticism he had endured from political columnists, many of whom unfairly compared him to his legendary predecessor, Truman remained upbeat and radiated confidence, which turned out to be justified and validated in 1948.

* * *

Surprisingly, Navy got into Army territory on its first two possessions, reaching the Army 45 on a 40-yard drive and then to the Cadets' 26-yard line after Davis had fumbled on Army's 32, only to lose the ball on a fumble by Navy quarterback Reaves Baysinger at the 36-yard line. Thereafter, Army totally dominated the first half. Following the fumble recovery, the Cadets marched 64 yards to their first touchdown that followed a 46-yard pass from Tucker to Davis, after which Davis took a pitchout from Tucker and raced 13 yards for what would be his 59th and last touchdown—that total is still an Army record. Jack Ray converted to make it 7–0.

Then Navy took the ensuing kickoff and drove 81 yards for a touchdown with Baysinger scoring on a quarterback sneak from less than a yard out. However, Bob Van Summern's extra-point attempt was blocked, leaving Army ahead by a point at 7–6.

Army immediately responded with a drive that also covered 81 yards, 52 of which came on Blanchard's first of two touchdowns in the half. Appearing fully recovered from his knee injury and no doubt motivated by the knowledge that this was his last game, Mr. Inside burst through the right side of the Army line, swerved to his right past a linebacker and, flashing his remarkable speed for a big fullback, sprinted down the right sideline for a touchdown. After Ray's conversion made it 14–6, Army center Bill Yeoman intercepted a Baysinger pass on the Navy 38-yard line. Three plays later, with the ball at the Middies' 27-yard line, Davis fired a pass down the middle to Blanchard on what would mark the fifth and last time they would combine on a touchdown. Fittingly, it was a dazzling play with Blanchard racing downfield then stopping at the 10 as if to receive a short pass—that Davis had feigned—and then whirling and bolting into the end zone to snare a perfectly thrown pass. After Ray's third extra point made it 21–6 at halftime, the likelihood in the minds of most of the huge crowd was that Army, after its dominance in the first half, would expand that lead over the final two quarters. Few in the crowd could have expected what was coming, though, in the second half, perhaps the most drama-filled 30 minutes in the history of the long rivalry.

With Tucker having aggravated his knee injury early in the game, he was unable to drop back to set up and pass, leaving the passing to Davis, who had become an efficient passer. Tucker's lack of mobility also forced Blaik to remove one of his best defenders early in the game, which as Blaik was to say, "contributed to our misadventures in the second half."

Navy's defense, so porous all season and, to a considerable extent in the opening half, stiffened markedly after the halftime break. After Army had been stopped by the fired-up Middie defense at the Navy 32, the Midshipmen drove 78 yards for their second touchdown, with reserve fullback Bill Hawkins hammering over from the 2-yard line then missing his extra-point attempt to leave Navy trailing 21–12.

What seemed to be surprisingly poor judgment by Blaik paved the way for Navy's third touchdown. Late in the final quarter, with Army at its own 35-yard line and in a fourth-and-inches to go coming up for a first down, Blaik elected to go for it, only to have Blanchard stopped for no gain, enabling Navy to take over deep in the Cadets' territory. Seizing the opportunity, the Middies scored early in the final period on a pass from halfback Bill Earl to captain Leon Bramlett, which evoked delirium among the 3,500 midshipmen in the stands along with thousands of others rooting for Navy. Again, though, Hawkins could not convert to leave Army ahead 21–18 with about 10 minutes left to play and Jack

Ray's three successful extra points and Navy's three failed conversions made the difference at this late juncture of what was turning into a surprisingly close battle.

Midway through the final quarter, Army, realizing that its three-point lead might hardly be sufficient against a Navy team that decidedly now had the momentum, reached the Middies' 39-yard line after Davis had shot around left end and raced 29 yards down the sideline before being stopped. But the Cadets' drive stalled and Navy took over at its own 37 with 7:00 to play and most of the 100,000-plus spectators standing with hearts pounding. Seemingly unstoppable by a vaunted Army defense that had held powerful and unbeaten Notre Dame scoreless three weeks earlier, Navy drove 67 yards to the Army 3-yard line, with the key play a fourth-down, do-or-die, 20-yard dash to the Army 3-yard line by halfback Lynn Chewning. Incredibly, Army, which hadn't lost since falling to Navy 13–0 in the last game of the 1943 season, found itself confronted with a Navy team in a first-and-goal-to-go at the Cadets' 3-yard line with 90 seconds left in the game.

In the press box, from which they communicated with Red Blaik, assistant coaches Herman Hickman and Andy Gustafson found themselves unable to look down on the field, with Hickman looking down at the floor and Gustafson staring into space. *Oh, God, don't let it happen,* Hickman said to himself. *Please don't let it happen.* In the din in the stands beneath them, neither Hickman nor Gustafson could hear Blaik calling by phone, nor could they bring themselves to answer.

On first down Chewning hit Army's right side but was stopped in his tracks by end Hank Foldberg and tackle Goble Bryant. On second down the 215-pounder got the call again only to have Barney Poole stop him cold for no gain. In a huge break for Army, the Midshipmen then were penalized five yards to the Cadets' 8-yard line for taking an illegal extra timeout. Now it was third down and still goal to go from the Army 3-yard line with only eight seconds remaining—time for only one more play. By then thousands of the huge throng of frenzied spectators had breached security men and come down from the stands and crowded along the sidelines.

On what would be the final play of the drive and of the game—and one of the most dramatic and memorable in Army football history—Hawkins, outstanding all afternoon, both on offense and defense, took a pitchout from quarterback Baysinger, faked a drive into the left side of the Navy line, and flipped a lateral to halfback Pete Williams who was headed the other way. As Williams raced towards the goal line with the crowd in an uproar, Barney Poole, aware that Army's three-year-long winning streak and perhaps another national championship were on the line, spun around from his left end position to avoid a block and lunged at Williams as he was about to cross the plane of the goal line. As Poole stopped Williams' progress but did not bring him down, most of the rest of the Army defenders led by linemen Joe Steffy, Hank Foldberg, Goble Bryant, and Jim Enos joined Poole to push back and finally bring him down about a foot from the goal line as the game ended. On the sideline, the usually stoic Red Blaik breathed a sigh of relief and, in a rare display of emotion, threw up in his arms in exultation, while in the press box Herman Hickman and Andy Gustafson both bellowed in delight.

As the Army players on the field ran to the sideline, they were engulfed by their teammates, particularly the first classmen like Blanchard, Davis, Poole, Enos, and Ug Fuson, the center and halfback. In the stands amid the delirious Corps of Cadets and also President Truman, who had won his $20 bet, the Army band struck up "On, Brave Old Army Team," which resonated with the rest of the Corps as perhaps never before, knowing that Army had barely escaped what would have been a crushing defeat and would have ended Army's winning streak in the last game for Army's first classmen, including the Cadets' greatest players, Doc Blanchard and Glenn Davis.

16

★ ★ ★

The Last Hurrahs

I N THE IMMEDIATE AFTERMATH OF THE SPINE-TINGLING FINISH OF the Army-Navy game, how, it was being asked in newspapers, on radio sportscasts, in bars and grills, around office water-coolers, and of course at West Point, could the weakest Navy team in years come so close to upsetting one of Army's best teams of all time? No one seemed to come up with a logical explanation, other than to rely on the old chestnut reasoning that anything could happen in the quintessential traditional college football game between the longtime rival service academies. It was one thing for Navy to put up a good fight when it lost to Army in a game that decided the national championship in 1944. But that year Navy had come into the game undefeated with one of its best teams ever. Yet, in 1946, the Middies, who had won only 1-of-8 games and lost their last seven, had come within inches of upsetting another unbeaten Army team that was possibly on the verge of winning its third straight national championship in perhaps the most exciting game ever played in the long rivalry. As Red Blaik recalled his feelings in the final seconds of the game, "It would be just like the Navy, I thought, to swallow a bitter, almost poisoning ending. Then much of what all this courageous team had done would be forgotten."

Indeed, the performance of what was considered a forlorn Navy team against one of the two best college teams in the country may have cost Army its third straight national championship. (Notre Dame was picked as the national champion in most major polls, including the most respected poll by the Associated Press.) Still, some people asked how could Notre Dame be rated ahead of Army when it had tied the Cadets, the defending national champion who had gone undefeated for the third straight year? The answer apparently was that Notre Dame had played what was regarded as a more rigorous schedule, even though, like Army, the Irish had played only one top-10 team. Admittedly though, Notre Dame had finished much stronger, following the tie with Army with impressive victories over Northwestern, Tulane, and 16th-ranked Southern California while giving up only six points in the game against USC in Los Angeles before a crowd of 103,000 people. Notre Dame shut out five opponents, including Army, while yielding just 26 points on four touchdowns. Still, some people in college football's inner circle agreed with several lesser polls that gave the top-ranking to Army and listed Notre Dame second. One of them was Red Blaik who said, "It is not clear to me on what basis the poll majority arrived at that decision." In Blaik's opinion, Army, though having been tied by Notre Dame, should have remained the undefeated champion. Maybe undefeated, but no longer the national champion.

For the third year in a row, Blanchard and Davis were named to the Associated Press All-American team, the most highly regarded poll, along with end Hank Foldberg, who as a "yearling" still had two more years of eligibility. Johnny Lujack edged out Arnold Tucker as the All-American first-team quarterback, although Tucker was chosen ahead of Lujack in some polls. Joe Steffy, Barney Poole, and guard Art

Gerometta were also named to some second team All-American teams, while Red Blaik was named Coach of the Year.

The biggest individual honor went to Glenn Davis who followed Blanchard, the 1945 winner, when he won the prestigious Heisman Trophy, emblematic of the best college player of the year. Tucker also captured a highly coveted honor when he was awarded the Sullivan Award as the most outstanding amateur athlete of the year Blanchard had become the first college football player to win the Sullivan the year before. During their last season, the duo of Blanchard and Davis had become so famous that they appeared on the cover of both *Time* and *Life* magazines, and it is believed to be the first, and perhaps only time a football player—or two in this case—had been on the cover, along with feature stories, in those two publications.

Davis had finished with a four-year total of 59 touchdowns (still an Army record), 43 rushing, 14 by receiving, and two on punt returns, while also setting still-standing Army records of 20 touchdowns in a season, in 1944; points scored (354), touchdowns responsible for (71); average yards gained per carry (8.5); interceptions (14), and a remarkable single-season, offensive record average of 11.5 yards per carry in 1944, which still stood as an NCAA record in 2014.

Blanchard, who played one less season than Davis, scored 38 touchdowns—26 by rushing, seven on passes (five of them from Davis), four on pass interceptions, and one on a kickoff return. Collectively, the 1945 team set Army records of 49 touchdowns and an average per carry of 7.64 yards, which in 2014 still stood for an NCAA record. Years later, Blanchard was still perturbed by the outcome of the 1946 tie game with Notre Dame. "It was the most boring game I've ever played in," he said of the game in which he and Davis together gained only 82 yards on 35 carries. "I think Blaik and Leahy were more worried about losing than winning."

* * *

Unlike in 1945, Army was receptive following the 1946 season to a bid to play undefeated and fourth-ranked UCLA in the Rose Bowl, in what was the most prestigious postseason game at the time, on New Year's Day. However, the year before Rose Bowl officials had signed a contract with the Pacific Coast Conference and the Big Ten Conference whereby the winners of those two conferences would meet in the game at Pasadena, California, but the Big Ten refused a request by Rose Bowl officials to step aside for one year to permit Army to play UCLA, which they knew would be a far better national attraction. Such a game, of course, would have been a homecoming of sorts for Glenn Davis, whose hometown of Claremont was only about 30 miles from Pasadena, who in four years had played only one game outside of the Northeast, in Ann Arbor, Michigan, in his final season. As it was, Army would not play in a bowl game until 1984. (Notre Dame, which had played in the Rose Bowl in 1925, disdained bowl invitations thereafter until 1969, after which it frequently played in bowl games.)

It was considered unlikely that Army would ever again field teams like the ones of 1944, 1945, and 1946 when squads were loaded with talented transfers who had already played at other colleges, such as Blanchard, Tucker, and Poole, or had in effect been recruited from army service like Tex Coulter. That, of course, gave Army, and also Navy to a lesser extent, a huge advantage against most opponents from 1943 through the 1945 seasons when the football teams from the majority of the schools the Cadets played during that period lost many of its best players to military service. Because most of those players were back in school in 1946, Army's success that year seemed to validate the teams' greatness, even though Notre Dame, denuded of many of its players, had been crushed by the Cadets in 1944 and 1945, was able to more than hold its own with the return of players like Johnny Lujack, George Connor, and Emil Sitko, along with its coach, Frank Leahy. Admittedly, though, no one seemed to complain about Army's supremacy during its championship years; if anything, the Cadets teams were more beloved than ever, perceived as they were by many Americans as a symbol of America's military might, although the players were not yet actually in the army and some never would be.

Of the past three seasons, Blaik said, "As their coach, I have great pride in the record of the 1944 squad," which had won all nine games and which Blaik often called his best "qualitative" team because of its depth. "I have great pride in the record of our 1945 team, which was definitely our best team. But I reserve the warmest affect and the greatest respect for the 1946 team, which in the face of adversities, playing the best of college opposition, completely and thoroughly demonstrated its right to be classed as great."

Several days after the Army-Navy game, Notre Dame and West Point, in a joint statement, announced that the 33-year series between the two schools' football teams would end, at least temporarily, after a game in 1947 at Notre Dame Stadium, which would mark the first time Army had ever played the Irish in South Bend. The statement indicated that the decision to terminate the series for at least a while was a joint one, but in fact Notre Dame did not want it to end, mainly because of its huge following in the metropolitan New York area, which in addition to its Subway Alumni included thousands of actual alumni and prospective students, plus the national attention the games attracted. The series would be resumed, albeit on a limited basis, in 1957 when Notre Dame would beat Army 23–21 at Philadelphia's Municipal Stadium during a season in which the Irish, with a 7–3 record, would finish ranked 10th while Army, after losing only to Notre Dame and Navy, would be ranked 18th. The following year, Blaik's last, the eventually undefeated Cadets, captained by All-American halfback and Heisman Trophy winner Pete Dawkins, would beat Notre Dame 14–2 in South Bend and finish third in the national rankings. After that, through the 2013 season, no Army team had been ranked in the top 10. After playing one another intermittently after 1947, Notre Dame demonstrated why Army no doubt had decided to end the long series when the Irish won 14 times in a row starting in 1965, with most of the victories by lopsided scores as the Cadets de-emphasized football and lost far more games than they would win.

In addition to its de-emphasis, Army's football program was hampered by the unpopular Vietnam War in the 1960s, when the U.S. Army found itself on the losing side and ignominiously had to abandon its efforts and hurriedly leave Vietnam. Other reasons include the high admission standards—a Scholastic Aptitude Score of at least 1,200 is usually required to gain admission; the difficult academic grind, the Academy's stringent rules of conduct, and the five-year military commitment required of graduates, which is two years more than what was required in the mid-1940s. That has discouraged most high school football stars from applying to the Academy when they can attend schools on full scholarships with far less rigorous academic curricula, and in many cases, earn millions of dollars playing in the National Football League, often without having to graduate from college.

Many of Army's players in the mid-1940s became career military men in either the army or the Air Force. That was ironic since most of them had shown no interest in going to West Point after graduating from high school and wound up at other colleges before being recruited to play football at the Military Academy. Among them were two of Army's greatest players, Blanchard and Arnold Tucker, both of whom served more than 20 years in the Air Force, which was known as the Army Air Corps until it became a separate branch of the U.S. armed forces in 1947 following World War II and before the Air Force Academy was established in Colorado Springs in Colorado in 1954.

Another outstanding player, Ed "Rafe" Rafalko, one of the few who went directly to West Point out of high school, served 22 years as a bomber pilot after learning how to fly at Stewart Field in Newburgh, New York, which was donated to West Point by the city of Newburgh early in World War II and thus became a training ground for prospective pilots in the Army Air Corps. Rafalko, Tucker, and Blanchard all eventually served briefly as assistant coaches under Red Blaik, as did Glenn Davis, while Rafalko, who retired as a major general, later became the athletic director at the Air Force Academy. Tucker, an outstanding all-round athlete, as were a number of his classmates, also played alongside Davis on the basketball team that he captained during the 1946–47 season, and competed in the broad jump and javelin on the track team. Following his discharge, Tucker spent two years as the athletic director at the University of Miami, where had played one season before transferring to West Point.

Idolized as players by thousands of fans and army personnel, Blanchard and Davis came under severe criticism in the press and by others when they requested that they be granted four-month deferments following their graduations in order to play in the NFL where they were coveted by several teams, and four-month deferments the following three years. Their requests were approved by West Point superintendent General Maxwell Taylor but denied by the War Department, a predecessor of the Pentagon. However, during their furlough after graduation, Blanchard and Davis were given permission to appear in a movie based on their West Point careers, titled *Spirit of West Point*. While not critically acclaimed in light of their lack of acting training, the movie did well at the box office and also by Blanchard and Davis who each earned $20,000 for about a week's worth of work. While making the movie, Davis, who had never missed a game during his four years at West Point, suffered a knee injury while playing football during a simulated game, an injury that was further aggravated later when he played for a team of college All-Stars against the New York Giants in a benefit football game at the Polo Grounds in New York that fall.

In 1948, while Davis was on furlough in California, he was introduced to 16-year-old Elizabeth Taylor, who had become a starlet at the
age of 12 in *National Velvet* and had appeared in two other films, *Lassie
Come Home* and *The White Cliffs of Dover*. When they began to date,
their relationship became the sort of love story that many newspaper
and magazine readers feasted on, involving a beauteous movie star and a
handsome army officer who recently had been the most famous football
player in the country, and the two were often photographed together.
After Davis left for a year's tour of duty in Korea, Taylor was photographed looking longingly at a photo of Davis on a table in her Los
Angeles home, which appeared in newspapers and magazines throughout the country. Rumors about their romance were further fueled when
Davis returned home in 1949 and was met at the Miami airport, where
a photo was taken of Taylor removing lipstick from Davis' face after
kissing him while the young lieutenant reportedly gave her a cultured
pearl necklace. The photo ran in *Life* magazine, and later in hundreds
of newspapers, leading to speculation that the relationship was serious
and rumors that they had become engaged. In fact, Taylor was by then
dating 28-year-old William Pawley Jr., who later had a brief film career
and whose wealthy father had been the American ambassador to Brazil
and Peru. They eventually became engaged but never married. As to
rumors that Taylor had previously been engaged to Glenn Davis, years
later Davis said, "It never happened. She had started dating that rich
guy, and I just said, 'Screw it,' and left."

However, Taylor and Davis remained friends to the extent that
Taylor asked Davis to escort her to the Academy Awards in 1949
while he was still in the army and still striking looking in a tuxedo.
Few, if any other, actors attracted as much attention that night as Taylor and Davis. "Liz was a nice person but naïve, and we had a lot of
fun together," Davis said. "Her mother had a great influence on her.
She really pushed her children. If she hadn't been so pushy, Liz would

have been a happier person." That assessment of Taylor's mother led many people to believe that she had been responsible for their breakup and Taylor's eventual relationship with Pawley, whom Taylor's mother may have favored because of his family's wealth. Davis also dated another well-known actress of the era, Ann Blyth, who had won an Oscar in 1946 for best supporting actress in her role as the daughter of Joan Crawford in the movie *Mildred Pierce* and became friendly with Debbie Reynolds.

Following his discharge in 1950, Davis spent two seasons with a powerful Los Angeles Rams team in 1950 and 1951 before retiring because of the knee injury he had sustained in 1947 that hampered his running ability, although he was still good enough to lead the Rams with a 4.2 yards per carry rushing average in 1950 when they reached the NFL Championship Game and lost 30–28 to the Cleveland Browns. In that game, Davis scored the Rams' first touchdown when quarterback Bob Waterfield connected with Davis on an 82-yard touchdown play. Davis also played in the title game in 1951 when the Rams avenged that loss to the Browns. That Rams team included Hall of Famers Waterfield, Norm Van Brocklin, Elroy "Crazy Legs" Hirsch, Tom Fears, and Andy Robustelli. "I was a mere image of what I had been," Davis said. "I was a better player my senior year in high school than I was with the Rams." That was not only due to his chronically bad knee but because his skills had markedly diminished after not having played football for four years. Still, during his two seasons with the Rams, Davis ran back 17 kickoffs for 346 yards for an average of 20 yards per return, and he caught 50 passes for 682 yards while also completing 4-of-7 passes for 102 yards and two touchdowns. Davis tried to return to the Rams in 1952 but re-injured his knee in a preseason exhibition game and decided to retire.

Davis subsequently went to work for the *Los Angeles Times* in 1954 as assistant director of special events, and later as the director in charge of the paper's charity sports events until he retired in 1987 when he was 62 years old. Though he did not become Elizabeth Taylor's first husband, in 1953 he married another well-known actress, Terry Moore, who was nominated for an Oscar as best supporting actress for her role in *Come Back, Little Sheba*, but the marriage lasted less than a year. Then in 1953 he married Harriett Lancaster Slack, whose husband had been killed during World War II when his plane was shot down in Europe. After she bore Davis' only child, a son named for his brother, Ralph, she died in 1955. The following year he married Yvonne Ameche, the widow of former Baltimore Colts fullback Alan Ameche, who also won a Heisman Trophy in 1954. Her marriage to Davis in 1956 made Mrs. Davis—the mother of four sons and two daughters—the only woman to have been married to two Heisman Trophy winners. "I was blessed twice," she said of her two marriages. Appropriately enough, the couple had met earlier that year at the annual Heisman Trophy presentation to which all Heisman winners and their family members are invited every year.

Mrs. Davis recalled an amusing set of circumstances involving Davis and two previous Heisman Trophy winners, halfbacks Tom Harmon of Michigan and Les Horvath of Ohio State, who had finished ahead of Davis and Blanchard in the Heisman voting in 1944. Having seen Horvath's Heisman Trophy and been told by her husband of its significance, the couple went to dinner parties at the homes of both Harmon and Davis in the 1950s, where Ruby Horvath saw their Heisman Trophies on display. "I thought you said getting the Heisman was a very special honor, and yet in a couple of weeks I've seen the same trophy in Tom Harmon and Glenn Davis' homes," Ruby Horvath said. Horvath, of course, had to explain what great players Harmon and Davis had also been.

* * *

Asked about Davis' relationship with Elizabeth Taylor, Yvonne Davis said in February 2014, "He never really talked about it. I think most of what was written was rumor, nothing else." Of his relationship with Debbie Reynolds, Mrs. Davis said, "I once met Debbie on a plane and she said she dated Glenn, but he said that he had merely spent time with her and other actors and actresses at parties arranged by movie studios."

Mrs. Davis went on to say, "Glenn lived a charmed and sweet life. He never talked about himself and was proudest of his graduation from West Point. He was a very happy guy."

Not surprisingly, Davis, who lived with his wife close to a golf course in La Quinta, California, became an excellent golfer with a three handicap who played golf with former president Gerald Ford and was also invited to play at a number of celebrity golf events, including one held by Bob Hope and another by Bing Crosby, both avid golfers.

Blanchard, who had somehow been rejected for the navy's pre-flight program while he was at North Carolina, flew 84 missions as a fighter-plane pilot during the Vietnam War. While stationed in England, Blanchard was cited for bravery by the Air Force after his jet fighter burst into flames and smoke filled his cockpit over an English village as he was approaching a landing field and managed to land it safely rather than bail out. "There was only thing I could do since otherwise the plane would have hit the village or one of the other nearby heavily populated areas," Blanchard said. In citing the then Major Blanchard for bravery, an Air Force spokesman said, "It was one of the finest flying jobs I ever saw." Blanchard retired from the Air Force in 1971 with the rank of colonel, and with his wife, who he had met while in basic training in Texas before being recruited by West Point, settled in San Antonio where they raised a family of three children and also had seven grandchildren.

Even after his Heisman Trophy season in 1946, Davis was hardly through as an athlete at West Point. In the spring of 1947, he had another outstanding year both as a centerfielder, hitter, and base-stealer. During World War II, the Brooklyn Dodgers and their Triple A farm team, the Montreal Royals, did their preseason training at Bear Mountain, just south of West Point, after baseball commissioner Kenesaw Mountain Landis decreed that, starting in 1943, big league teams could not train in Florida as most of them did, and still do. While at Bear Mountain, the Dodgers and Royals often practiced in the West Point field house and played a number of games against Army, as did the New York Giants and the New York Yankees. In one game against the Royals, Davis beat out a bunt for a single—one of his two hits—and then stole second, third, and home to the amazement of the Royals. So impressed was he by Davis' baseball ability, that Dodgers general manager Branch Rickey reportedly offered Davis a contract and asked him to write in his own asking price to sign. Davis, of course, had to remind Rickey that he was committed to serve in the army for three years and thus could not sign.

Even after his discharge in 1950, Davis was still in demand as a baseball player. "I was offered a couple of baseball contracts, but I knew the boat had sailed on that," he said. "I figured I'd need three or four years in the minors to make the grade, and by then I'd be close to 30. The one thing I had left to sell was football."

In his farewell appearance, or appearances as it turned out, as an athlete at West Point, Davis outdid even himself on a Saturday in May 1947 when an Army baseball team that had won 17 games and tied one, played its final game against Navy while the two academies competed against one another in a track meet about a half mile from Doubleday Field, which was named for Abner Doubleday, a West Point graduate said to have been the inventor of baseball. In that game, Davis, already hitting better than .400, bunted safely for a single—one of his two hits in four times at-bat—but Army lost 8–4. Immediately after the game, Davis hurried to a waiting car and was driven to the track meet while changing quickly into a track uniform and borrowed track shoes. Davis, who had not competed in an outdoor track meet in 1947, arrived just in time to compete in the 100-yard dash, and won it in 9.7 seconds, the second fastest time in a college track meet that year. Called for a false start, Davis was cautious in coming out of the blocks the second time, breaking late, but he easily caught up with and passed the racers ahead of him to win the race, according to football teammate Bob Folsom. Shortly afterward, Davis was back in the starting blocks for the 220-yard dash, and won it in 20.9 seconds, a new Army record. To top off his remarkable spring day, Davis took third place in the broad jump, which he had never competed in before at West Point. "And he did it all with borrowed shoes," Folsom said. As it turned out, Davis' outstanding performance helped make the difference as Army beat Navy in the meet.

In need of a sprinter, Army track coach Leo Novak had asked Davis if he would compete in the meet against Navy even though Davis had a baseball game the same day. Davis' only preparation consisted of going to the West Point track a week earlier to be fitted for track spikes and then trotting around the quarter-mile track to make certain the shoes fit. Davis had clearly demonstrated how fast he was, even off the football field, when, during an indoor meet at Madison Square Garden a few months earlier, Davis beat Barney Ewell, the silver medalist in the 100-meter race at the 1948 Olympics, in the 60-yard dash. Desirable as he was to Novak as a sprinter, Davis preferred to play baseball during the spring at West Point.

Blanchard also spent several seasons with the track team as a shot-putter, something he had never done before arriving at West Point. Ralph Davis, Glenn's brother, was a star in the sport and took Blanchard under his wing. At first, Blanchard could barely throw the shot about 30', about 20' less than Ralph Davis. Within a month, however, Blanchard was heaving the heavy metal ball more than 40', and two months later he won an indoor event that included the best shot-putters in the East with a toss of 48'3". In the first of two track meets with Navy Blanchard was barely beaten by Ralph Davis after a throw of 49'5". In the second meet, Blanchard set a West Point record with a heave of 51'10¾" to edge Ralph Davis, his shot-put mentor, whose best toss was also over 50' at a time when few shot-putters in the world could reach 50'.

Neither Blanchard nor Davis distinguished themselves academically at West Point. However, Blanchard became in charge of his company when he was in his last year at the Academy and as a ranking cadet officer had the task of inspecting players before the football team left on road trips, while Davis became a regimental supply sergeant on the Academy staff. In a class of 310 graduates in June 1947, Blanchard ranked 296th and Davis 305. Had they not been so heavily involved in sports, particularly Davis, there's little doubt but they would have finished higher. However, both Blanchard and Davis turned out to be eminently successful beyond their football careers.

Blanchard and Davis rarely saw each other in later life, but their mutual respect lasted the rest of their lives. Apart from the reunion of the 1945 national championship team in 1995, they also were reunited in the fall of 1988 during a homecoming and alumni weekend at West Point where they received a hero's welcome at a football practice and then at a luncheon the day of the Army-Lafayette game. At the practice, Coach Jim Young gathered his team in a circle around himself, Blanchard, and Davis, and introduced them as "the greatest football players in the history of the Military Academy," an introduction that elicited cheers from the players.

After marching in the alumni parade the following Saturday, Blanchard, then 62, and Davis, 63, along with the other alums, were guests at a luncheon hosted by Academy superintendant Lieutenant General David Palmer at the venerable Thayer Hotel on the Academy grounds. Try as they might to blend in with the rest of the alumni, Blanchard and Davis were the center of attention as the alums recalled their wondrous feats of more than four decades ago. At one point

General Palmer called everyone to attention and said, "Ladies and gentlemen, I was unable to get Grant and Lee or Eisenhower and MacArthur for you today, but I do have another pair of Army heroes here, and I must call them a pair because that's certainly what they were. Will you join me in welcoming Glenn Davis and Doc Blanchard." The room erupted with applause as the other guests rose to their feet to give Mr. Inside and Mr. Outside a standing ovation as they stood to acknowledge the tribute. As the applause continued, they looked at one another and, with mutual respect and admiration, they both smiled. Neither Blanchard nor Davis were ever comfortable with public adulation off the football field, but this was different; they were West Pointers being honored by other West Pointers, where they had electrified so much of the nation as the greatest 1-2 running combination in college football history and in the process gave a huge lift to the morale of West Pointers the world over during World War II.

★　★　★

With Mr. Inside and Mr. Outside gone, along with Tucker, Poole, and a number of other starters, Army's football future in the next few years looked uncertain, to say the least. Still, the Cadets kept the undefeated streak going in 1947 by winning three of their first four games and tying Illinois in the fourth game. But then after outscoring one of Columbia's best teams, anchored by quarterback Gene Rossides and end Bill Swiacki 20–7 entering the fourth quarter at Baker Field in the fifth game, the Lions scored twice in the final period to upset Army 21–20 for the Black Knights' first loss since they were beaten by Navy in the final game of the 1943 season. "I had a premonition we were in for it," Blaik was to say of the game that Columbia came into with a 2–2 record. "I tried to warn our players of the danger we would be in, but I could not seem to get through to them. After our Friday afternoon workout in Baker Field, I told my assistants 'This team is not ready, and neither are you coaches.'" Strangely enough, Blaik seemed unwilling to share what blame there might have been. Following a 27–7 defeat by Notre Dame at South Bend in the last scheduled game of the series, Army finished with a record of 5–2–2.

Proving that they could win in peacetime as well as in war, when the team was loaded with experienced players from other colleges, the Cadets bounced back to go unbeaten in 1948, when Blaik instituted a two-platoon system, and again in 1949. Then in 1950, after extending its unbeaten streak to 28 games, Army, on the verge of a third consecutive unbeaten season, was defeated by Navy 14–2 in the Cadets' final game of the season when Army wound up ranked second behind Oklahoma.

In what became the most devastating experience during Blaik's 18 years as the Army coach—he would retire following the 1958 unbeaten season when Army finished ranked third in the country— West Point officials announced on August 3, 1951, that 90 cadets had been expelled for an "infraction" of West Point's stringent honor code, including 37 members of the football team, among them Blaik's son, Bob, the Army quarterback. Because of what became known as the "cribbing scandal," which was a front-page story in newspapers across the country, a decimated Army team won only 4-of-18 games in 1951 and 1952. Blaik, who said he had considered resigning because of the involvement of members of the football team, thought the expulsions were unduly harsh, as did his friend General Douglas MacArthur, by then retired and living at the Waldorf-Astoria Hotel in New York. "It could have been settled quickly and quietly by a reprimand from the superintendent," MacArthur said. "That was all that would have been needed, except in the case of two of the boys. And they could have been helped by a kick in the pants." Following the dismissals, Blaik went to Washington and met for about a half hour with President Truman, a big fan of Army football teams. "The president told me he was not at all satisfied with the way the case had been handled," said Blaik, who maintained that during the investigation at West Point the cadets who were expelled were "handled in a manner to discredit them."

"He said his sympathies were with the boys, but that it was too late for him to take any action, too late for the Army to undo what had been done," Blaik said of his meeting with President Truman.

Army's football fortunes rose again in 1953 when the team began a stretch of six consecutive winning seasons through 1958, Blaik's last season, when Pete Dawkins was an All-American halfback and Blaik had end Bill Carpenter line up far from the rest of the linemen on offense, and rarely come into a huddle, which earned him the nickname of "the Lonely End." "The expulsion affair was the kind of thing a man never gets completely out of his system," Blaik wrote in his biography. "I believe, however, that I shelved aside much of my bitterness and became imbued with an unshakable determination to build back football at West Point as a result of unmistakable evidences that developed after the 1951 season."

The colonel-coach did just that, but by the early 1960s West Point, mainly due to its difficult entrance requirements, its academic curriculums, its service commitment following graduation, and the lure of the NFL to many top-tier high school prospects, was never able to match its Golden Age football accomplishments of the Blanchard-Davis era—and no doubt it never will.

EPILOGUE

A S MUCH AS THE WORLD HAD CHANGED BY 1947, TWO YEARS after the end of World War II, so had life at West Point. Hazing of first-year cadets, often cruel and dehumanizing, had been sharply curtailed, and by 1950 was prohibited, although some upperclassmen still tried to lord themselves over plebes. Cadets also were permitted to leave the Academy grounds more often compared with in the 1940s and 1950s when, apart from first-classmen (seniors in collegiate nomenclature), they were as a rule only able to leave for a break at Christmas and for brief summer breaks. By 2014 there were about 4,500 cadets at the Military Academy, compared with around 3,000 in the early and mid-1940s.

By the time Blanchard, Davis, Tucker, and some of their other teammates graduated in June 1947, the country was prospering again. Cars, trucks, refrigerators, meats of all kind, and even nylon stockings were all available. Rationing and price controls had ended, there were no major strikes, incomes for most Americans had increased, unemployment was relatively low, and more than 1 million veterans were attending college under the GI Bill of Rights.

President Truman, whose support among Americans had plummeted to as low as 32 percent in 1946, had risen to more than 60 percent, and he was now basking in a surge of popularity, largely due to the country's economy and the feeling that he had become a stronger leader after having been labeled as an "accidental president" who was indecisive, ineffectual, and even soft on Communism. By the spring of 1947, his leadership was particularly manifested by what became known as the Truman Doctrine, wherein he had proposed—and a Republican-dominated Congress agreed—to have the U.S. give approximately $400 million in relief to Greece and Turkey, whose economies had deteriorated to the point of becoming dangerously close to disintegration, making them ripe for a Communist takeover. His only regret was that because of a "red scare" that resulted in the formation of a House Committee on Un-American Activities, he was prompted, reluctantly, to subject all Federal employees to local checks and have the attorney general produce a list of possible subversive organizations. Of the more than 3 million Federal workers investigated, only about 200 lost their jobs because of questionable, albeit not proven, loyalty. During the "red scare" epidemic, Truman said, "I am not worried about the Communist Party taking over the government of the United States, but I am against a person whose loyalty is not to the government of the United States holding a government job."

One of Truman's closest advisors, Clark Glifford, said he felt Truman's stance was a "response to the temper of the times," and that the president had thought that the fear of Communists infiltrating the government "was a bunch of baloney." That was classic Truman straight-talk that epitomized the populism and the type of fighting spirit that eventually would endear him to more and more Americans and make his political comeback in 1948 one of the most spectacular in American presidential history.

America continued to return to normalcy in 1947. Most of the 16 million American veterans had returned from military service, and most, but certainly not all, had settled into content civilian lives where the average price of a house was less than $2,000 (the equivalent of about $22,000 in 2014), on average earn slightly less than $3,000 a year; buy a new car for about $1,300; a gallon of gas for 15¢; and a loaf of bread for around 13¢. Adjusted for inflation, all of those prices would be much more by today's monetary standards.

It was also the year of one of the most significant events in sports history, which occurred on April 15 when Jackie Robinson, a four-sport athlete at UCLA and former army lieutenant, became the first black in modern times to play in a Major League Baseball game when he took the field for the Brooklyn Dodgers at Ebbets Field in Brooklyn. Another great black athlete, Joe Louis, who had spent three years in the army during the war, barely retained his world heavyweight title with a 15-round split decision over Jersey Joe Walcott at Madison Square Garden in New York.

*　*　*

Indeed, Army could have used a football player like Robinson in the backfield in some of the postwar years. Apart from a few stretches of winning seasons, football at the United States Military Academy went into a precipitous decline after mostly successful seasons in the 1950s and 1960s. From 1973 through the 1983 season, the Black Knights had a winning record in only one of 11 seasons. Then after six winning records in seven years from 1985 through 1990 and appearances in three bowl games, Army, after appearing in a fourth bowl game in 1996, endured 13 consecutive losing seasons from 1997 through 2009. Despite all those losing seasons, the Cadets continued to attract capacity crowds of about 42,000 fans at every game, drawn by the pregame parade of Cadets on The Plain in the heart of the Academy and the pageantry before the games when several Cadet companies march onto the field at Michie Stadium, along with the West Point band, followed by a parachute jump onto the field by an army paratrooper who is cradling the game ball. On the sideline during games at Michie Stadium overlooking Lusk Reservoir—regarded as one with the most beautiful settings of any college stadium in the country—stand the team's mascots, two army mules, and a cannon that is fired after each Army touchdown. Then there is the halftime show featuring both the Academy and visiting team's marching bands, along with the Army cheerleaders—once all male but co-ed since 1974.

In addition to Blanchard and Tucker, about two dozen of the players from the 1944, 1945, and 1946 teams remained in the army well beyond their three-year commitments with more than a few, including Ed "Rafe" Rafalko, becoming generals. Three other players who did not graduate—Barney Poole, Tex Coulter, and Shorty McWilliams, whose West Point career lasted only one year—later played in the National Football League. Glenn Davis was also one of the few who played in the league after fulfilling his military commitments. Most of those who did not stay in the military beyond their commitments became successful in a variety of businesses and in a few cases became coaches at the college or high school level. Most of Blaik's assistant coaches during the Blanchard and Davis era went on to become head coaches at other schools—Herman Hickman at Yale, Andy Gustafson at Miami, Stu Holcomb at Purdue, and Sid Gillman at Cincinnati and later with the Los Angeles Rams of the NFL. Blaik's most famous former assistant, Vince Lombardi, was at West Point from 1949 until 1953. He left to become the offensive coach for the New York Giants and later became a legendary head coach with the Green Bay Packers and the Washington Redskins. After Blaik retired following the 1958 season, Army had 13 head coaches over the next 54 years, most of them with losing seasons.

* * *

After living comfortably with his wife, Yvonne, alongside the LaQuinta Country Club in Southern California, Glenn Davis developed prostate cancer and died of complications following surgery in March 2005. In his obituary of Davis, Mike Cupper of the *Los Angeles Times* wrote that Davis was one of the finest all-around athletes ever to come out of

Southern California, and Davis and Doc Blanchard "remain to this day college football's most famous running back combination."

Fittingly enough, and at his request according to Yvonne, Army's greatest football star and probably its best all-around athlete was buried at the West Point Cemetery—only a few yards away from Red Blaik, who had died in 1989. A number of Davis' former teammates, including Joe Steffy, Ed Rafalko, Doug Kenna, and Goble Bryant, were among the approximately 200 mourners along with Pete Dawkins, a retired general and Army's last Heisman Trophy winner who was the third Cadet to win the prestigious award after Blanchard in 1945 and Davis in 1946. A surprise mourner was Joe Bellino, who won the Heisman Trophy in 1960 following his spectacular career as a halfback with Navy. Somehow it seemed a fitting coda that one of Navy's greatest football stars would pay tribute to the greatest football player ever to play for Navy's arch-rival. Blanchard would follow Davis in death four years later when he died of pneumonia at his home in Bulverde, Texas, in April 2009 at the age of 84.

* * *

Ralph Davis never aspired to try to follow in his father's footsteps, a seemingly impossible task for any son, although he was a halfback on his high school team, and like his dad was a sprinter on the track team. "My father would throw passes to me and give me advice, but he was never pushy," Ralph Davis said. "He let me go my own way and didn't try to convince me to keep playing football." One of Ralph Davis' greatest joys as a young man was getting to know Doc Blanchard. "Doc was very outgoing—a great storyteller, and a great guy who was fun to be around," Ralph said in a 2014 interview.

While at West Point, Blanchard was fun-loving, gregarious, a prankster, and a self-styled ladies man who went into Manhattan as often as he could to date models and actresses and attract attention as one of the country's most famous sports stars. But following his retirement from the Air Force, he lived quietly in the San Antonio area with his wife and two children and seven grandchildren. Though still friendly and outgoing, Blanchard kept his own counsel and rarely attracted any attention outside of San Antonio. Ironically, by comparison, Davis was often in the limelight as a result of his celebrity romances and later through his participation in charity celebrity golf tournaments. "Glenn liked playing with celebrities like presidents Eisenhower and Ford, and with Bob Hope and Bing Crosby. But he was so well-known and liked that they liked playing with him as much as he did with them," Jim Hardy, a close friend and neighbor, said.

Davis, of course, also was a major attraction on the Los Angeles Rams football team in 1950 and 1951, while Blanchard, having opted to make the Air Force a career, never did. Nor, he often said, did he regret it. "The only thing I do regret," he once said with a smile, "is that I didn't sign a big contract and make all that money. But then I'd had enough because in '46 I got hurt the second or third game, and I played the whole season with a bad knee."

Mr. Inside, of course, hardly had to validate his credentials by playing in the NFL. Neither did Mr. Outside, although he more than held his own during his two seasons with the Rams while playing on a bad knee that had nullified much of his speed and curtailed his dazzling whirling-dervish maneuvers in the open field.

Davis and Blanchard last saw each other at a ceremony in Dallas in 2004 when Davis received the Doak Walker Legends Award, named in honor of the former Southern Methodist University halfback and 1948 Heisman Trophy winner. The award is given predominantly to halfbacks who exemplify extraordinary contributions to their team and display outstanding sportsmanship. By then Davis had been treated for prostate cancer, a brain tumor, kidney failure, and a number of other medical issues, according to his wife, Yvonne.

Even in his later years, Davis remained a larger-than-life sports figure—the handsome, easygoing, and likable All-American boy who never grew old, while Doc Blanchard was content to live a private but rewarding life out of the public eye in a small San Antonio suburb.

"Glenn was the fiercest competitor I ever knew but also the classiest and nicest human being you could ever meet," longtime friend Jim Hardy, the former NFL quarterback, said in echoing sentiments expressed by every one of Davis' former teammates interviewed for this book. "He had nerves of steel on the golf course and hated to lose, but he also had a super sense of humor and was the most genuinely modest guy I ever met. He never seemed to change and stayed youthful-looking through the years. Everyone liked him, and why not? He was a very special person."

Very special indeed. Davis was a lifelong All-American boy and an athlete for the ages, who along with Doc Blanchard gave a lift to much of the nation with their spectacular exploits during and immediately after World War II.

ACKNOWLEDGMENTS

A S WAS THE CASE WITH MY FIVE PREVIOUS BOOKS, MUCH
if indeed not most of my research was done in libraries, most notably the Westport Library in Connecticut, where I pored through about
a half-dozen microfilm versions of newspapers, some of which no longer
exist. For acquiring that microfilm and hard-to-find books, I am particularly indebted to Susan Madeo, the inter-library loan coordinator for the
Westport Library, who, like most librarians I've found, is always willing
to help. As in the past, I tried to read as much about my subject matter,
mainly in books, newspapers, and magazines, as I can, along with watching old film of games involving the teams or individuals I'm writing about.
Thanks are also in order to librarians at the Ferguson Library in Stamford
and the Norwalk Public Library, both in Connecticut, who served me well.

Extremely helpful, too, were staffers at the United States Military Academy Library at West Point, including Suzanne Christoff, the director of the
library's archives and special collections department, who aided me in my
research and obtaining photos, and Brian Shearer, the assistant video director who provided film of Blanchard and Davis in action. Others included
Kim McDermott, the communications director for the West Point Association of Graduates; Susan Lintelman, the manuscripts curator; Pauline
Mariani of the graduates office; and retired army colonel Morris Herbert,
the unofficial West Point historian who was a plebe when Blanchard and
Davis were in their last year at West Point and who worked in the graduates office until early 2014 when he retired. Others who helped were Mady
Salvani, assistant director of athletic communications and a veritable font
of information on Army sports, who provided materials, information, and
photos; Theresa Brinkerhoff, chief of the media relations office; and Bob
Kinney, the Academy's personable former sports information director who
I recall ran a very smooth operation in the press box—practically always
with a smile on his face—when I covered Army football games at Michie
Stadium in the 1980s and 1990s.

Of particular help were former Army football players who played with Glenn Davis and Doc Blanchard such as retired major general Edmund "Rafe" Rafalko, Arnold Tucker, Dick Walterhouse, Roland Catarinella, and Robert Woods, the only man to have played on both sides in the Army-Navy games. It was also a joy to interview Heisman Trophy winner and former All-American quarterback Johnny Lujack and his onetime Notre Dame teammate, Terry Brennan, who starred at halfback for the Fighting Irish in the mid-1940s and later served as the head coach at his alma matter. Their sharp and vivid memories of those players of games played seven decades ago, along with their memories of Davis and Blanchard, were invaluable during my research, as was Jim Hardy, a former National Football League quarterback and one of Davis' closest friends.

Others who helped were Scott Strassmeir, the sports information director at the U.S. Naval Academy; Carol Copley of the sports information office at Notre Dame; Jeff Williams, assistant director of championships at the National Collegiate Athletic Association; Zach Eisendrath of the sports information office at the University of Michigan; Bob Kelleher, the principal at Bonita High School in LaVerne, California, where Davis was a student before going to West Point; Judith Schiff, chief research archivist in the Yale University Manuscripts and Archives department; and two of Davis' former high school teammates, Dr. Dan Saint Claire and Charles Creighton.

It was also a pleasure talking with Yvonne Davis, Glenn Davis' widow, who provided me with information about Mr. Inside's later life and a treasure trove of photos and clippings. Thanks, too, to Paul McLaughlin of Norwalk, Connecticut, my computer guru who has guided me through numerous computer pitfalls since he was in high school and without whose help this book might never have made it into print.

Also a tip of the hat to Tom Bast, a longtime acquisitions editor at Triumph Books, who saw the merit of recalling the wondrous days of Mr. Inside and Mr. Outside and their great Army teams, for which I am grateful, and to Karen O'Brien, my editor on the project.

SOURCES

BOOKS

Blaik, Earl H. with Cohane, Tim. *You Have to Pay the Price*. New York: Holt, Rinehart and Winston, 1960.

Brady, John. *The Heisman: A Symbol of Excellence*. New York: Atheneum, 1984.

Cohane, Tim. *Gridiron Grenadiers*. New York: G.P. Putnam's Sons, 1948.

Drape, Joe. *Soldiers First*. New York: Times Books. Henry Holt and Company, 2012.

Feinstein, John. *A Civil War*. New York, Boston, Toronto, London: Little, Brown and Company, 1996.

Kearns Goodwin, Doris. *No Ordinary Time*. New York: Simon & Schuster Paperbooks, 1994.

Groom, Winston. *1942*. New York: Atlantic Monthly Press, 2005.

Mattox, Henry E. *Army Football in 1945*. Jefferson, North Carolina and London: McFarland & Company, 1990.

McCullough, David. *Truman*. New York: Simon & Schuster Paperbacks, 1992.

Morrison, Samuel Eliot. *The Oxford History of American People*. New York: Oxford University Press, 1965.

Roberts, Randy. *Team for America*. Boston, New York: Mariner Books, Houghton Mifflin Harcourt, 2012.

Sugar, Bert Randolph. *The 100 Greatest Athletes*. New York: Citadel Press, 1995.

Total Football. New York: HarperCollins, 1999.

NEWSPAPERS

New York Times
New York Daily News
New York Herald Tribune
New York Sun
New York World Telegram & Sun
Chicago Tribune
South Bend Tribune
Middletown (N.Y.) Times Herald-Record
Los Angeles Times
Philadelphia Inquirer
Washington Post
Baltimore Sun
Notre Dame Scholastic

MAGAZINES

Sports Illustrated
Time
Life
The Sporting News
Sport magazine
Army Football Media Guide
Notre Dame Football Media Guide
The Pointer (West Point publication)

INTERNET

Google
Wikipedia

INDEX